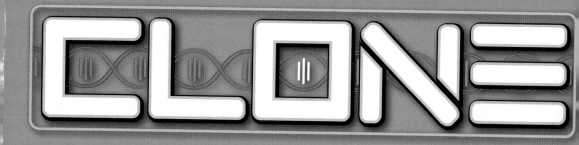

CREATED BY DAVID SCHULNER

DAVID SCHULNER
AARON GINSBURG
WADE MCINTYRE
WRITERS

JUAN JOSE RYP
ARTIST

ANDY TROY
COLORIST

RUS WOOTON
LETTERER

SEAN MACKIEWICZ
EDITOR

JUAN JOSE RYP
AND ANDY TROY
COVER

CREATED BY DAVID SCHULNER

**IMAGE COMICS, INC.**
Robert Kirkman - Chief Operating Officer
Erik Larsen - Chief Financial Officer
Todd McFarlane - President
Marc Silvestri - Chief Executive Officer
Jim Valentino - Vice-President

Eric Stephenson - Publisher
Ron Richards - Director of Business Development
Jennifer de Guzman - Director of Trade Book Sales
Kat Salazar - PR & Marketing Coordinator
Jeremy Sullivan - Digital Marketing Coordinator
Jamie Parreno - Online Marketing Coordinator
Emilio Bautista - Sales Assistant
Braewyn Bigglestone - Senior Accounts Manager
Emily Miller - Accounts Manager
Jasmine Dudas - Administrative Assistant
Tyler Shainline - Events Coordinator
David Brothers - Content Manager
Jonathan Chan - Production Manager
Drew Gill - Art Director
Meredith Wallace - Print Manager
Monica Garcia - Senior Production Artist
Vincent Kukua - Production Artist
Jenna Savage - Production Artist
Addison Duke - Production Artist
IMAGECOMICS.COM

**SKYBOUND**
For SKYBOUND ENTERTAINMENT

Robert Kirkman - CEO
J.J. Didde - President
Sean Mackiewicz - Editorial Director
Shawn Kirkham - Director of Business Development
Helen Leigh - Office Manager
Brian Huntington - Online Editorial Director
Lizzy Iverson - Administrative Assistant

For international rights inquiries,
please contact: foreign@skybound.com

WWW.SKYBOUND.COM

# CHAPTER 6

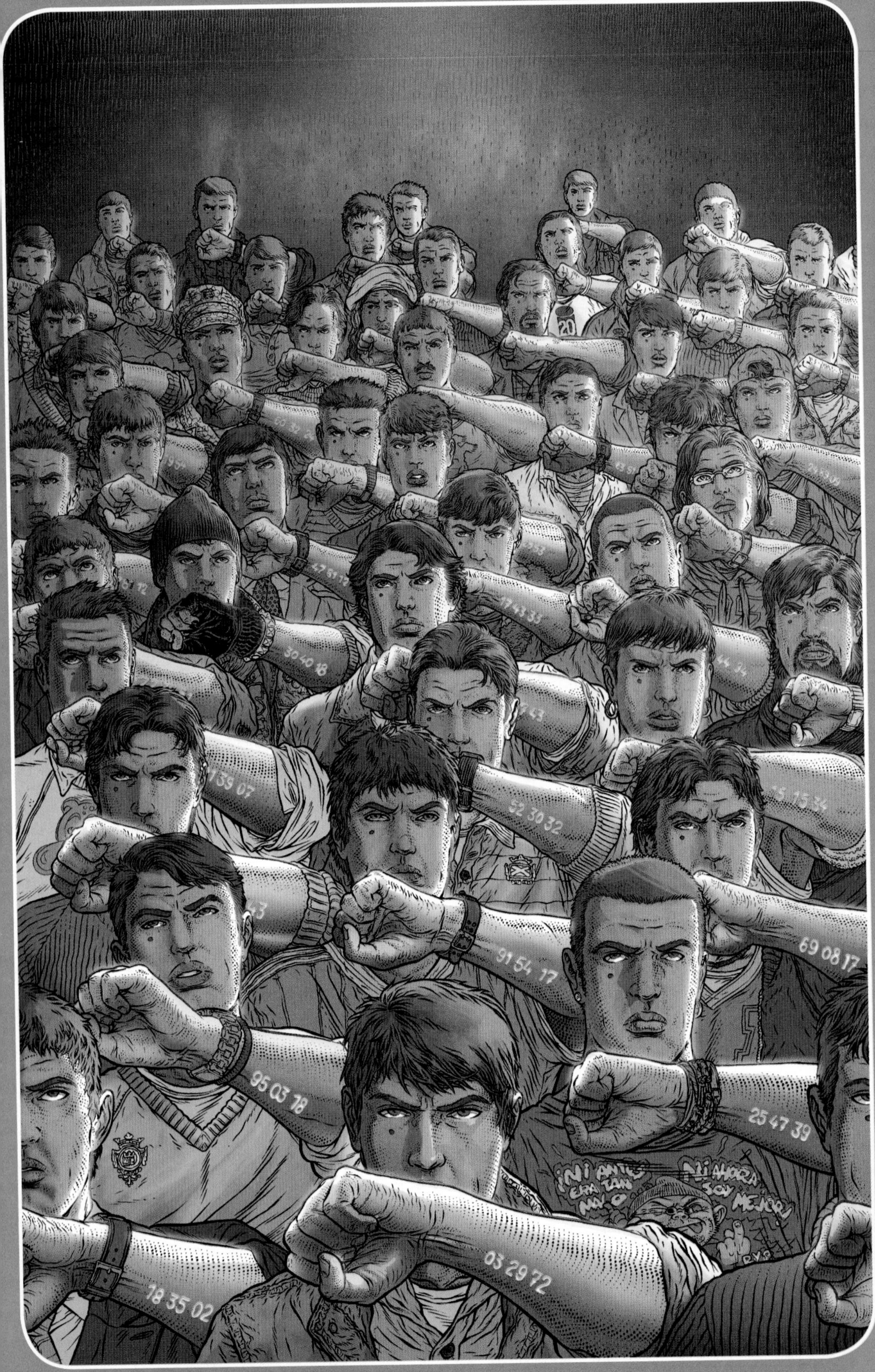
17 43 33
30 40 18
52 30 32
91 54 17
69 08 17
95 03 78
25 47 39
03 29 72
18 35 02

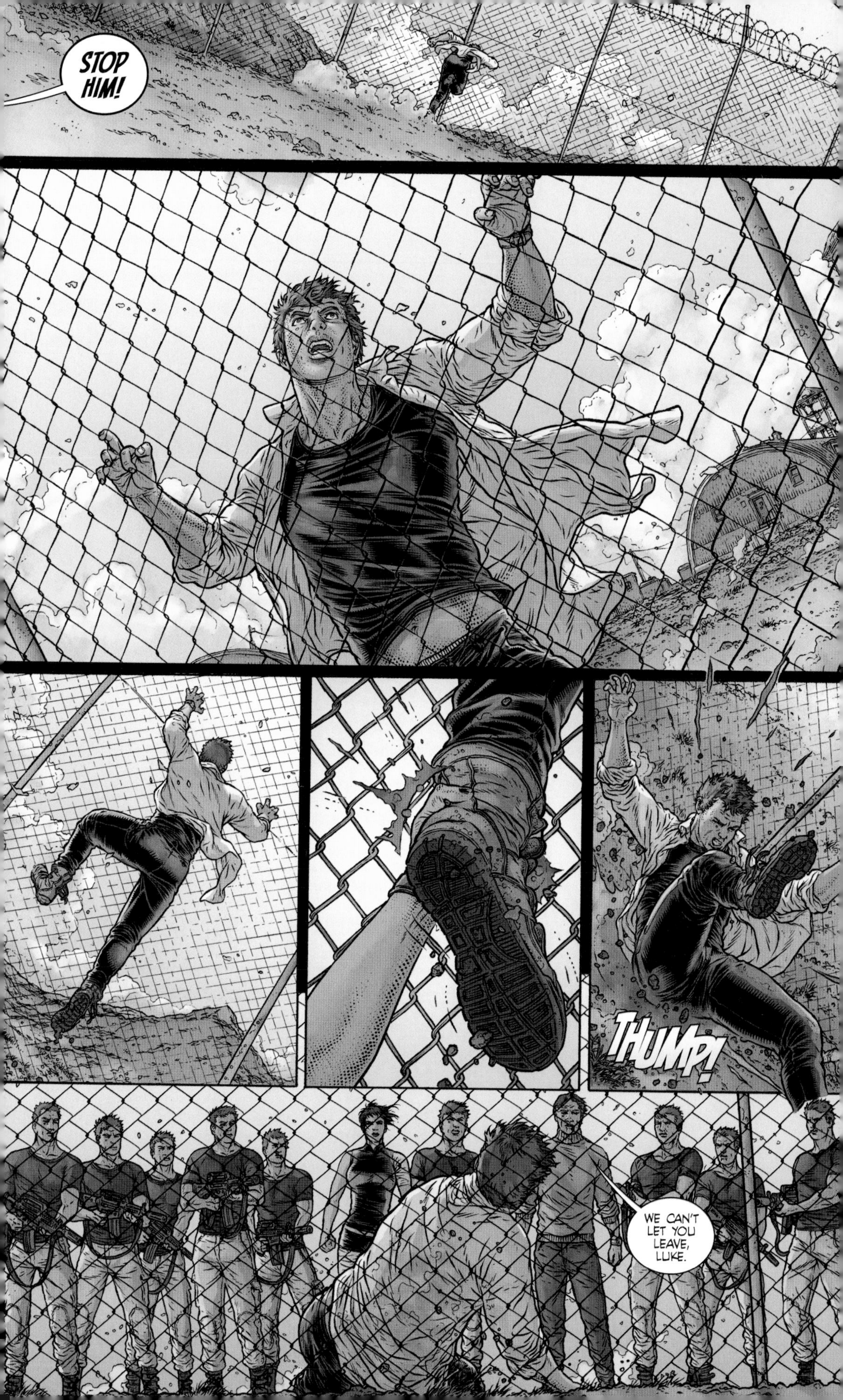
STOP HIM!
THUMP!
WE CAN'T LET YOU LEAVE, LUKE.

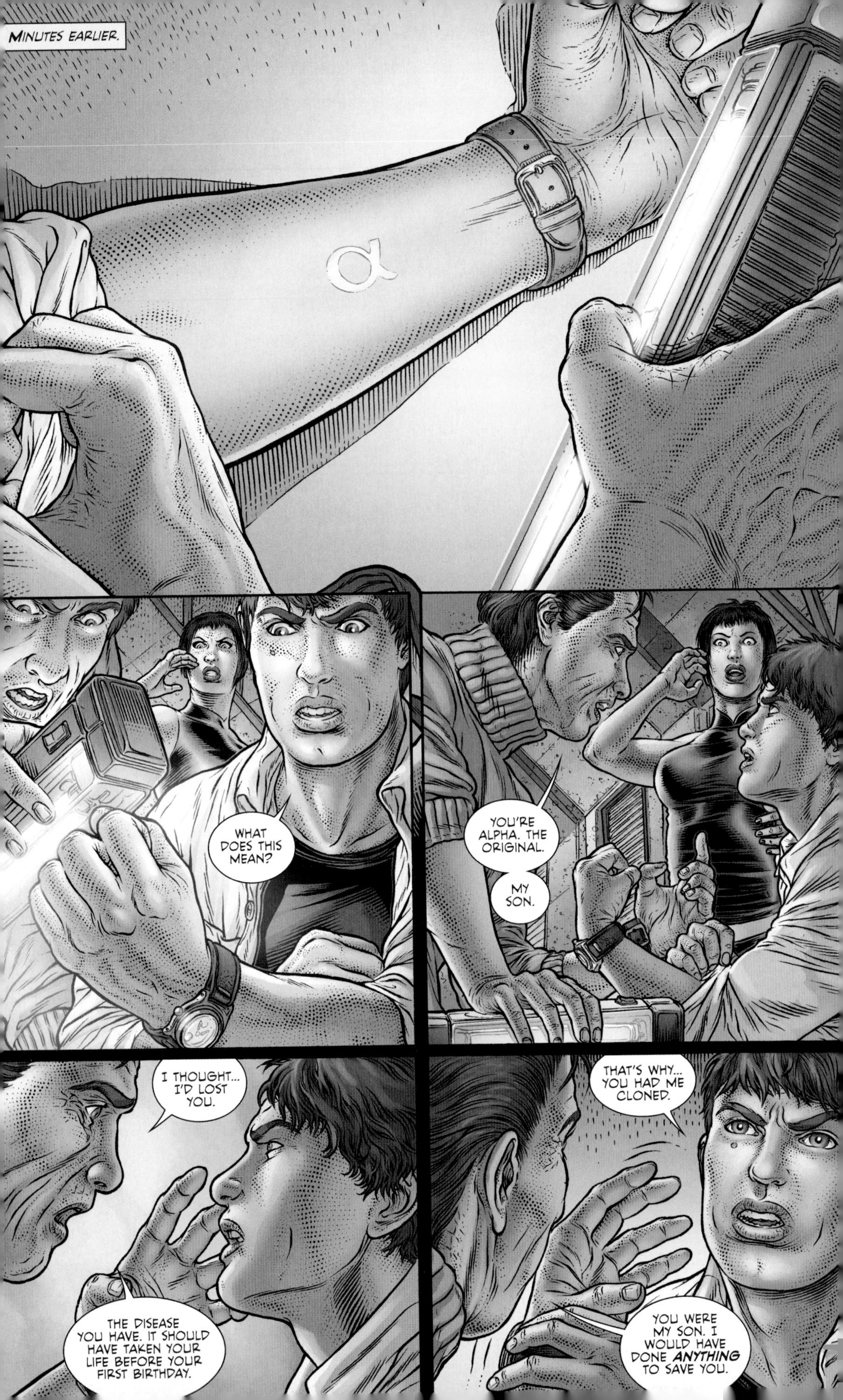
MINUTES EARLIER.
WHAT DOES THIS MEAN?
YOU'RE ALPHA. THE ORIGINAL.
MY SON.
I THOUGHT... I'D LOST YOU.
THE DISEASE YOU HAVE. IT SHOULD HAVE TAKEN YOUR LIFE BEFORE YOUR FIRST BIRTHDAY.
THAT'S WHY... YOU HAD ME CLONED.
YOU WERE MY SON. I WOULD HAVE DONE ANYTHING TO SAVE YOU.

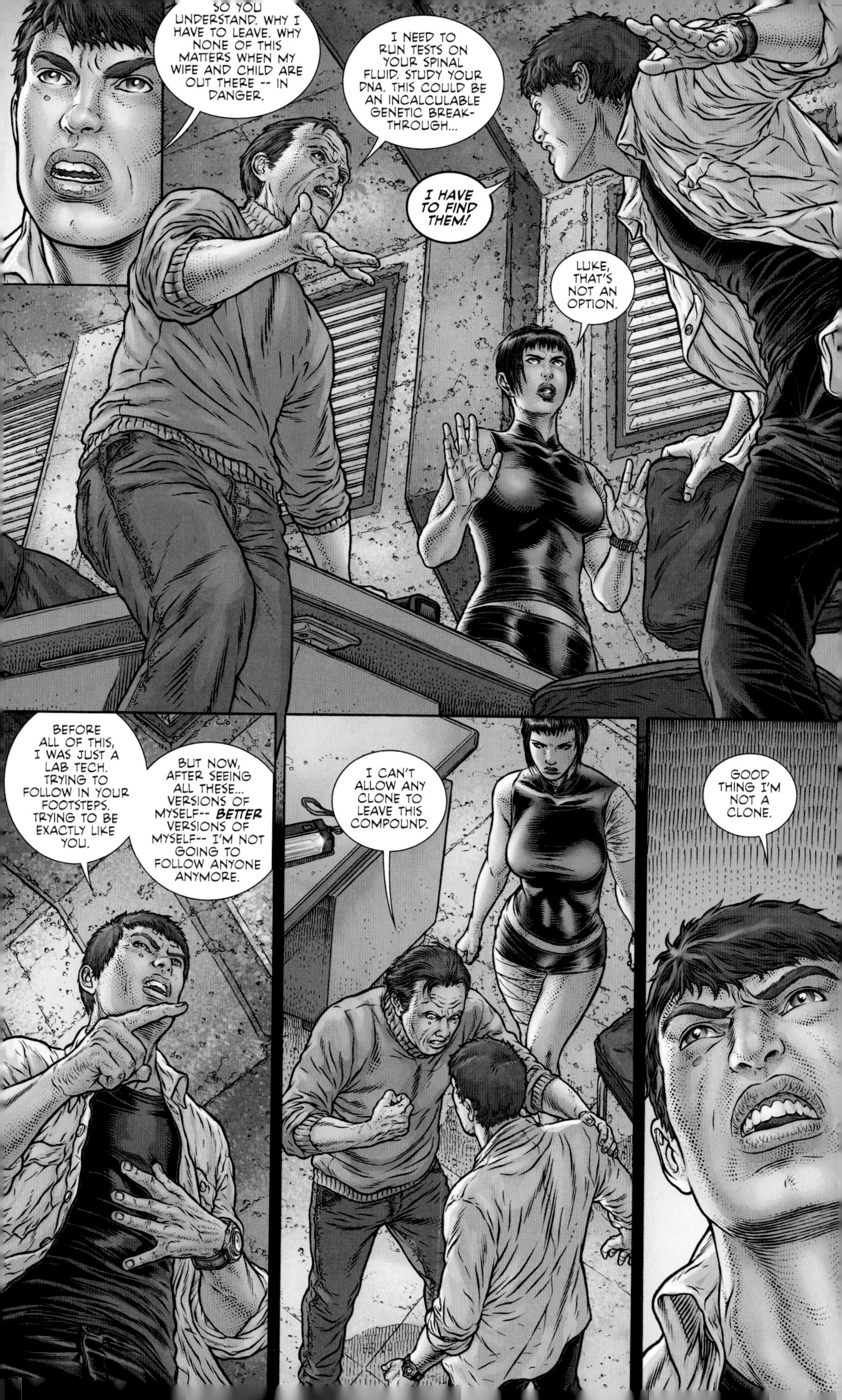
SO YOU UNDERSTAND. WHY I HAVE TO LEAVE. WHY NONE OF THIS MATTERS WHEN MY WIFE AND CHILD ARE OUT THERE -- IN DANGER.
I NEED TO RUN TESTS ON YOUR SPINAL FLUID. STUDY YOUR DNA. THIS COULD BE AN INCALCULABLE GENETIC BREAK-THROUGH...
I HAVE TO FIND THEM!
LUKE, THAT'S NOT AN OPTION.
BEFORE ALL OF THIS, I WAS JUST A LAB TECH. TRYING TO FOLLOW IN YOUR FOOTSTEPS. TRYING TO BE EXACTLY LIKE YOU.
BUT NOW, AFTER SEEING ALL THESE... VERSIONS OF MYSELF-- BETTER VERSIONS OF MYSELF-- I'M NOT GOING TO FOLLOW ANYONE ANYMORE.
I CAN'T ALLOW ANY CLONE TO LEAVE THIS COMPOUND.
GOOD THING I'M NOT A CLONE.

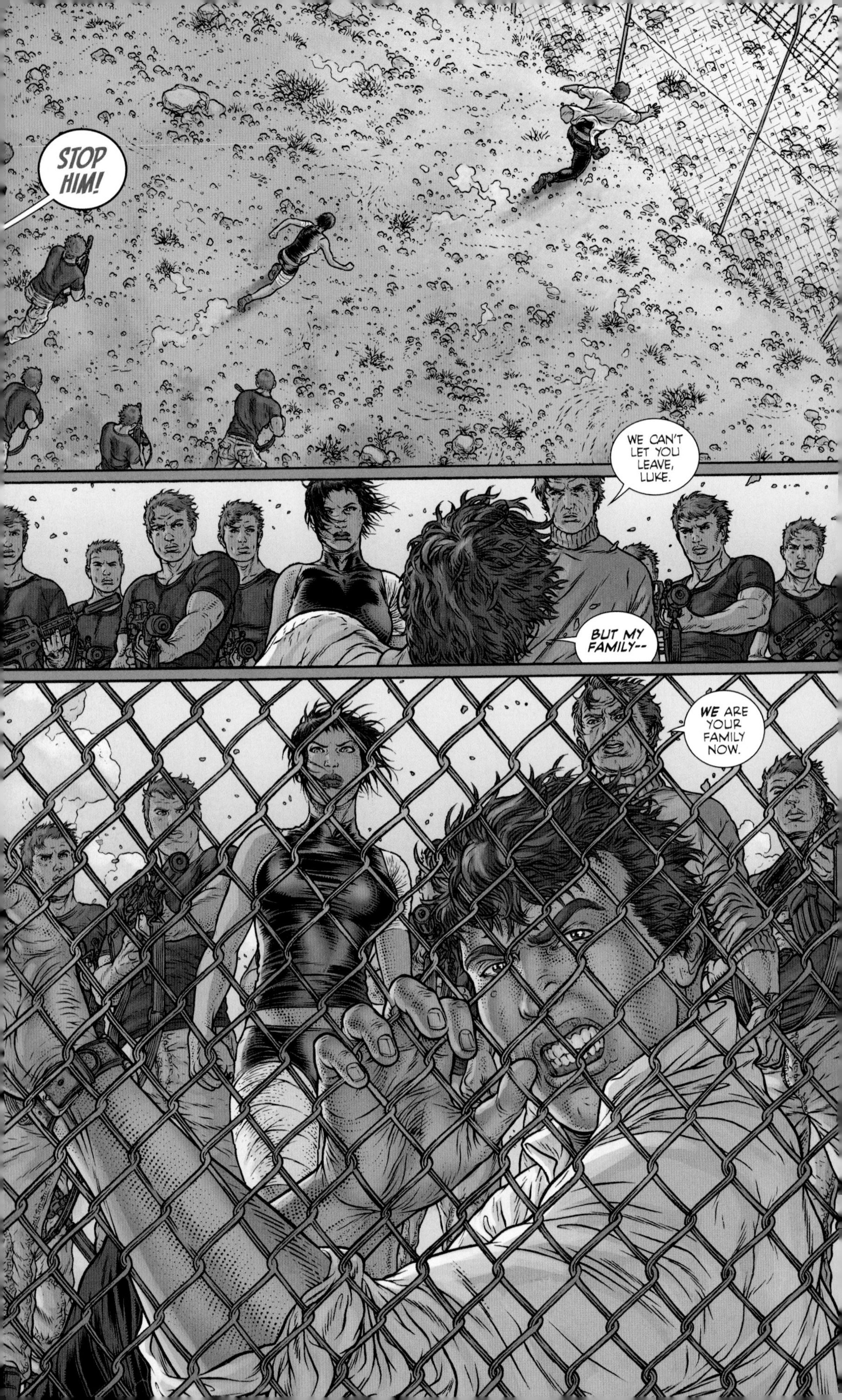
STOP HIM!
WE CAN'T LET YOU LEAVE, LUKE.
BUT MY FAMILY--
WE ARE YOUR FAMILY NOW.

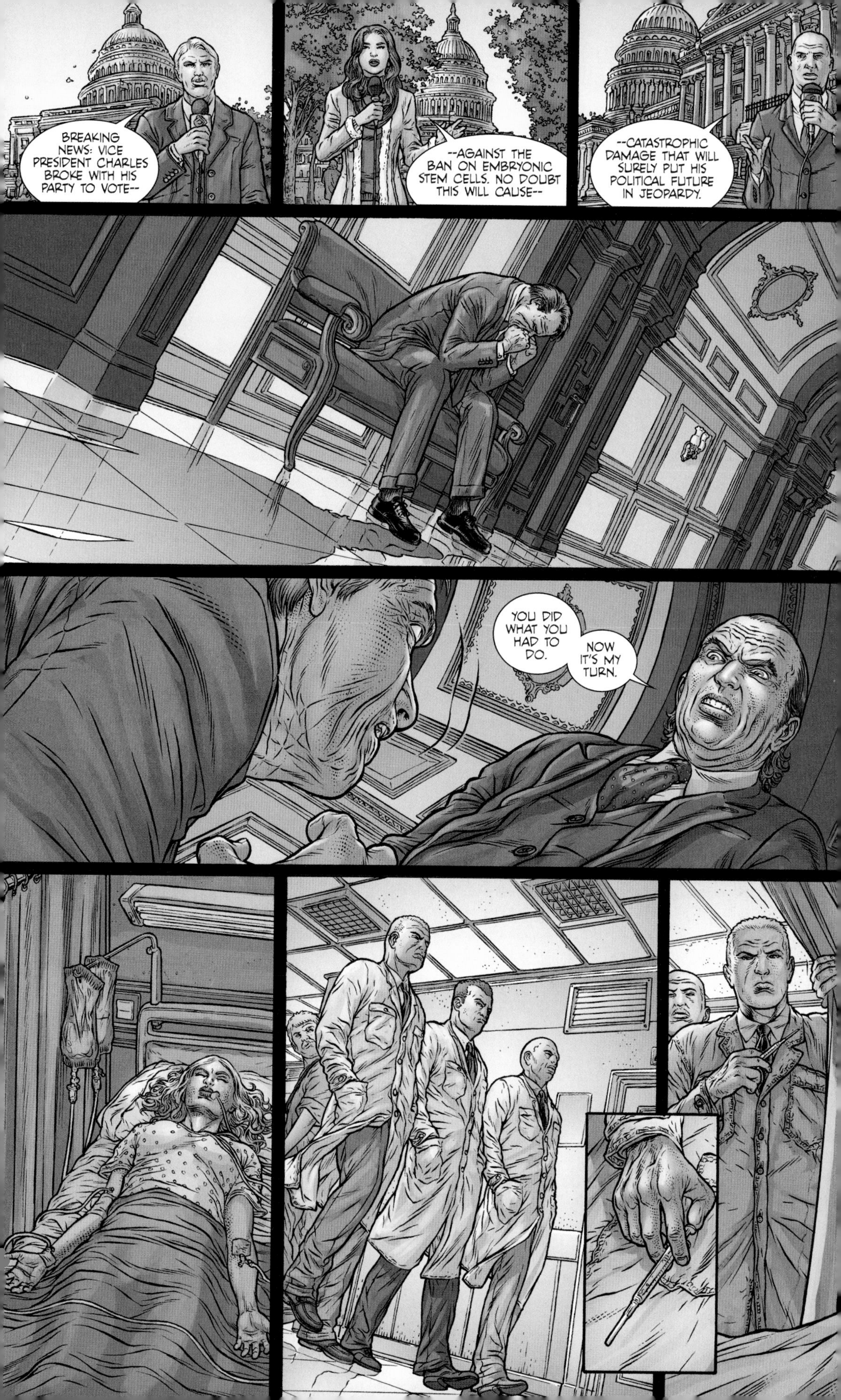
BREAKING NEWS: VICE PRESIDENT CHARLES BROKE WITH HIS PARTY TO VOTE--
--AGAINST THE BAN ON EMBRYONIC STEM CELLS. NO DOUBT THIS WILL CAUSE--
--CATASTROPHIC DAMAGE THAT WILL SURELY PUT HIS POLITICAL FUTURE IN JEOPARDY.
YOU DID WHAT YOU HAD TO DO.
NOW IT'S MY TURN.

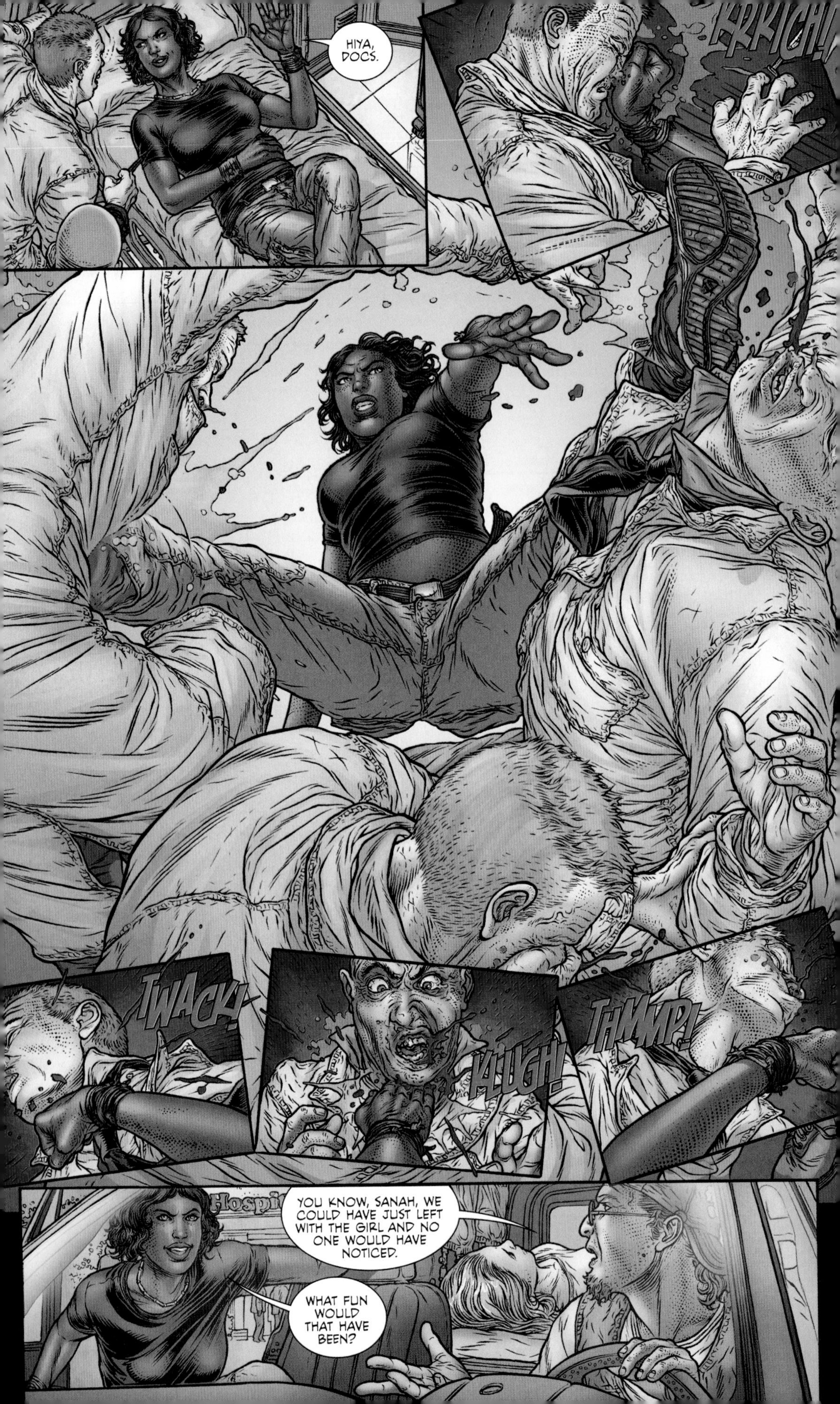
HIYA, DOCS.
TWACK!
KLUGH!
THMMP!
YOU KNOW, SANAH, WE COULD HAVE JUST LEFT WITH THE GIRL AND NO ONE WOULD HAVE NOTICED.
WHAT FUN WOULD THAT HAVE BEEN?

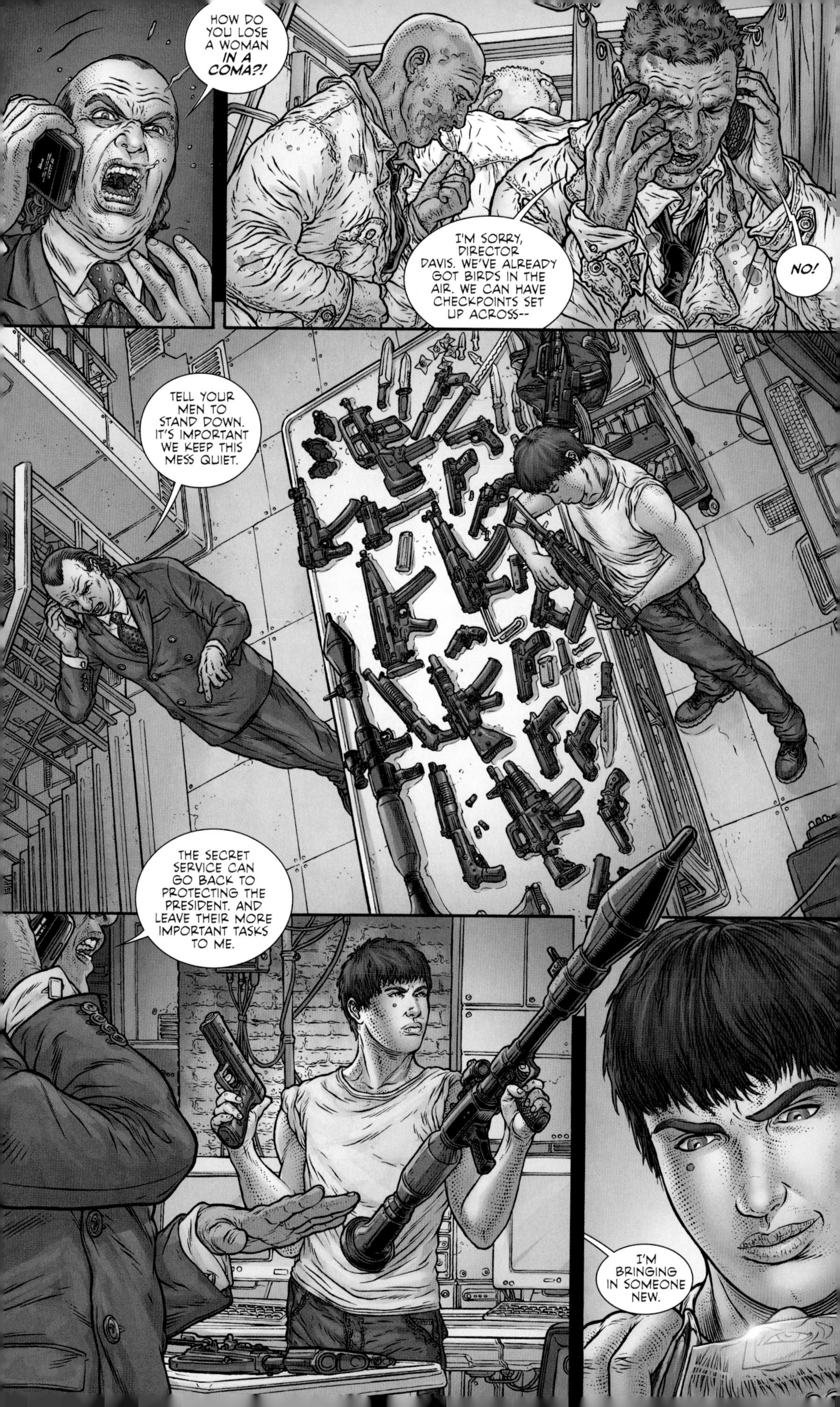
HOW DO YOU LOSE A WOMAN *IN A COMA?!*
I'M SORRY, DIRECTOR DAVIS. WE'VE ALREADY GOT BIRDS IN THE AIR. WE CAN HAVE CHECKPOINTS SET UP ACROSS--
*NO!*
TELL YOUR MEN TO STAND DOWN. IT'S IMPORTANT WE KEEP THIS MESS QUIET.
THE SECRET SERVICE CAN GO BACK TO PROTECTING THE PRESIDENT. AND LEAVE THEIR MORE IMPORTANT TASKS TO ME.
I'M BRINGING IN SOMEONE NEW.

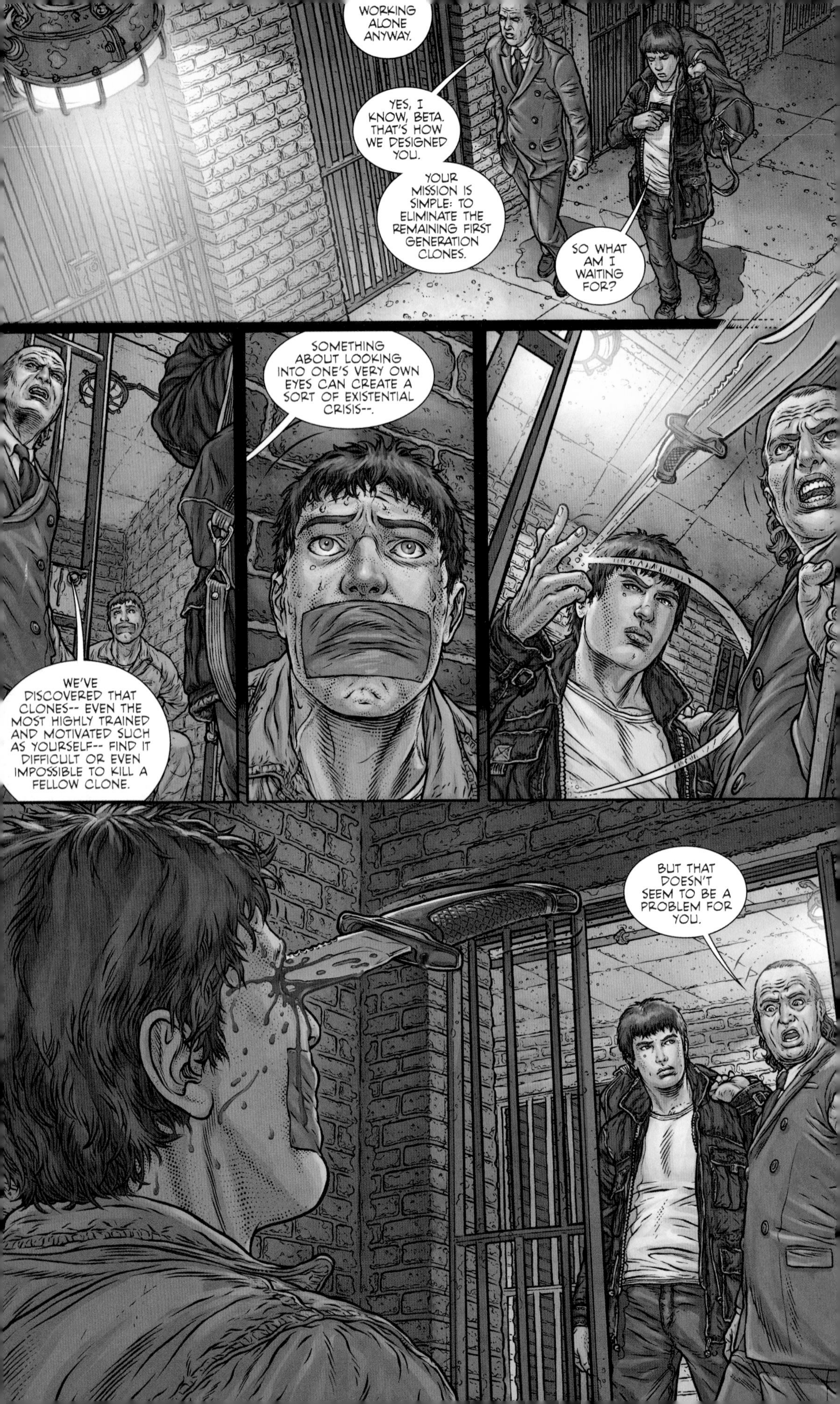
WORKING ALONE ANYWAY.
YES, I KNOW, BETA. THAT'S HOW WE DESIGNED YOU.
YOUR MISSION IS SIMPLE: TO ELIMINATE THE REMAINING FIRST GENERATION CLONES.
SO WHAT AM I WAITING FOR?
WE'VE DISCOVERED THAT CLONES-- EVEN THE MOST HIGHLY TRAINED AND MOTIVATED SUCH AS YOURSELF-- FIND IT DIFFICULT OR EVEN IMPOSSIBLE TO KILL A FELLOW CLONE.
SOMETHING ABOUT LOOKING INTO ONE'S VERY OWN EYES CAN CREATE A SORT OF EXISTENTIAL CRISIS--.
BUT THAT DOESN'T SEEM TO BE A PROBLEM FOR YOU.

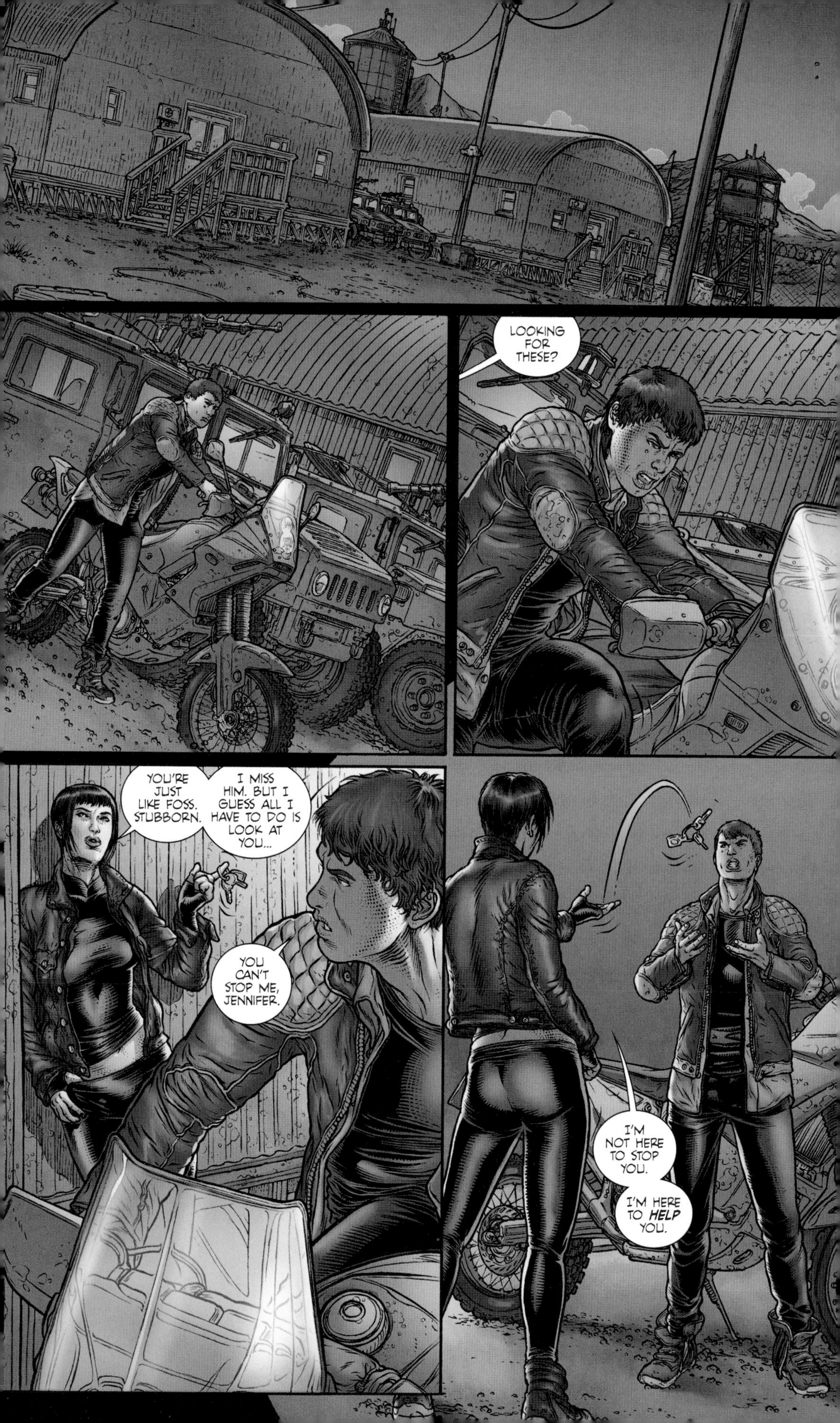
LOOKING FOR THESE?
YOU'RE JUST LIKE FOSS. STUBBORN.
I MISS HIM. BUT I GUESS ALL I HAVE TO DO IS LOOK AT YOU...
YOU CAN'T STOP ME, JENNIFER.
I'M NOT HERE TO STOP YOU.
I'M HERE TO *HELP* YOU.

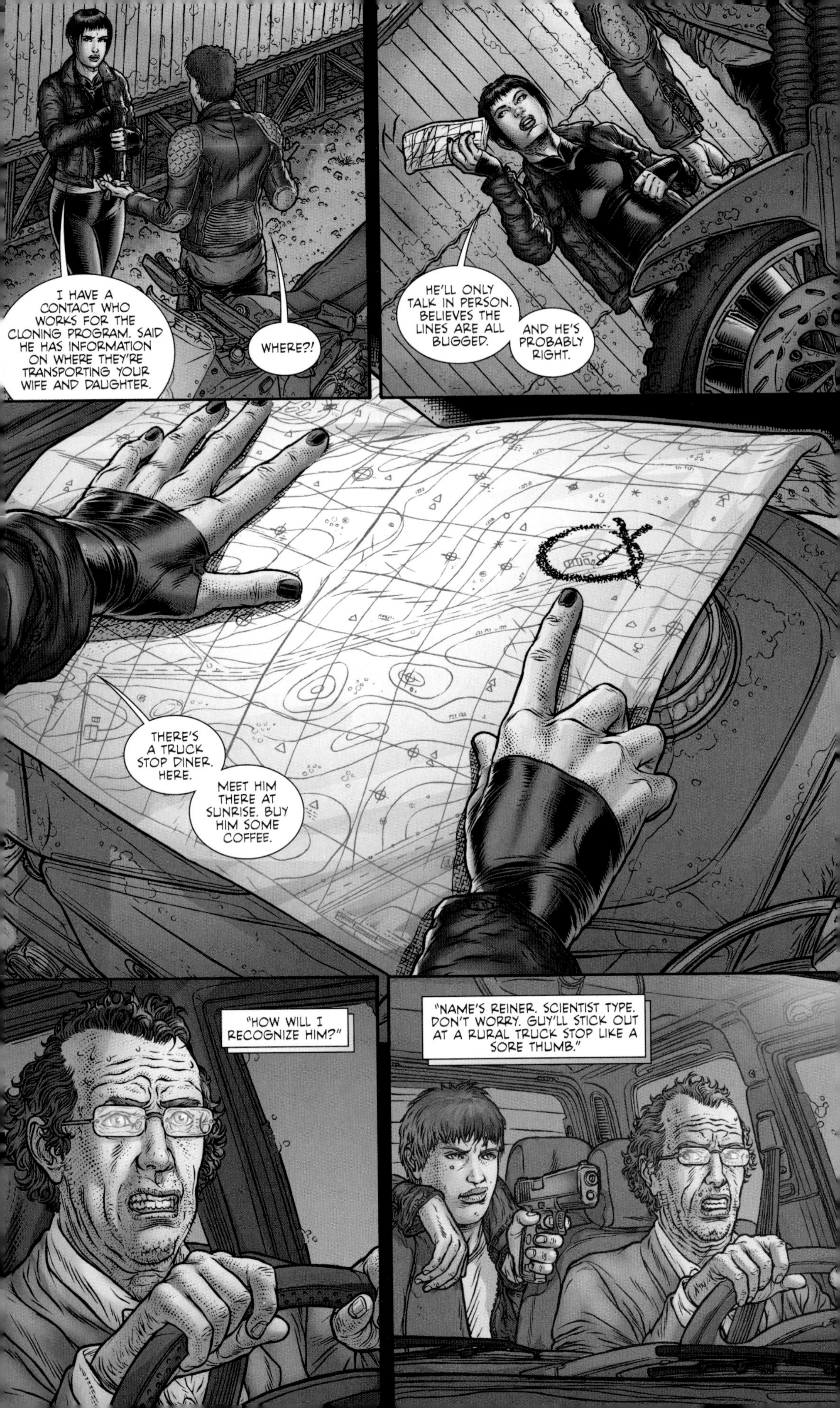
I HAVE A CONTACT WHO WORKS FOR THE CLONING PROGRAM. SAID HE HAS INFORMATION ON WHERE THEY'RE TRANSPORTING YOUR WIFE AND DAUGHTER.
WHERE?!
HE'LL ONLY TALK IN PERSON. BELIEVES THE LINES ARE ALL BUGGED.
AND HE'S PROBABLY RIGHT.
THERE'S A TRUCK STOP DINER. HERE.
MEET HIM THERE AT SUNRISE. BUY HIM SOME COFFEE.
"HOW WILL I RECOGNIZE HIM?"
"NAME'S REINER. SCIENTIST TYPE. DON'T WORRY. GUY'LL STICK OUT AT A RURAL TRUCK STOP LIKE A SORE THUMB."

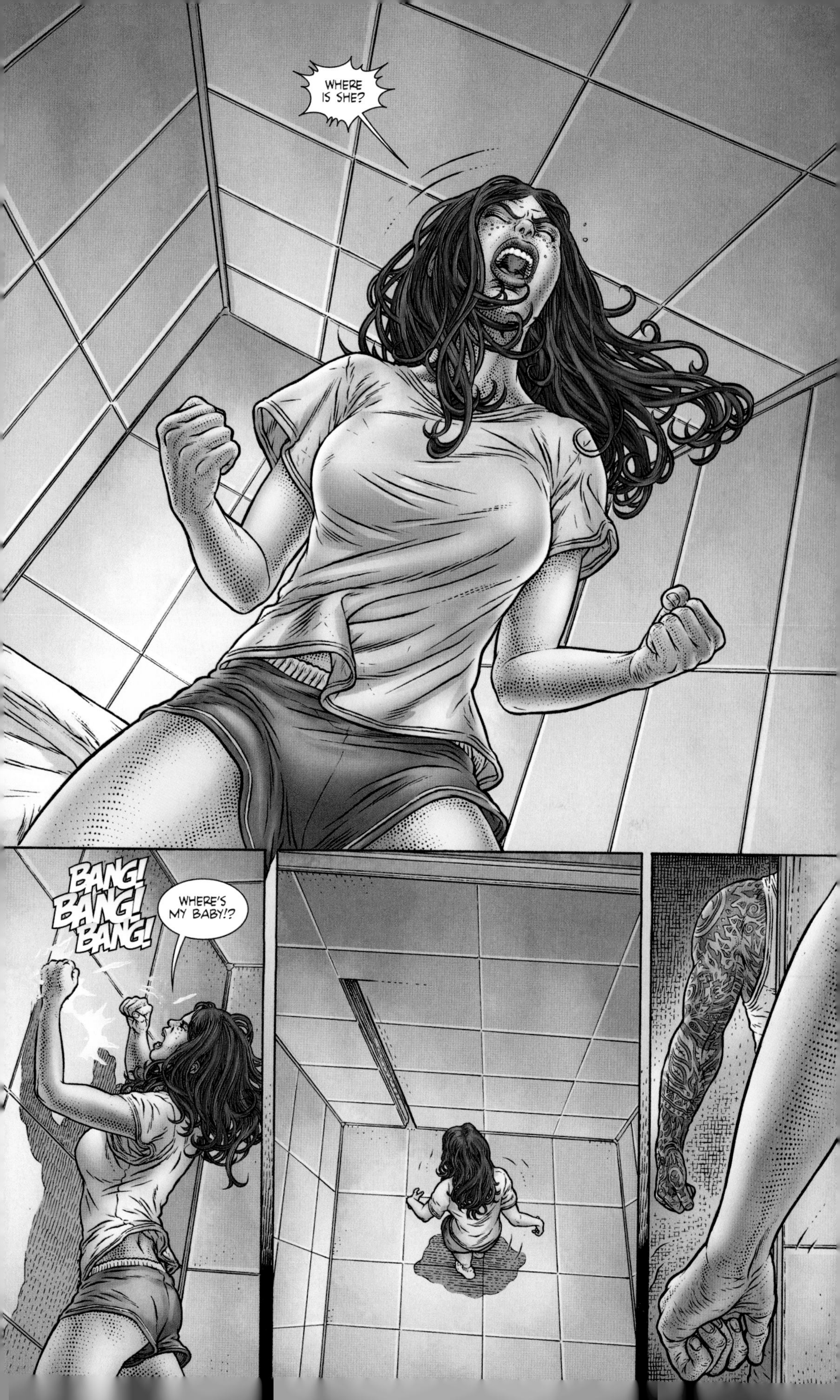
WHERE IS SHE?
BANG! BANG! BANG!
WHERE'S MY BABY!?

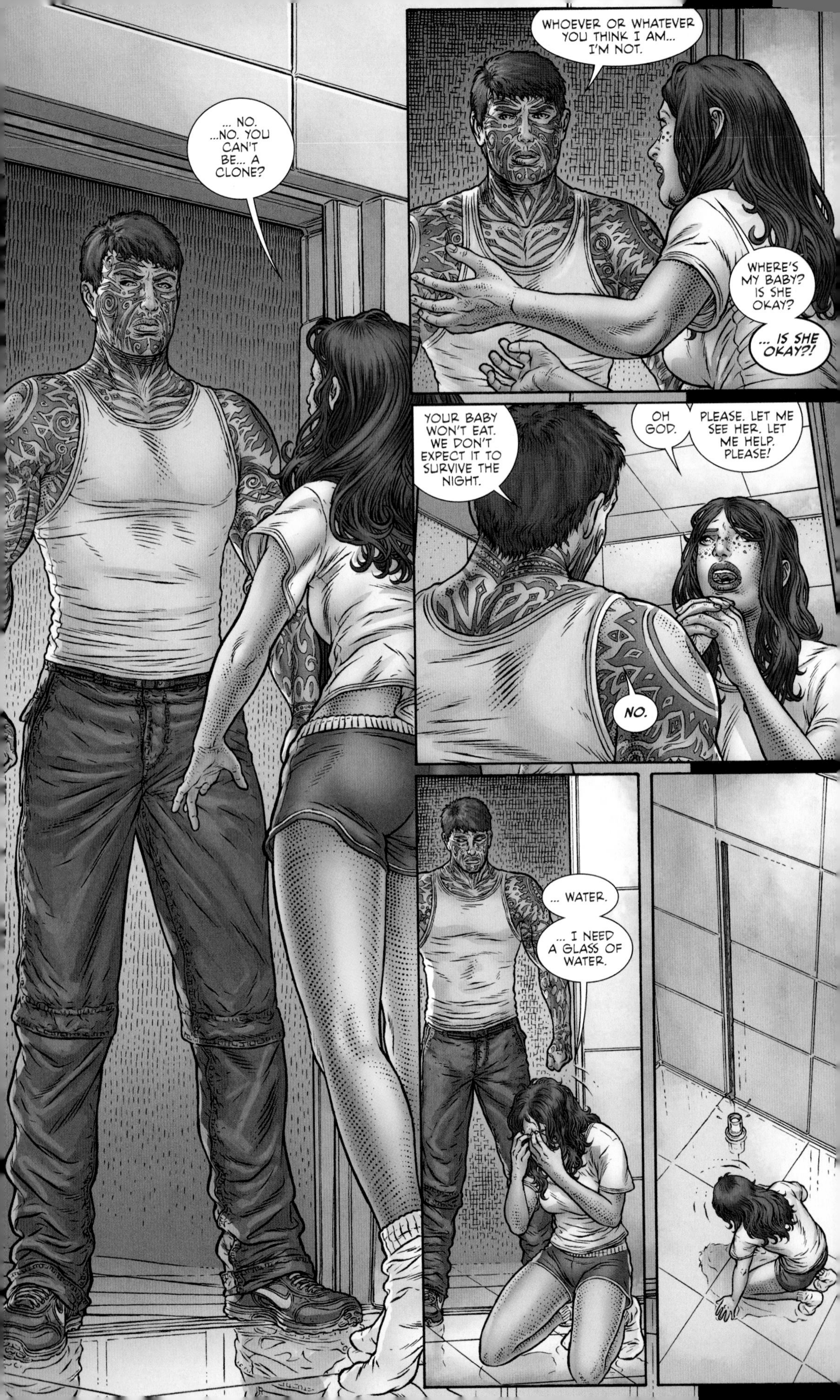
... NO.
...NO. YOU CAN'T BE... A CLONE?
WHOEVER OR WHATEVER YOU THINK I AM... I'M NOT.
WHERE'S MY BABY? IS SHE OKAY?
... IS SHE OKAY?!
YOUR BABY WON'T EAT. WE DON'T EXPECT IT TO SURVIVE THE NIGHT.
OH GOD.
PLEASE. LET ME SEE HER. LET ME HELP. PLEASE!
NO.
... WATER.
... I NEED A GLASS OF WATER.

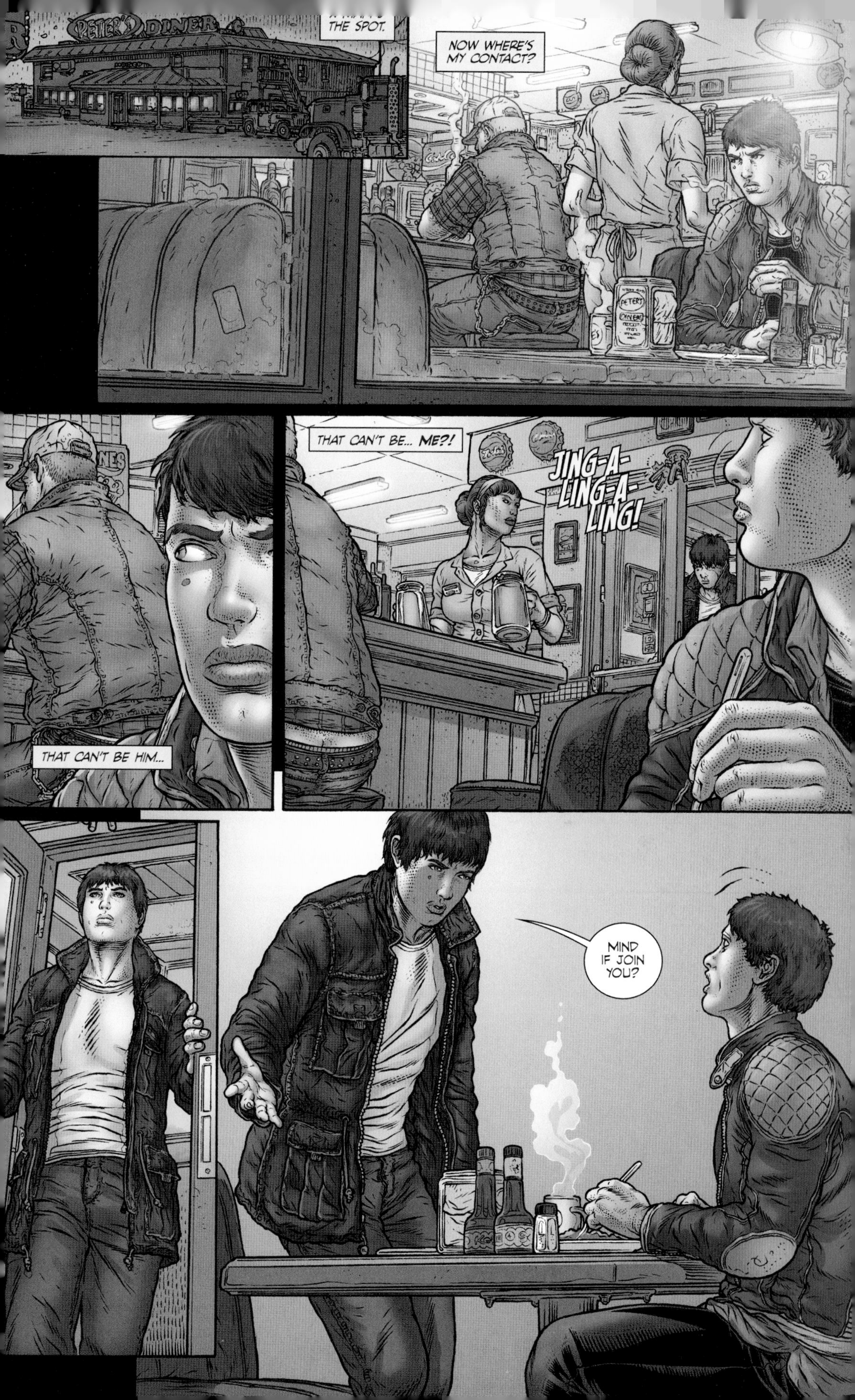
PETER'S DINER
THE SPOT.
NOW WHERE'S MY CONTACT?
THAT CAN'T BE HIM...
THAT CAN'T BE... ME?!
JING-A-LING-A-LING!
MIND IF JOIN YOU?

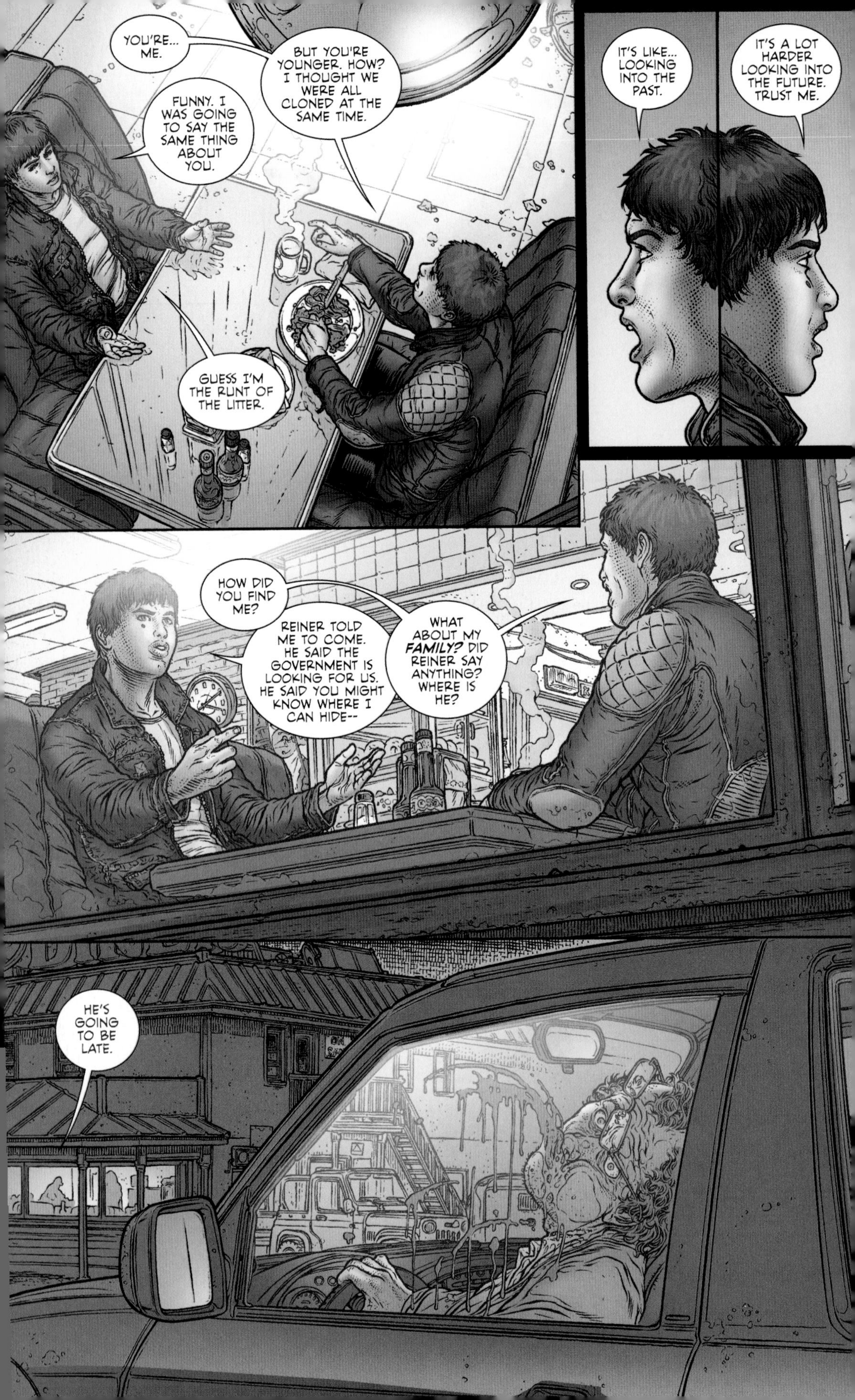

YOU'RE... ME.
BUT YOU'RE YOUNGER. HOW? I THOUGHT WE WERE ALL CLONED AT THE SAME TIME.
FUNNY. I WAS GOING TO SAY THE SAME THING ABOUT YOU.
GUESS I'M THE RUNT OF THE LITTER.
IT'S LIKE... LOOKING INTO THE PAST.
IT'S A LOT HARDER LOOKING INTO THE FUTURE. TRUST ME.
HOW DID YOU FIND ME?
REINER TOLD ME TO COME. HE SAID THE GOVERNMENT IS LOOKING FOR US. HE SAID YOU MIGHT KNOW WHERE I CAN HIDE--
WHAT ABOUT MY FAMILY? DID REINER SAY ANYTHING? WHERE IS HE?
HE'S GOING TO BE LATE.

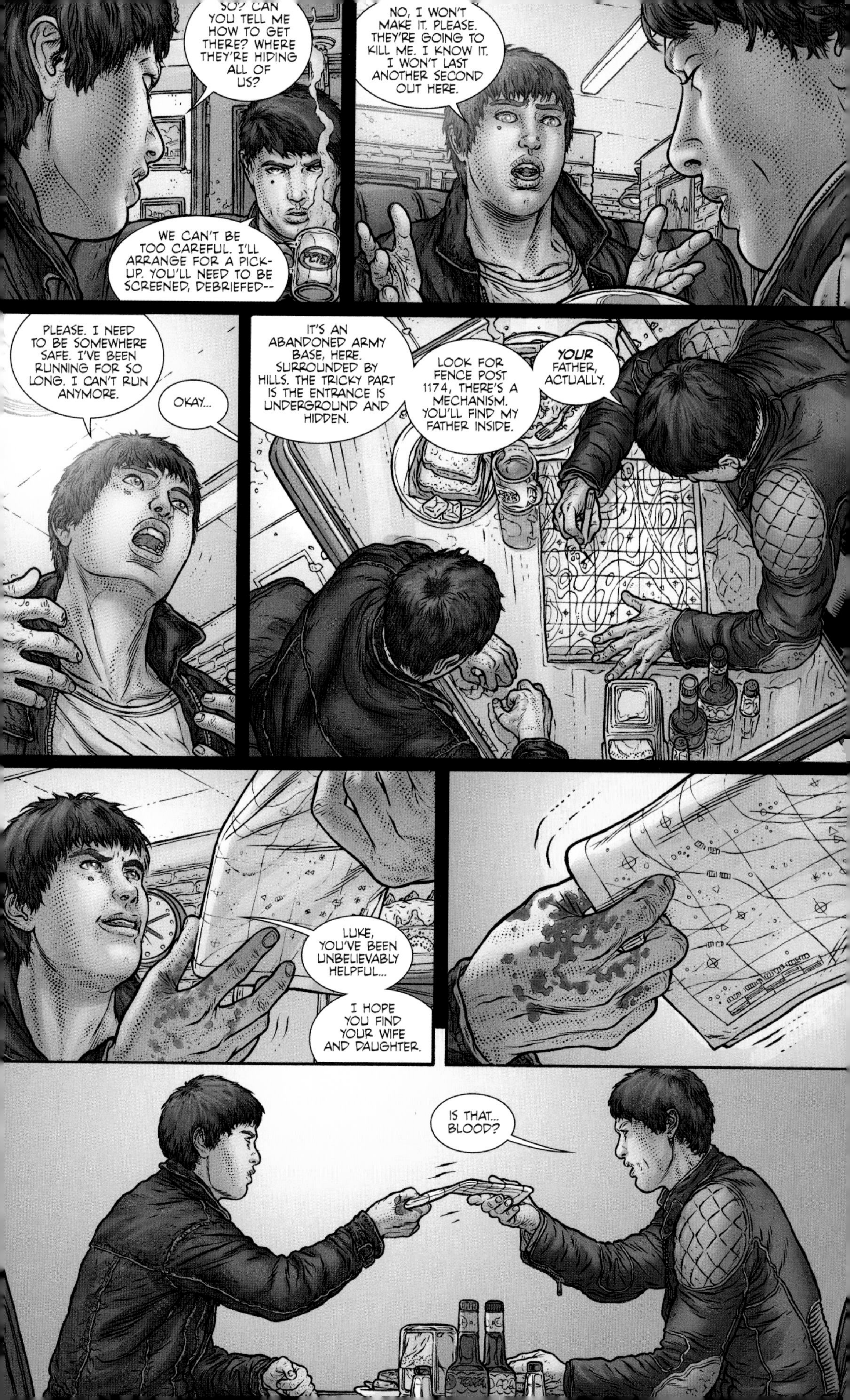
SO? CAN YOU TELL ME HOW TO GET THERE? WHERE THEY'RE HIDING ALL OF US?
WE CAN'T BE TOO CAREFUL. I'LL ARRANGE FOR A PICK-UP. YOU'LL NEED TO BE SCREENED, DEBRIEFED--
NO, I WON'T MAKE IT. PLEASE. THEY'RE GOING TO KILL ME. I KNOW IT. I WON'T LAST ANOTHER SECOND OUT HERE.
PLEASE. I NEED TO BE SOMEWHERE SAFE. I'VE BEEN RUNNING FOR SO LONG. I CAN'T RUN ANYMORE.
OKAY...
IT'S AN ABANDONED ARMY BASE, HERE. SURROUNDED BY HILLS. THE TRICKY PART IS THE ENTRANCE IS UNDERGROUND AND HIDDEN.
LOOK FOR FENCE POST 1174, THERE'S A MECHANISM. YOU'LL FIND MY FATHER INSIDE.
YOUR FATHER, ACTUALLY.
LUKE, YOU'VE BEEN UNBELIEVABLY HELPFUL...
I HOPE YOU FIND YOUR WIFE AND DAUGHTER.
IS THAT... BLOOD?

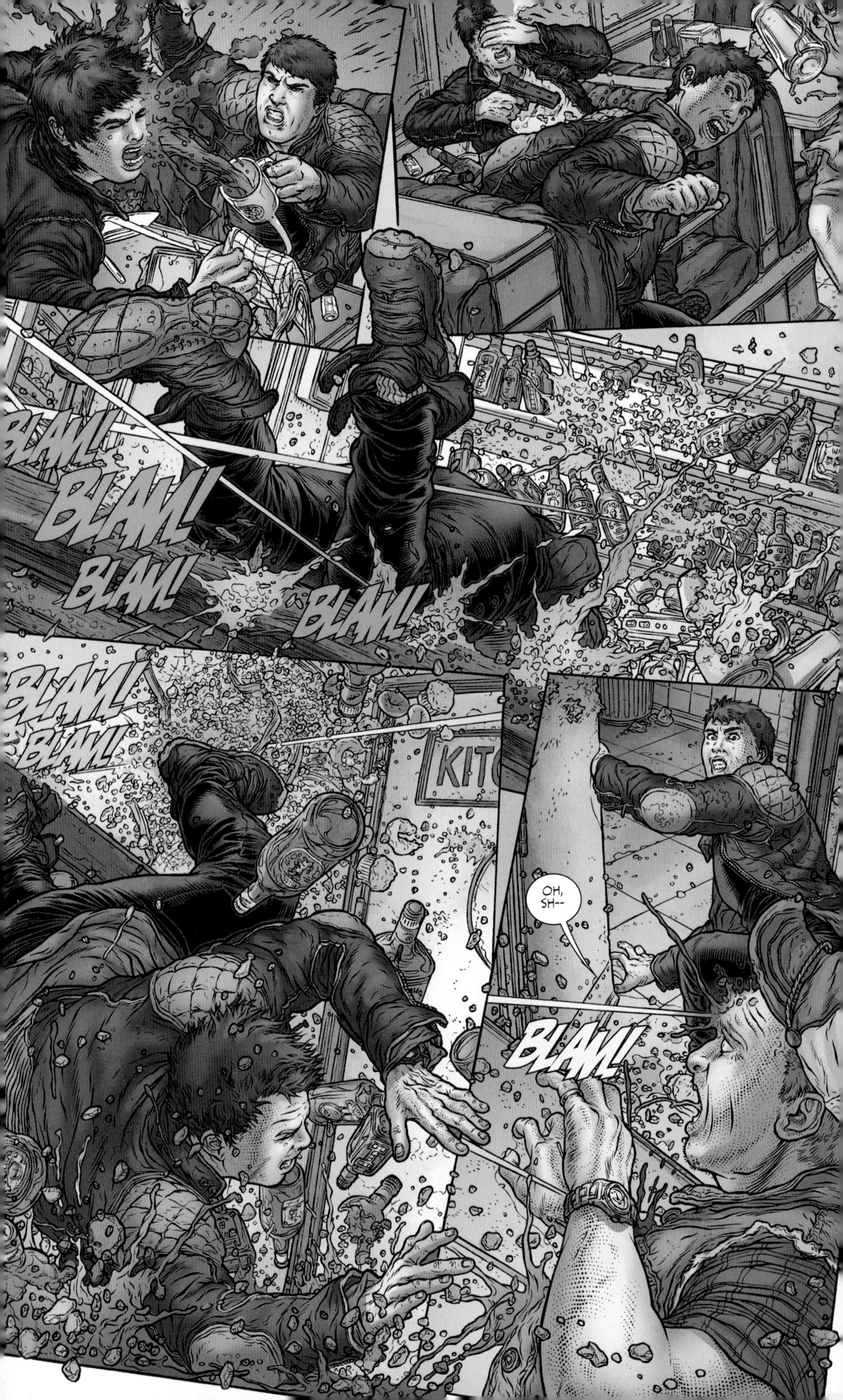
BLAM!
BLAM!
BLAM!
BLAM!
BLAM!
BLAM!
KITC
OH, SH--
BLAM!

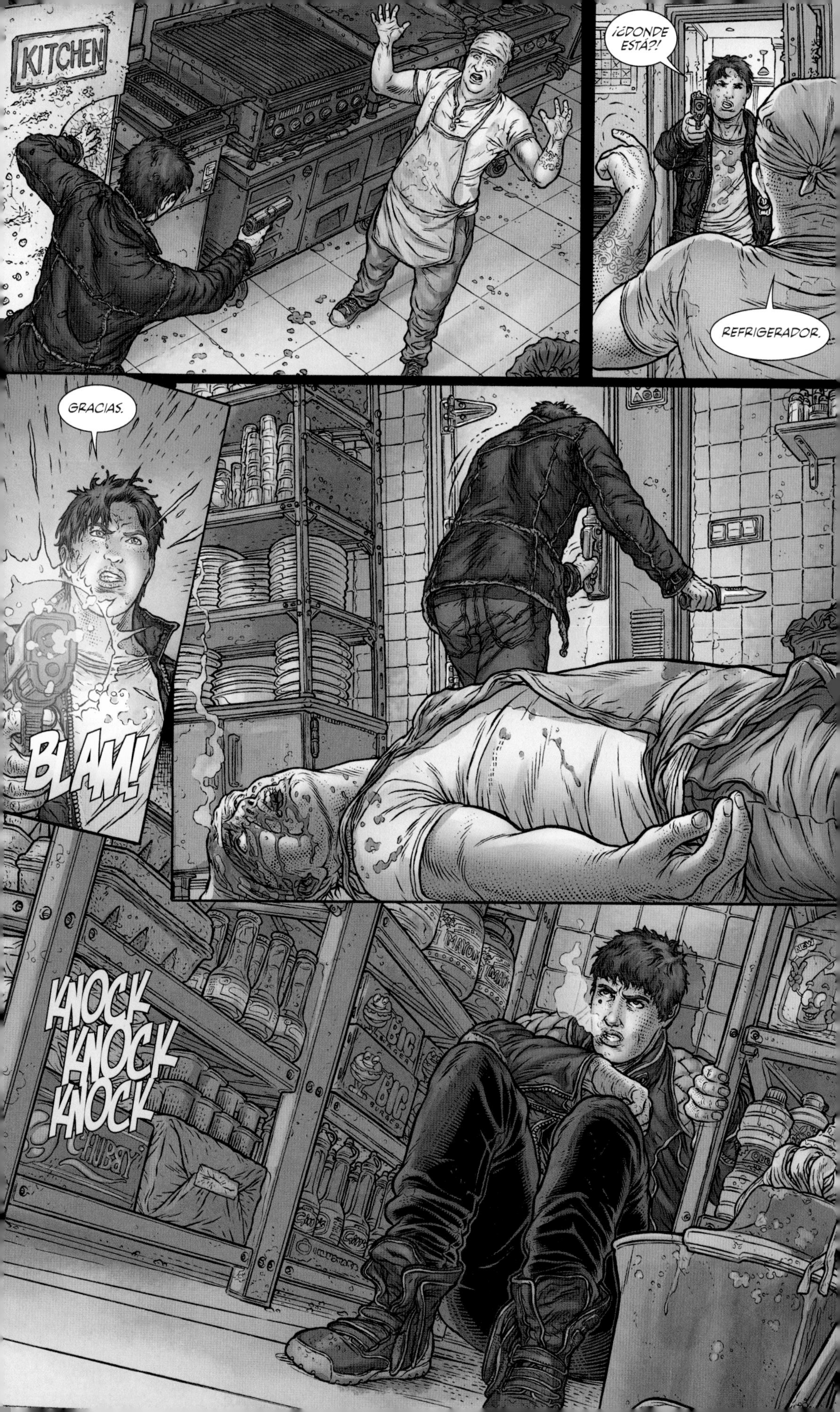
KITCHEN
¡¿DONDE ESTÁ?!
REFRIGERADOR.
GRACIAS.
BLAM!
KNOCK
KNOCK
KNOCK

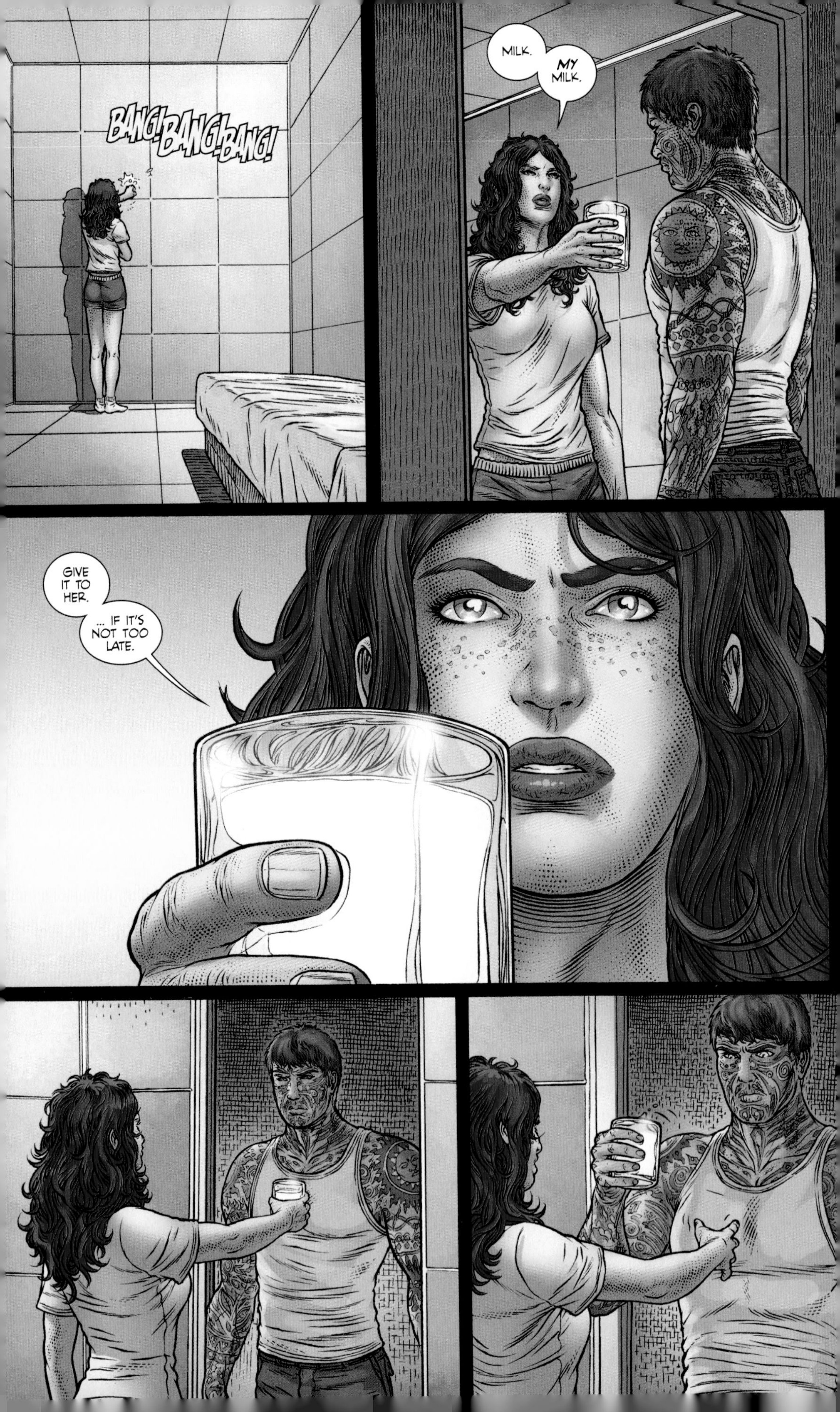
BANG! BANG! BANG!
MILK.
MY MILK.
GIVE IT TO HER.
... IF IT'S NOT TOO LATE.

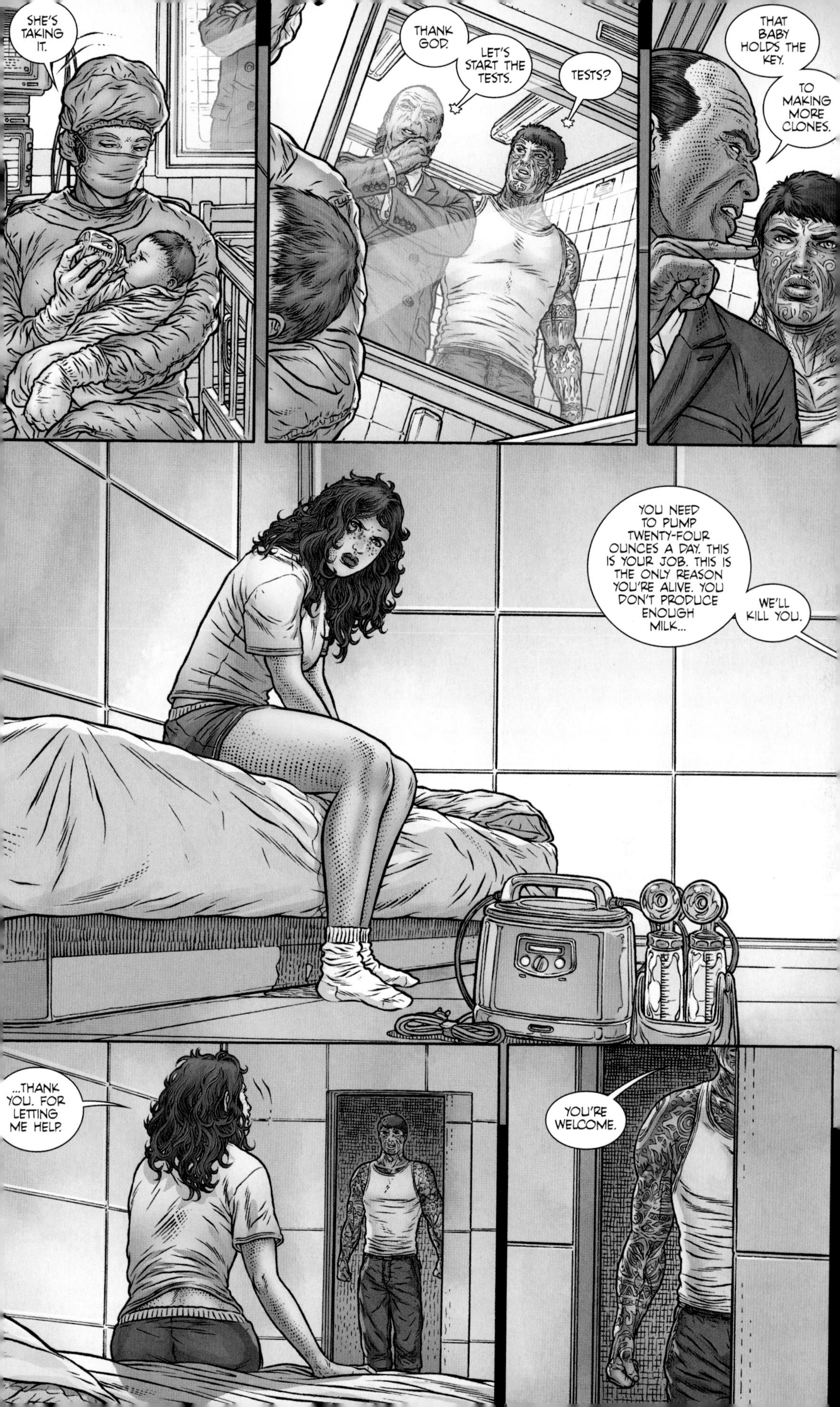
SHE'S TAKING IT.
THANK GOD.
LET'S START THE TESTS.
TESTS?
THAT BABY HOLDS THE KEY.
TO MAKING MORE CLONES.
YOU NEED TO PUMP TWENTY-FOUR OUNCES A DAY. THIS IS YOUR JOB. THIS IS THE ONLY REASON YOU'RE ALIVE. YOU DON'T PRODUCE ENOUGH MILK...
WE'LL KILL YOU.
...THANK YOU. FOR LETTING ME HELP.
YOU'RE WELCOME.

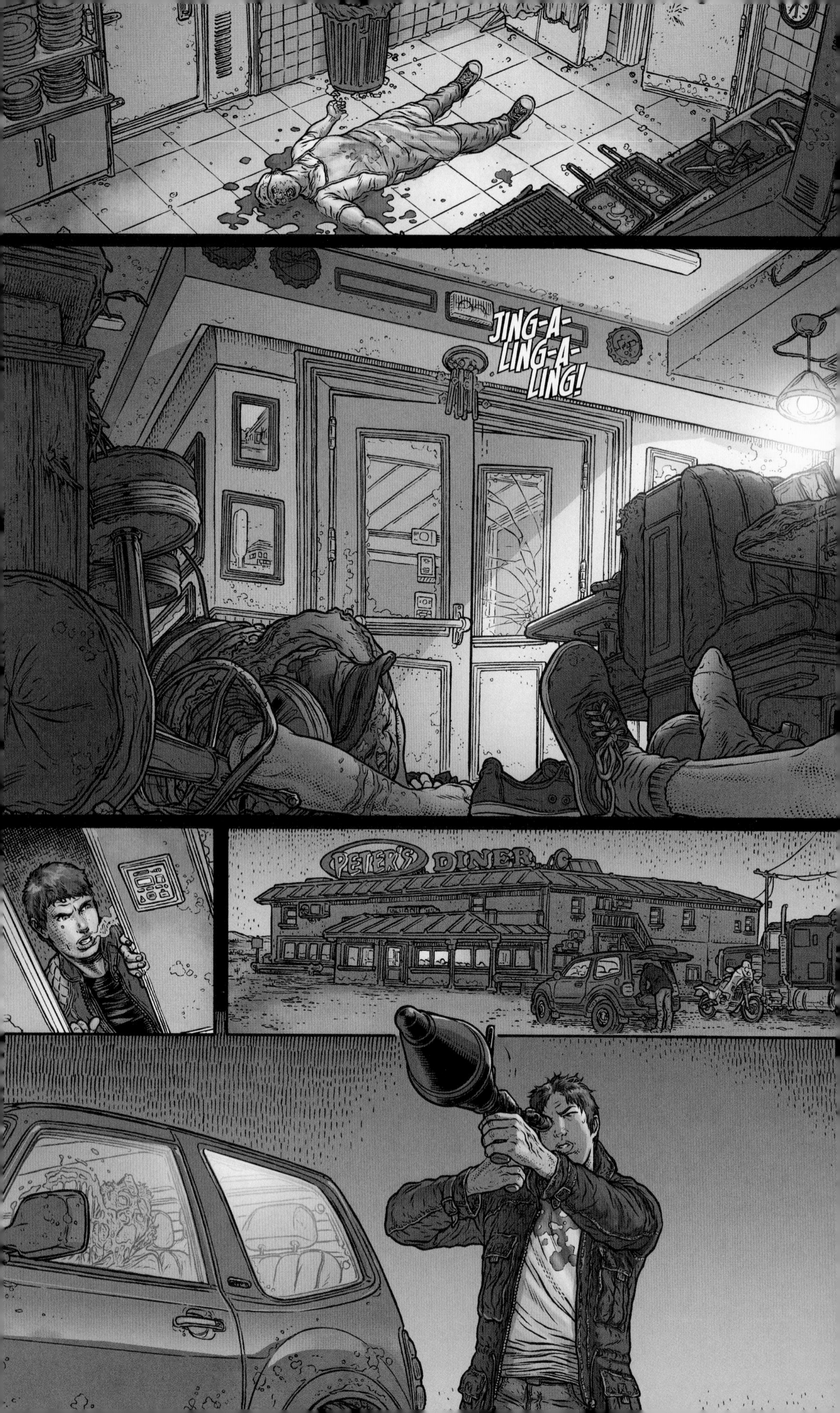
JING-A-
LING-A-
LING!
PETER'S DINER

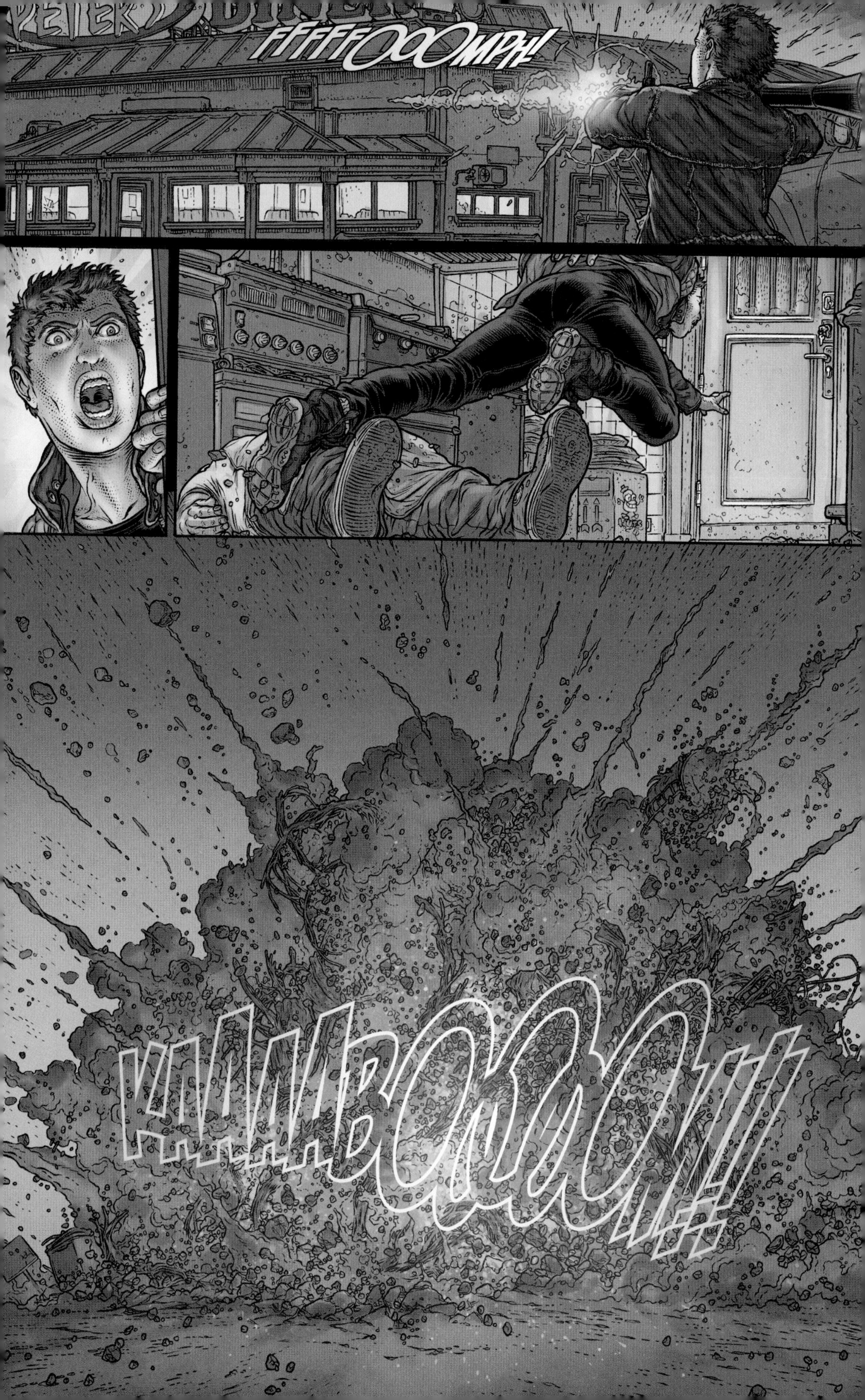
FFFFOOOMPH!
KWAMBOOOM!!

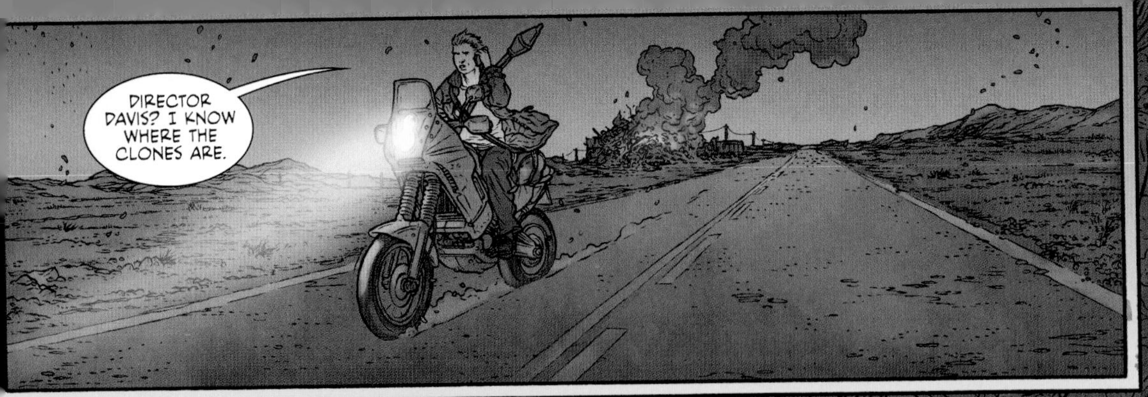
DIRECTOR DAVIS? I KNOW WHERE THE CLONES ARE.

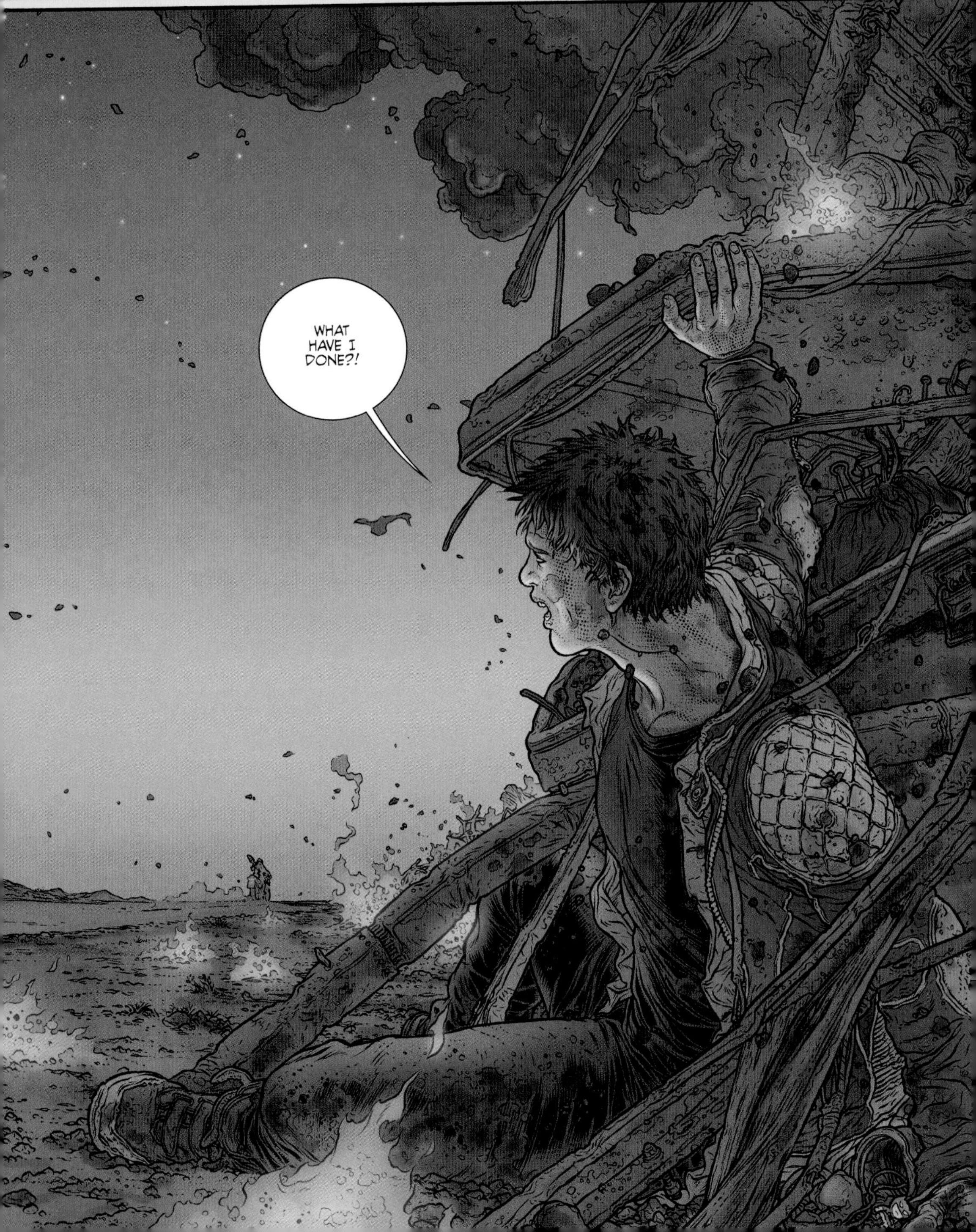
WHAT HAVE I DONE?!

# CHAPTER 7

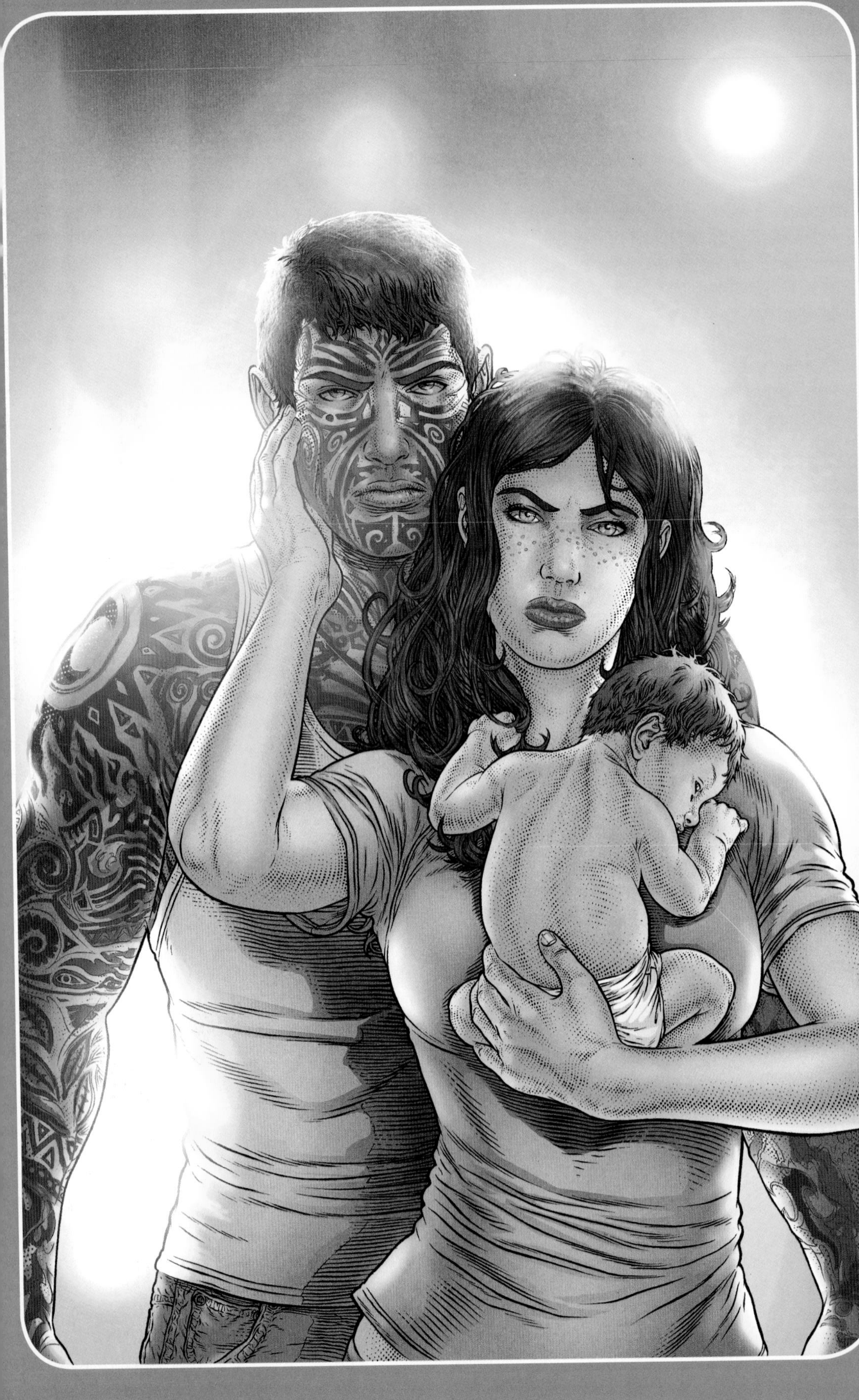

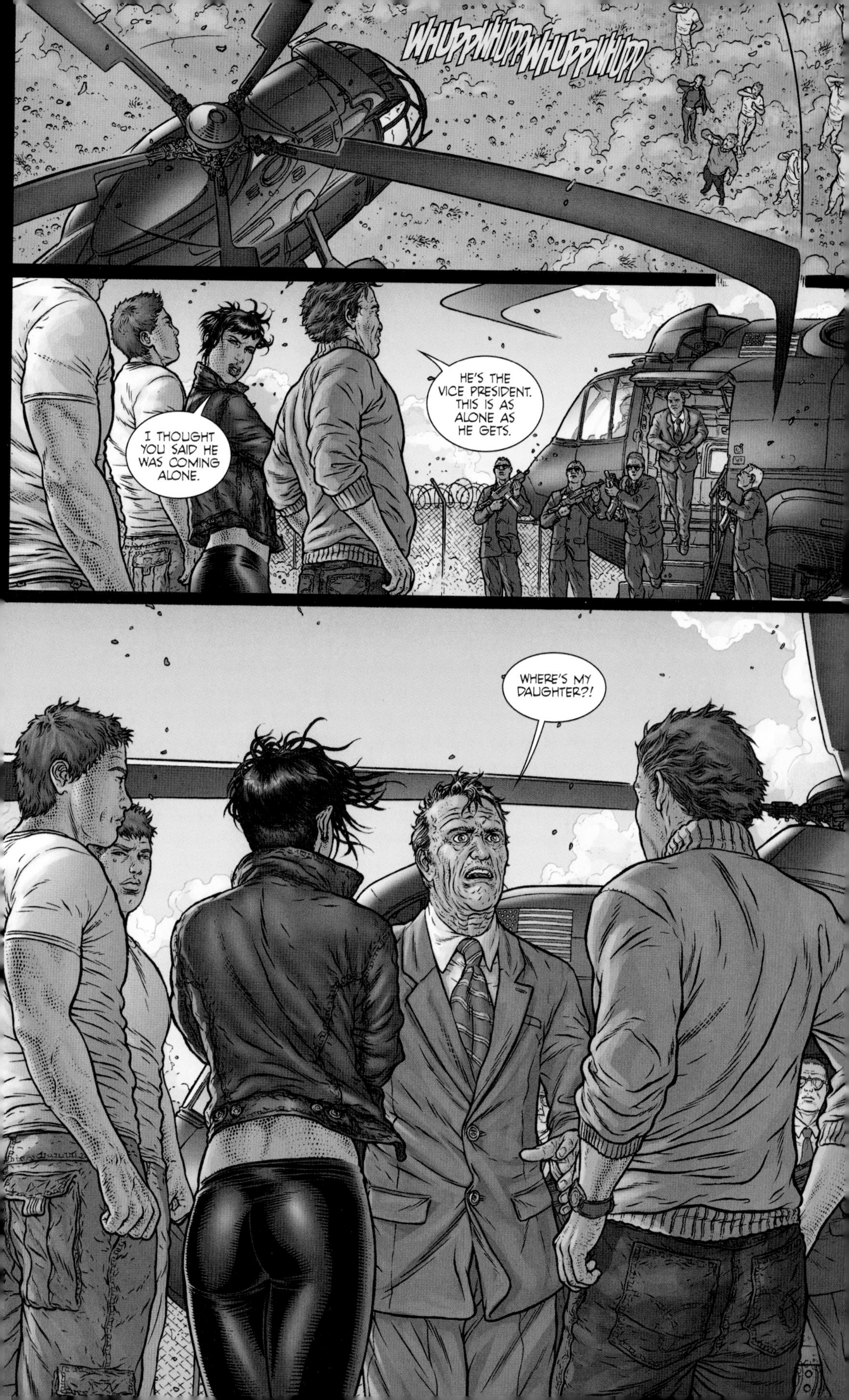
WHUPPWHUPPWHUPPWHUPP
I THOUGHT YOU SAID HE WAS COMING ALONE.
HE'S THE VICE PRESIDENT. THIS IS AS ALONE AS HE GETS.
WHERE'S MY DAUGHTER?!

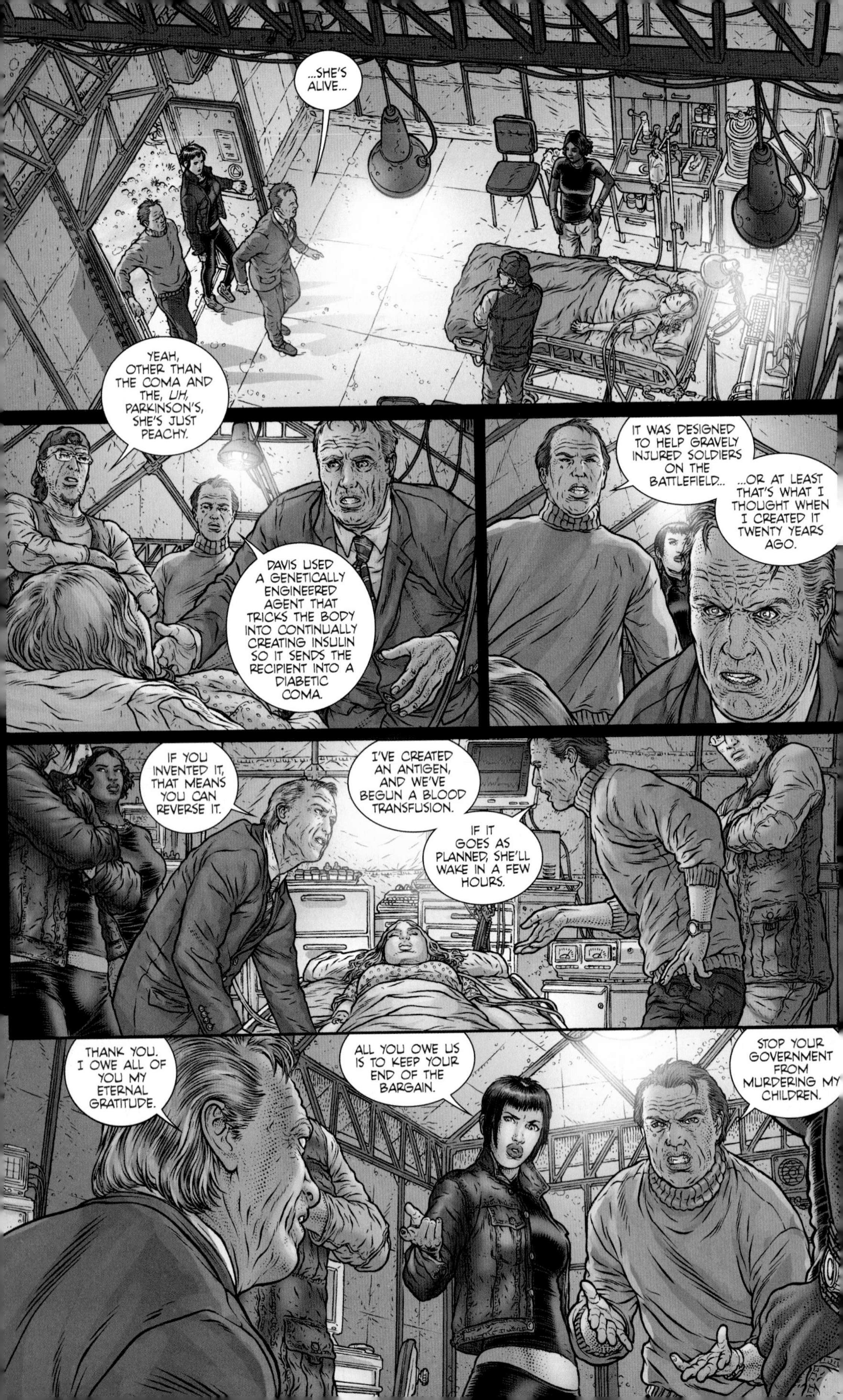
...SHE'S ALIVE...
YEAH, OTHER THAN THE COMA AND THE, UH, PARKINSON'S, SHE'S JUST PEACHY.
DAVIS USED A GENETICALLY ENGINEERED AGENT THAT TRICKS THE BODY INTO CONTINUALLY CREATING INSULIN SO IT SENDS THE RECIPIENT INTO A DIABETIC COMA.
IT WAS DESIGNED TO HELP GRAVELY INJURED SOLDIERS ON THE BATTLEFIELD...
...OR AT LEAST THAT'S WHAT I THOUGHT WHEN I CREATED IT TWENTY YEARS AGO.
IF YOU INVENTED IT, THAT MEANS YOU CAN REVERSE IT.
I'VE CREATED AN ANTIGEN, AND WE'VE BEGUN A BLOOD TRANSFUSION.
IF IT GOES AS PLANNED, SHE'LL WAKE IN A FEW HOURS.
THANK YOU. I OWE ALL OF YOU MY ETERNAL GRATITUDE.
ALL YOU OWE US IS TO KEEP YOUR END OF THE BARGAIN.
STOP YOUR GOVERNMENT FROM MURDERING MY CHILDREN.

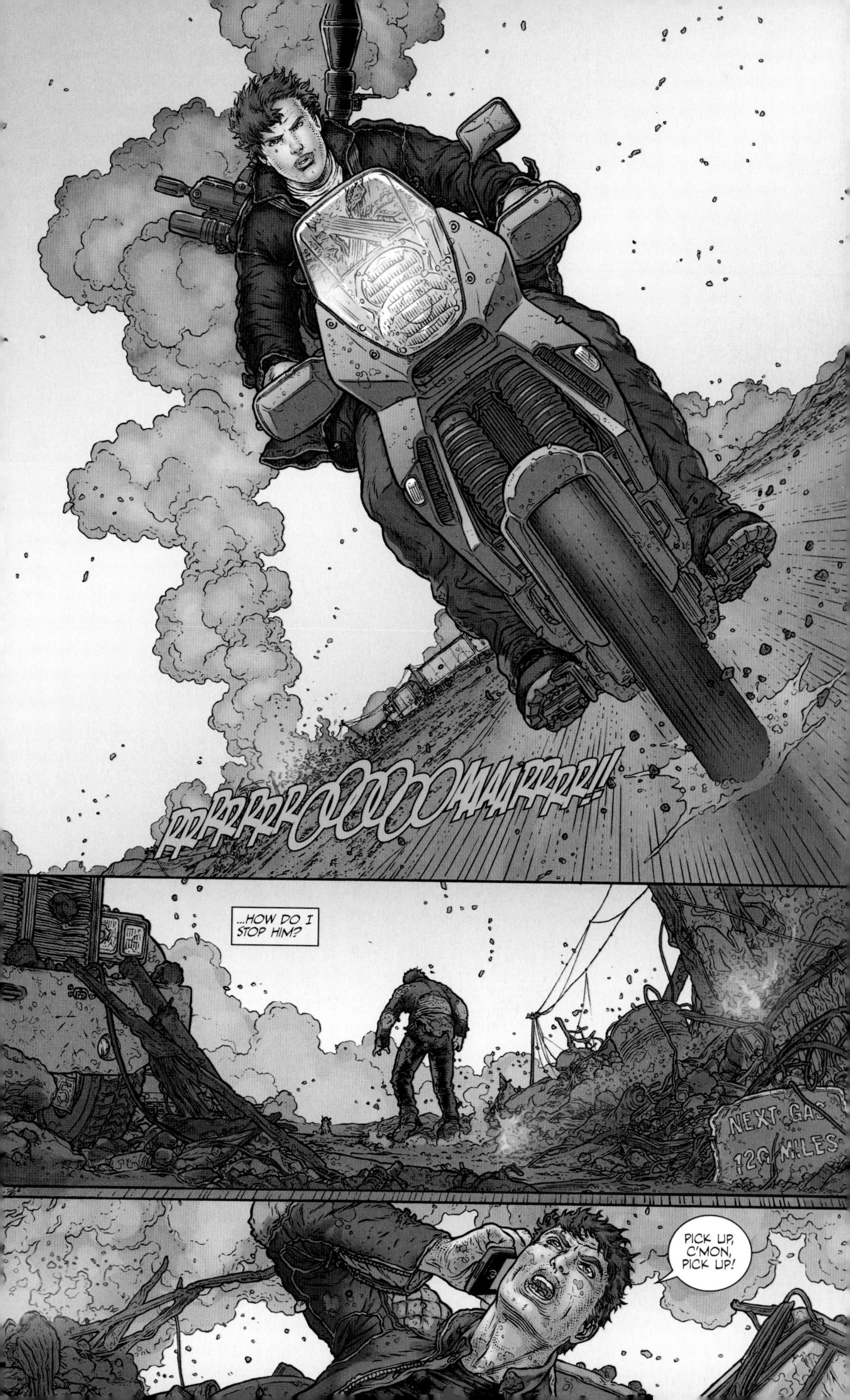
RRRRRRRRROOOOOOOOAAARRRR!!
...HOW DO I STOP HIM?
NEXT GAS 120 MILES
PICK UP, C'MON, PICK UP!

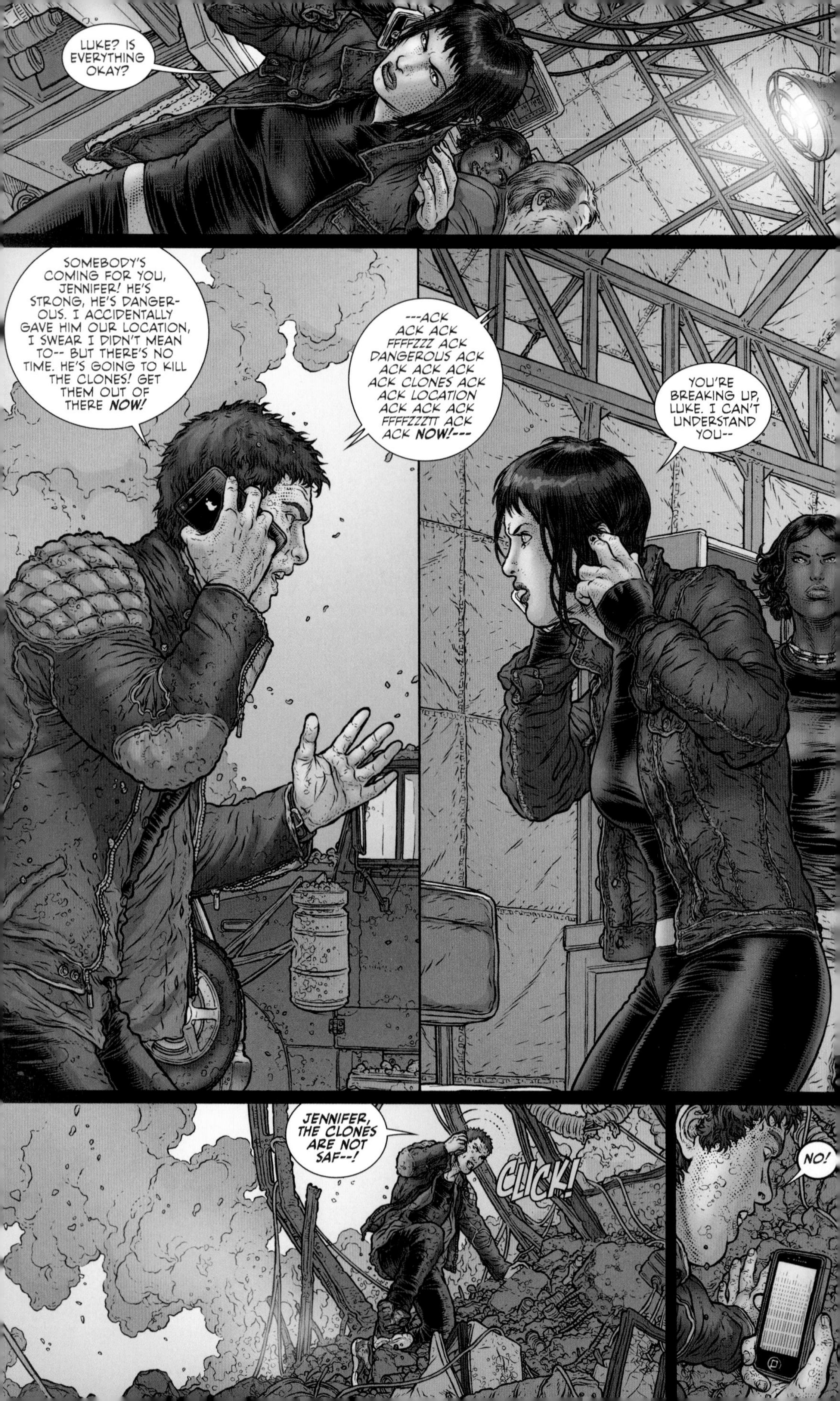
LUKE? IS EVERYTHING OKAY?
SOMEBODY'S COMING FOR YOU, JENNIFER! HE'S STRONG, HE'S DANGER-OUS. I ACCIDENTALLY GAVE HIM OUR LOCATION, I SWEAR I DIDN'T MEAN TO-- BUT THERE'S NO TIME. HE'S GOING TO KILL THE CLONES! GET THEM OUT OF THERE NOW!
---ACK ACK ACK FFFFZZZ ACK DANGEROUS ACK ACK ACK ACK ACK CLONES ACK ACK LOCATION ACK ACK ACK FFFFZZZTT ACK ACK NOW!---
YOU'RE BREAKING UP, LUKE. I CAN'T UNDERSTAND YOU--
JENNIFER, THE CLONES ARE NOT SAF--!
CLICK!
NO!

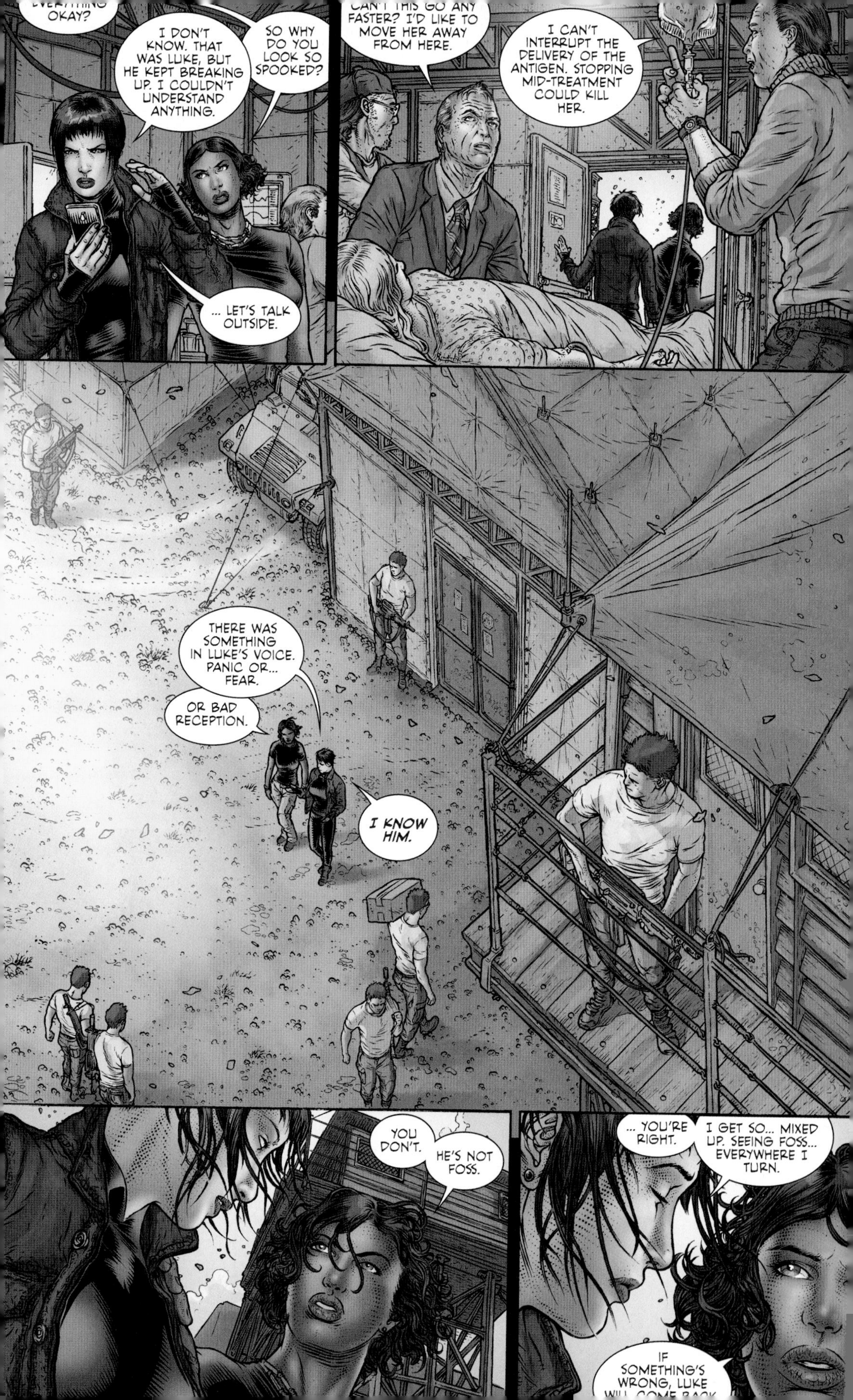
OKAY?
I DON'T KNOW. THAT WAS LUKE, BUT HE KEPT BREAKING UP. I COULDN'T UNDERSTAND ANYTHING.
SO WHY DO YOU LOOK SO SPOOKED?
... LET'S TALK OUTSIDE.
CAN'T THIS GO ANY FASTER? I'D LIKE TO MOVE HER AWAY FROM HERE.
I CAN'T INTERRUPT THE DELIVERY OF THE ANTIGEN. STOPPING MID-TREATMENT COULD KILL HER.
THERE WAS SOMETHING IN LUKE'S VOICE. PANIC OR... FEAR.
OR BAD RECEPTION.
I KNOW HIM.
YOU DON'T.
HE'S NOT FOSS.
... YOU'RE RIGHT.
I GET SO... MIXED UP. SEEING FOSS... EVERYWHERE I TURN.
IF SOMETHING'S WRONG, LUKE

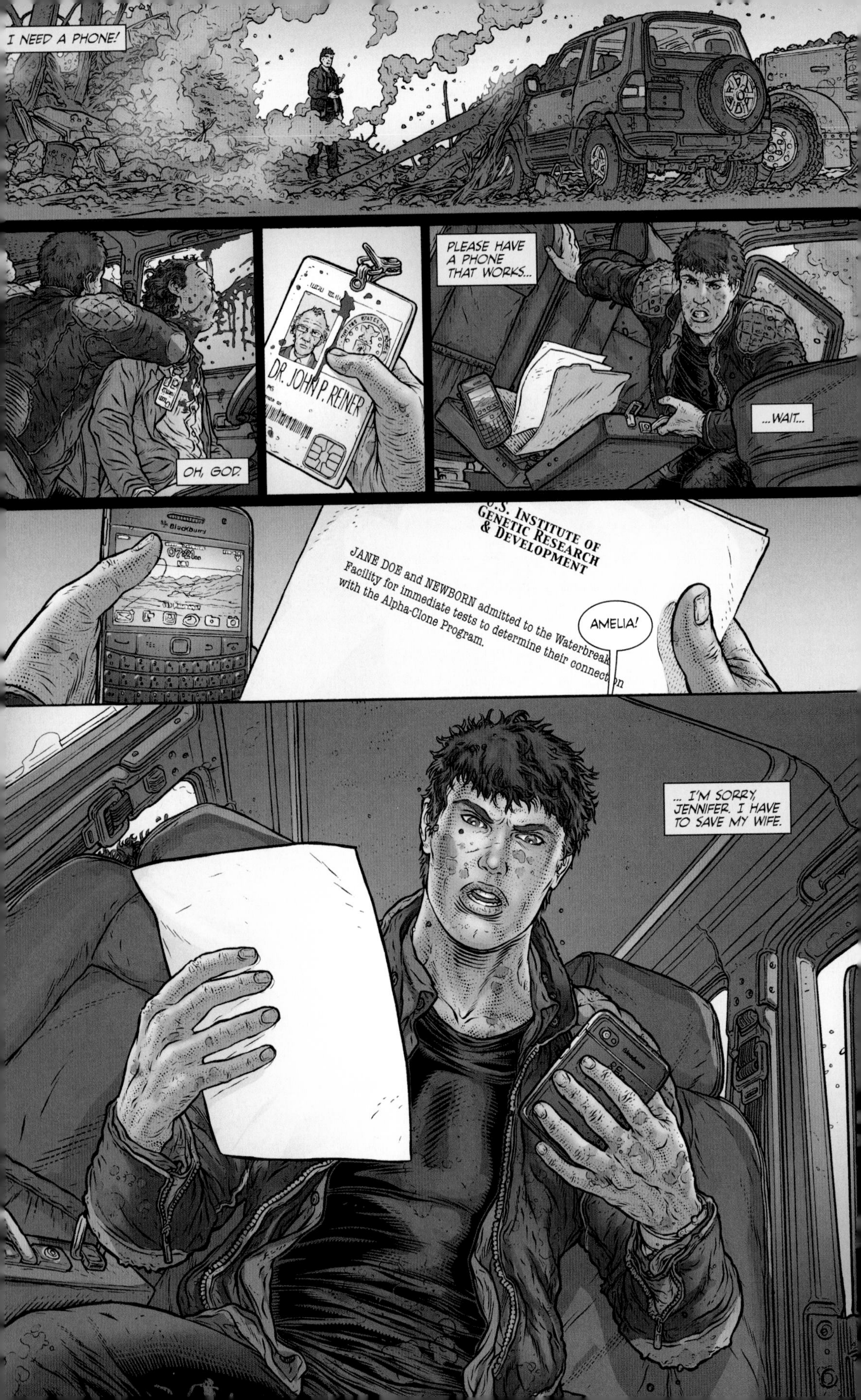
I NEED A PHONE!
OH, GOD.
DR. JOHN P. REINER
PLEASE HAVE A PHONE THAT WORKS...
...WAIT...
BlackBerry
07:21
S. INSTITUTE OF GENETIC RESEARCH & DEVELOPMENT
JANE DOE and NEWBORN admitted to the Waterbreak Facility for immediate tests to determine their connection with the Alpha-Clone Program.
AMELIA!
... I'M SORRY, JENNIFER. I HAVE TO SAVE MY WIFE.

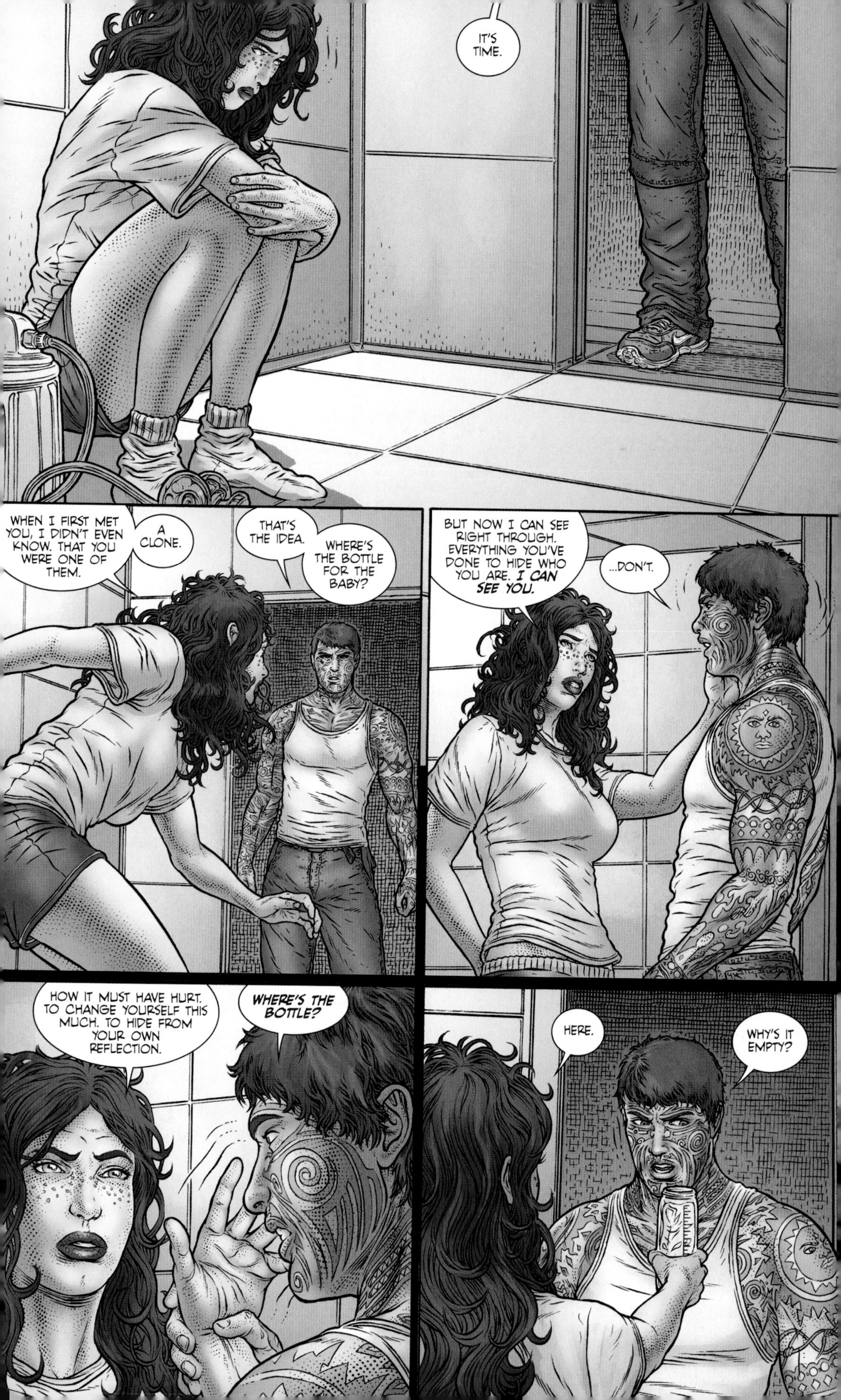

IT'S TIME.
WHEN I FIRST MET YOU, I DIDN'T EVEN KNOW. THAT YOU WERE ONE OF THEM.
A CLONE.
THAT'S THE IDEA.
WHERE'S THE BOTTLE FOR THE BABY?
BUT NOW I CAN SEE RIGHT THROUGH. EVERYTHING YOU'VE DONE TO HIDE WHO YOU ARE. *I CAN SEE YOU.*
...DON'T.
HOW IT MUST HAVE HURT. TO CHANGE YOURSELF THIS MUCH. TO HIDE FROM YOUR OWN REFLECTION.
*WHERE'S THE BOTTLE?*
HERE.
WHY'S IT EMPTY?

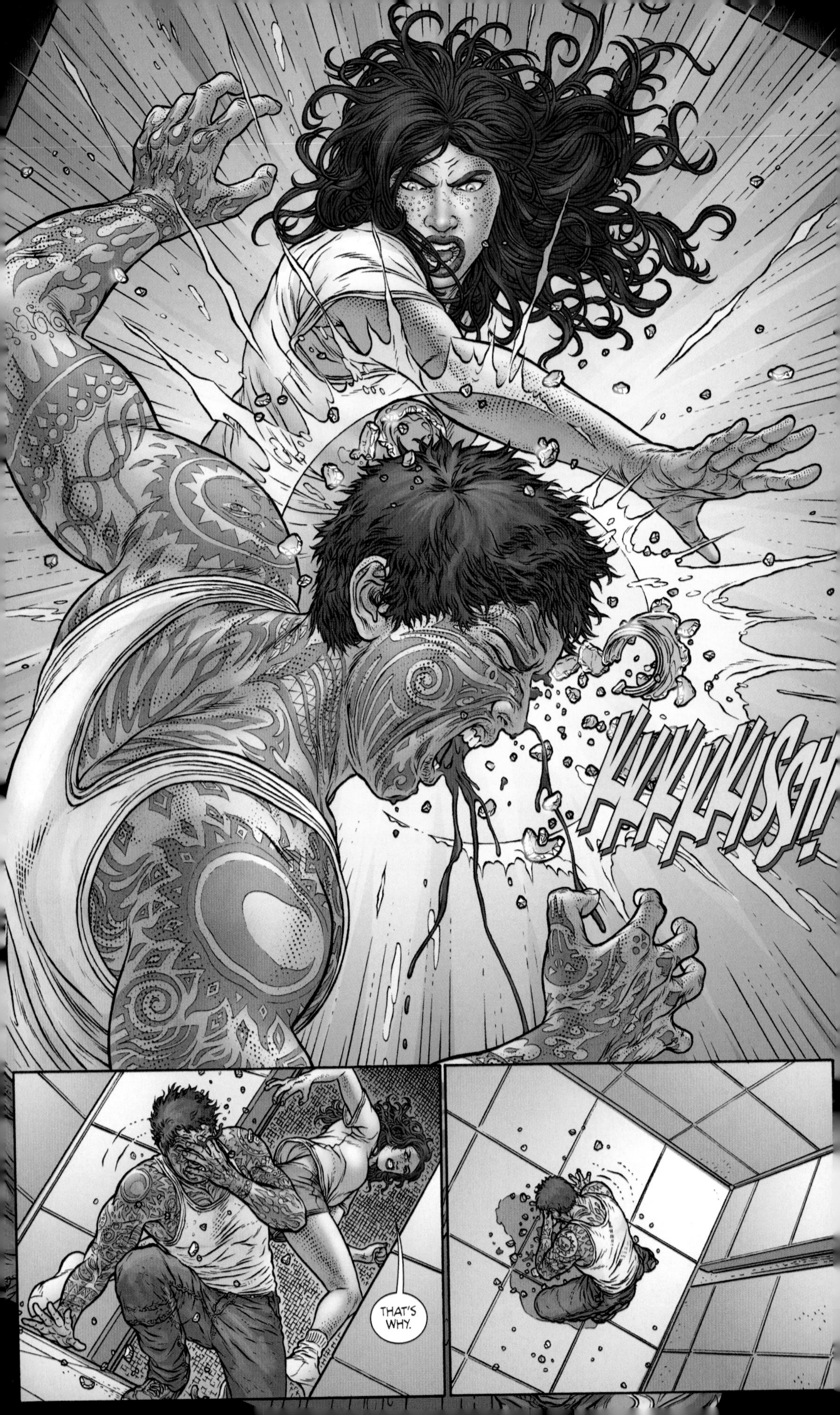
KHHHHUSH!!
THAT'S WHY.

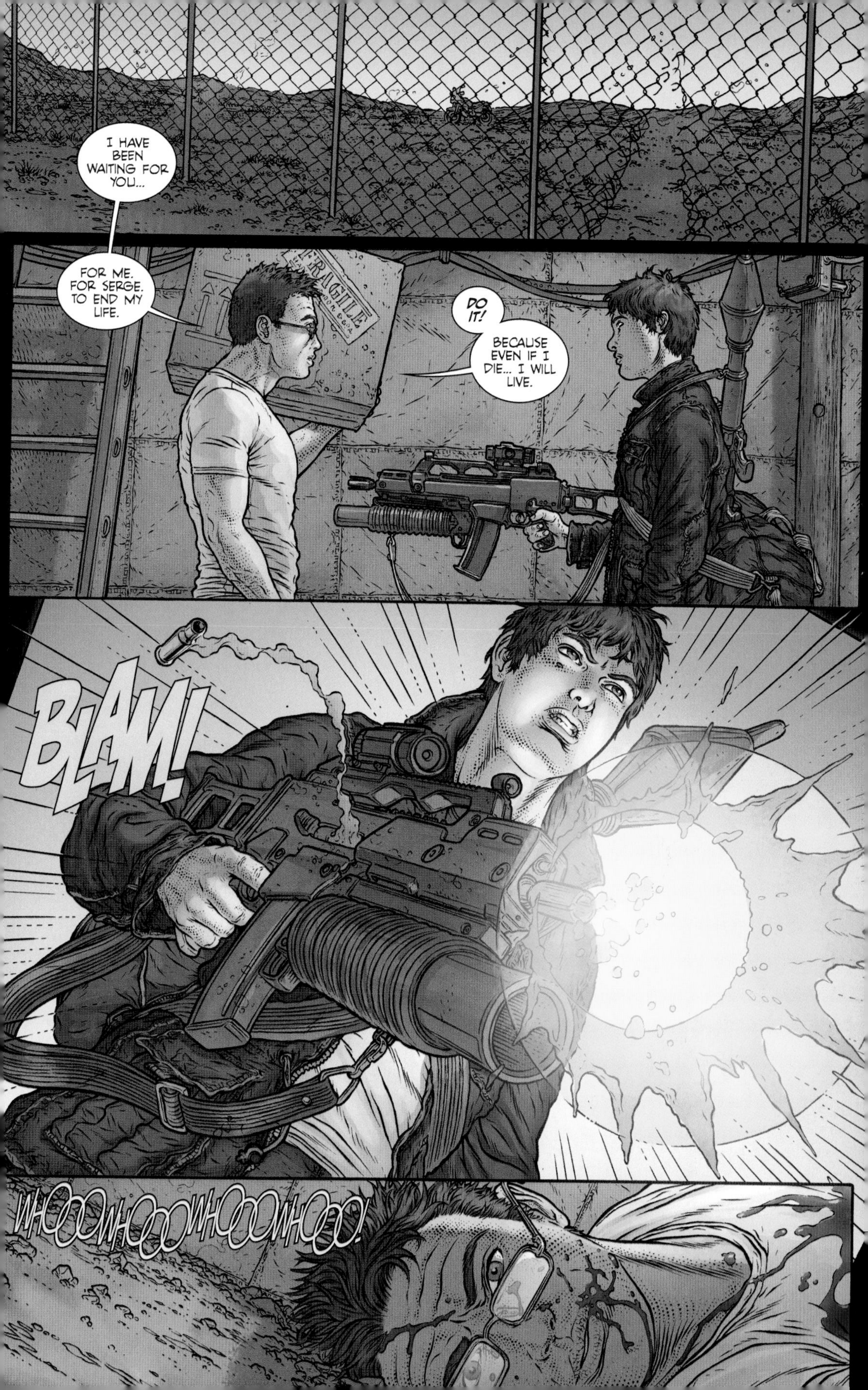
I HAVE BEEN WAITING FOR YOU...
FOR ME. FOR SERGE. TO END MY LIFE.
DO IT!
BECAUSE EVEN IF I DIE... I WILL LIVE.
BLAM!
WHOOOWHOOOWHOOOWHOOO!

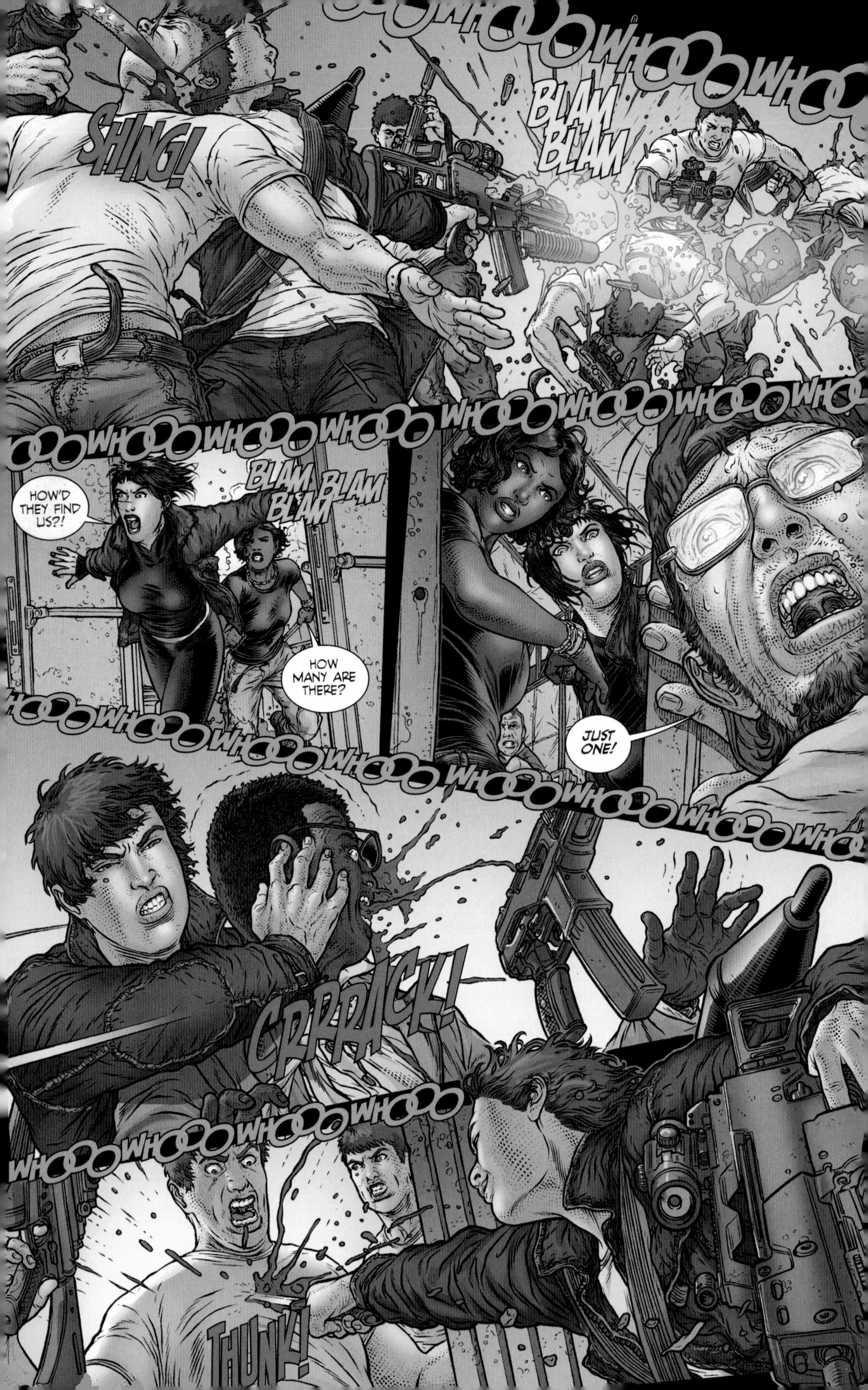
SHING!
BLAM
BLAM
HOW'D THEY FIND US?!
BLAM BLAM
BLAM
HOW MANY ARE THERE?
JUST ONE!
CRRRACK!
THUNK!

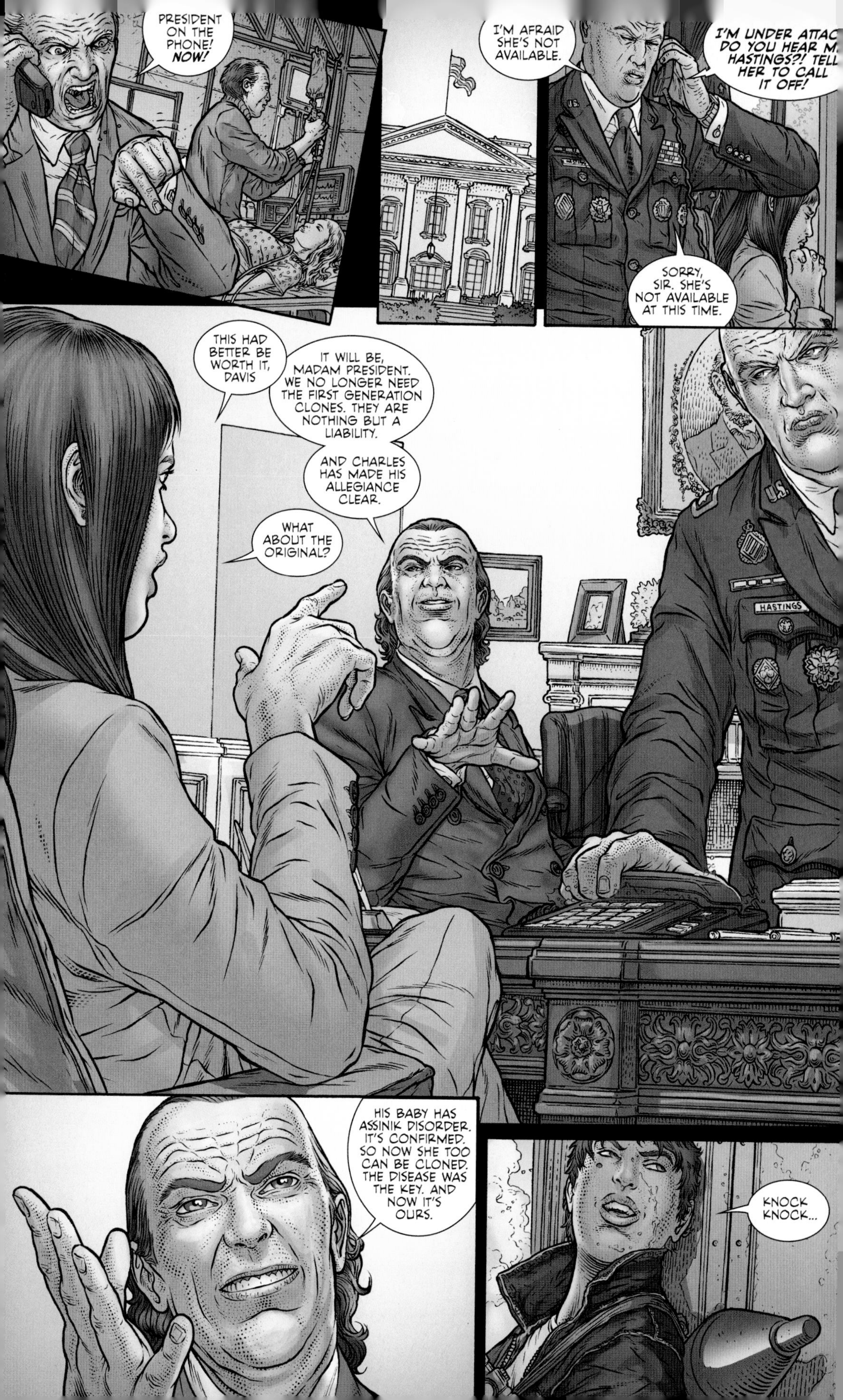
PRESIDENT ON THE PHONE! NOW!
I'M AFRAID SHE'S NOT AVAILABLE.
I'M UNDER ATTAC DO YOU HEAR M HASTINGS?! TELL HER TO CALL IT OFF!
SORRY, SIR. SHE'S NOT AVAILABLE AT THIS TIME.
THIS HAD BETTER BE WORTH IT, DAVIS
IT WILL BE, MADAM PRESIDENT. WE NO LONGER NEED THE FIRST GENERATION CLONES. THEY ARE NOTHING BUT A LIABILITY.
AND CHARLES HAS MADE HIS ALLEGIANCE CLEAR.
WHAT ABOUT THE ORIGINAL?
HASTINGS
HIS BABY HAS ASSINIK DISORDER. IT'S CONFIRMED. SO NOW SHE TOO CAN BE CLONED. THE DISEASE WAS THE KEY. AND NOW IT'S OURS.
KNOCK KNOCK...

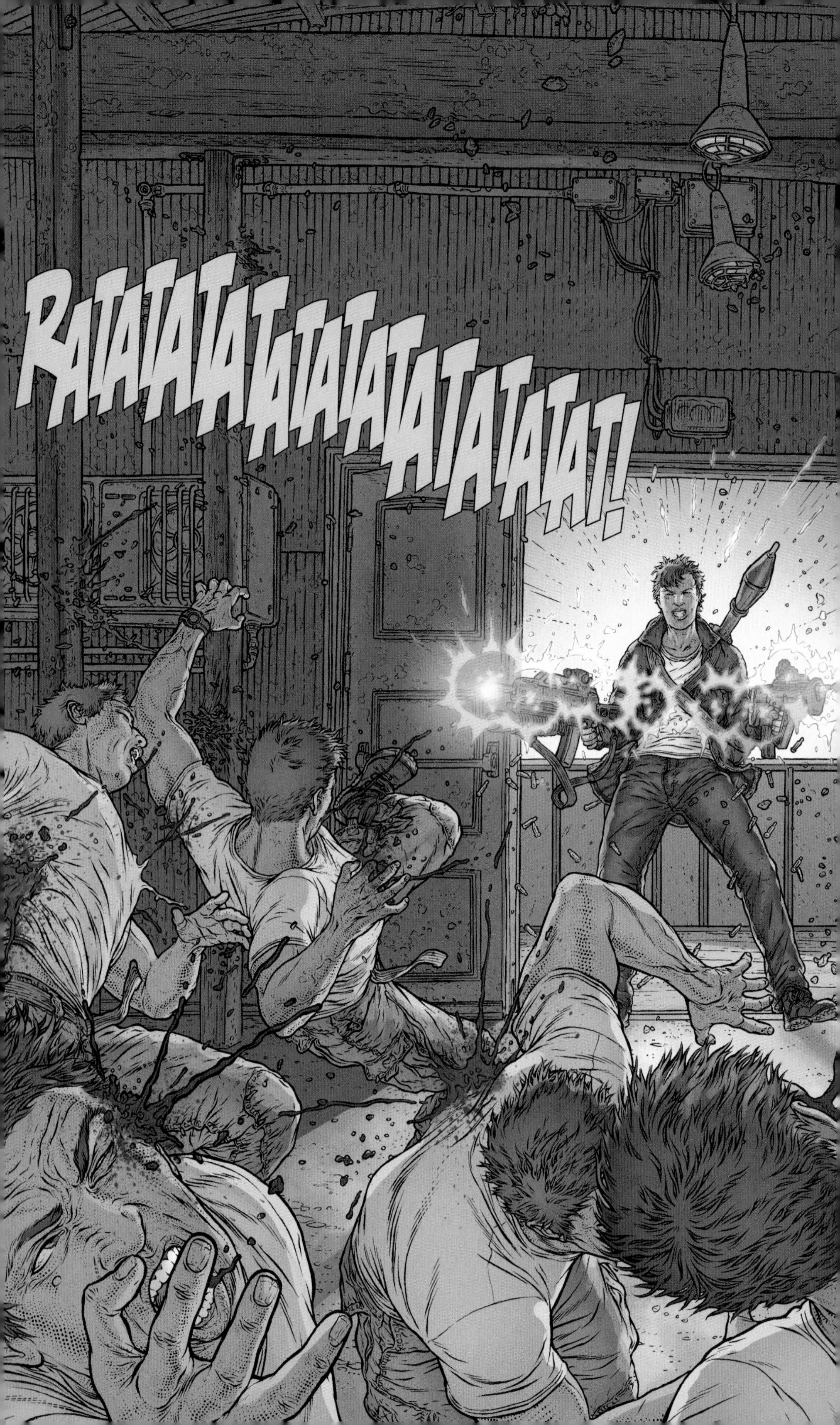
RATATATATATATATATATATATATAT!

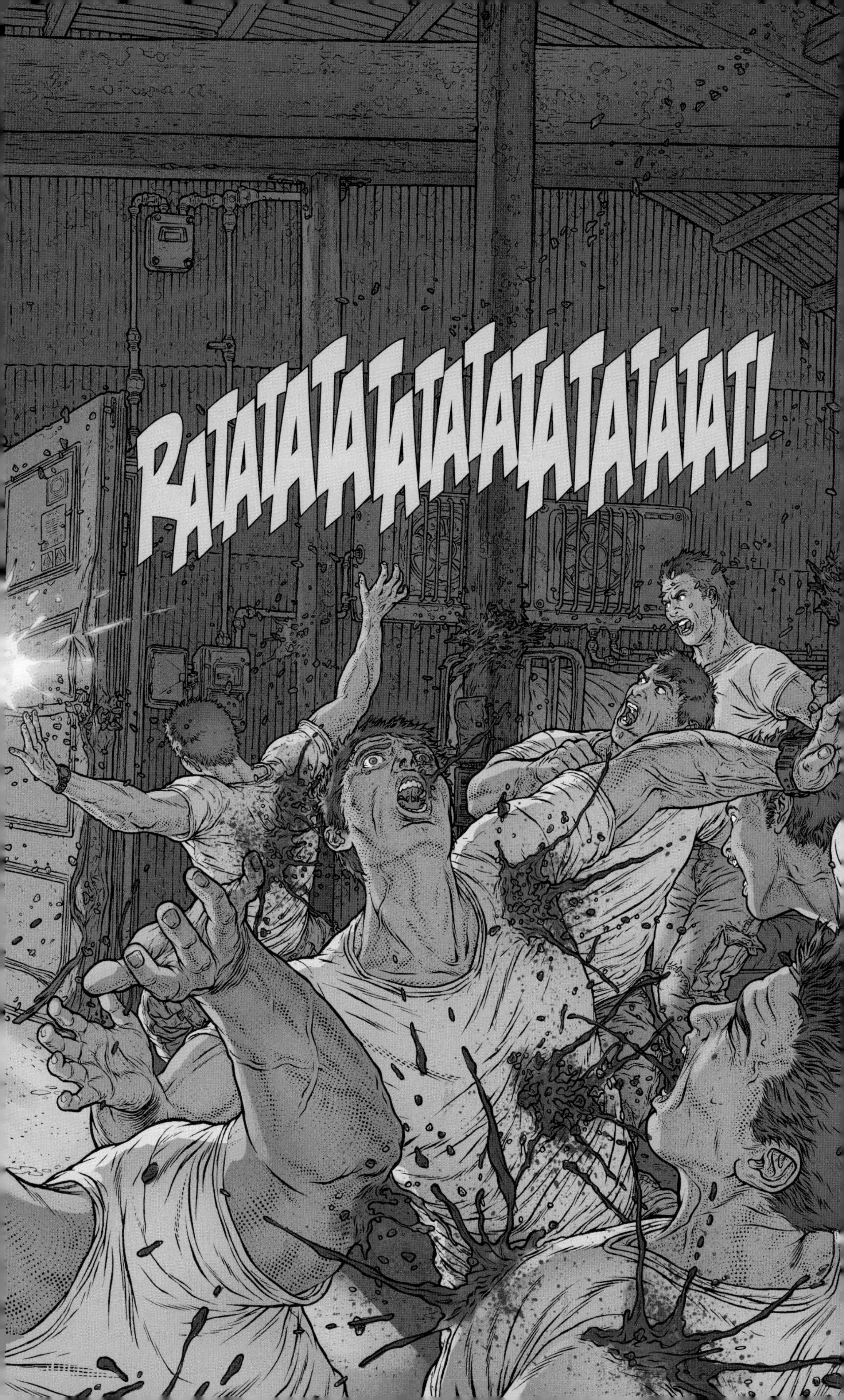
RATATATATATATATATATATAT!

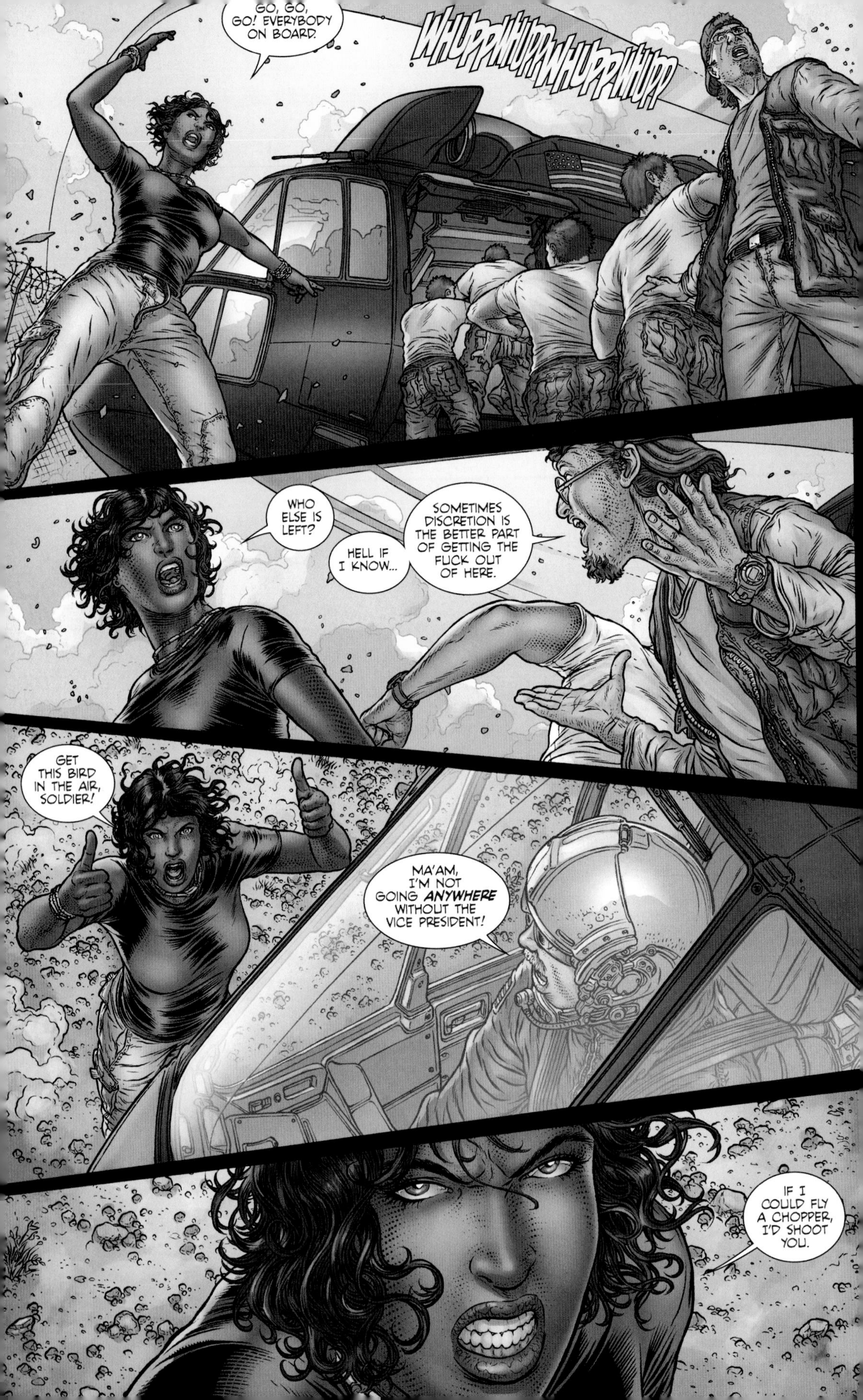
GO, GO, GO! EVERYBODY ON BOARD.
WHUPPWHUPPWHUPPWHUPP
WHO ELSE IS LEFT?
HELL IF I KNOW...
SOMETIMES DISCRETION IS THE BETTER PART OF GETTING THE FUCK OUT OF HERE.
GET THIS BIRD IN THE AIR, SOLDIER!
MA'AM, I'M NOT GOING ANYWHERE WITHOUT THE VICE PRESIDENT!
IF I COULD FLY A CHOPPER, I'D SHOOT YOU.

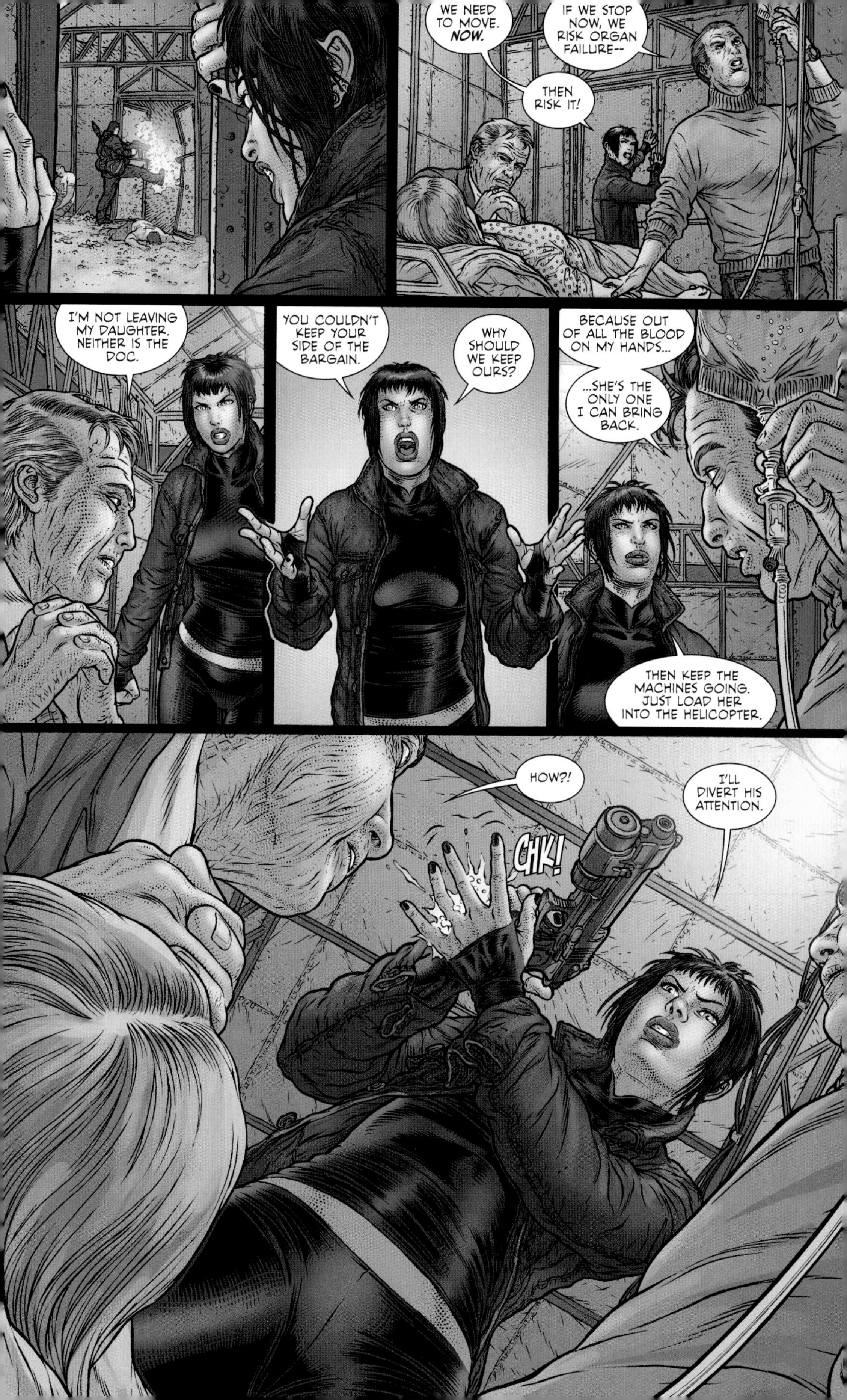
WE NEED TO MOVE. NOW.
IF WE STOP NOW, WE RISK ORGAN FAILURE--
THEN RISK IT!
I'M NOT LEAVING MY DAUGHTER. NEITHER IS THE DOC.
YOU COULDN'T KEEP YOUR SIDE OF THE BARGAIN.
WHY SHOULD WE KEEP OURS?
BECAUSE OUT OF ALL THE BLOOD ON MY HANDS...
...SHE'S THE ONLY ONE I CAN BRING BACK.
THEN KEEP THE MACHINES GOING. JUST LOAD HER INTO THE HELICOPTER.
HOW?!
CHK!
I'LL DIVERT HIS ATTENTION.

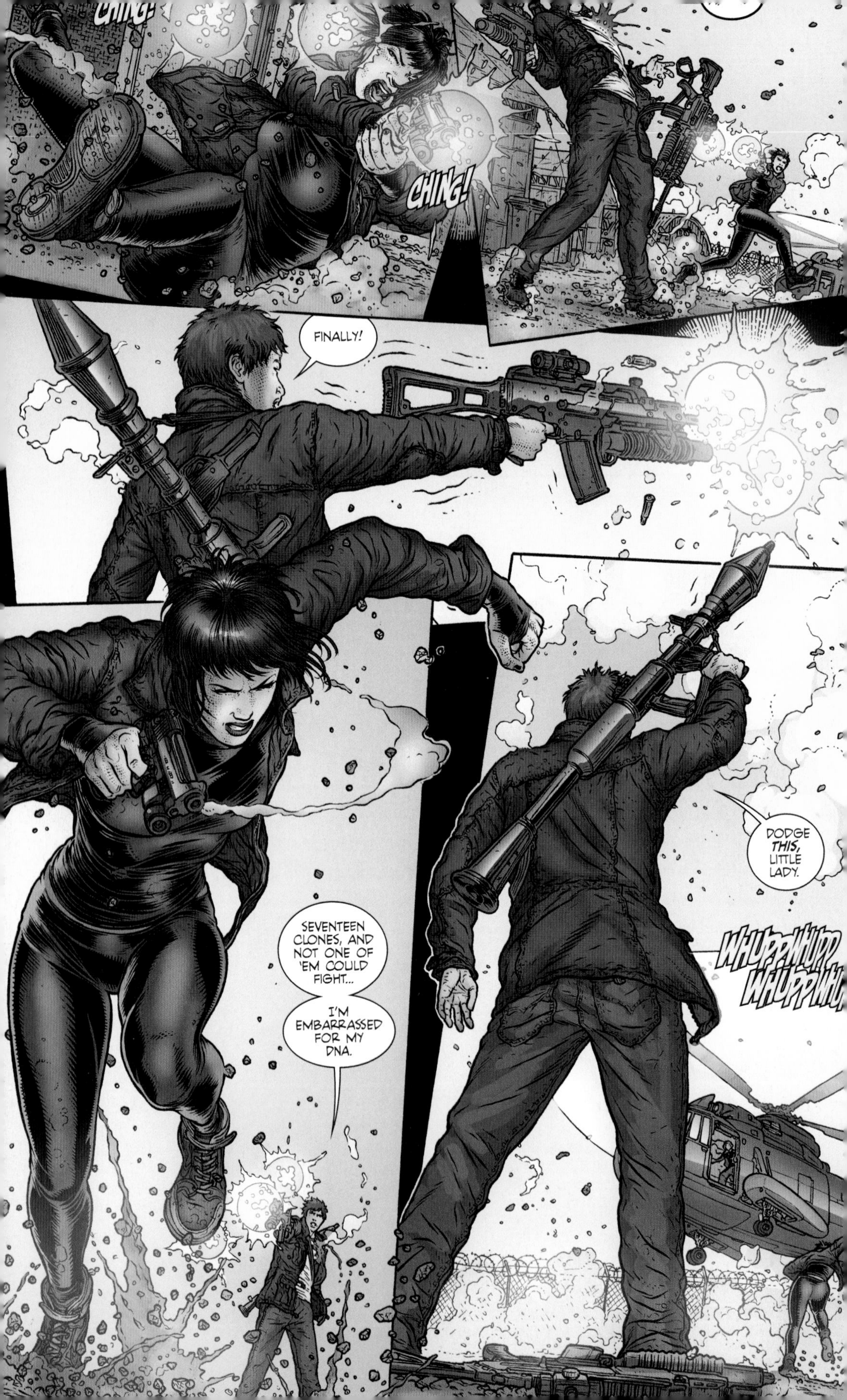
CHING!
CHING!
FINALLY!
DODGE THIS, LITTLE LADY.
SEVENTEEN CLONES, AND NOT ONE OF 'EM COULD FIGHT...
I'M EMBARRASSED FOR MY DNA.
WHUPPWHUPP WHUPPWHU

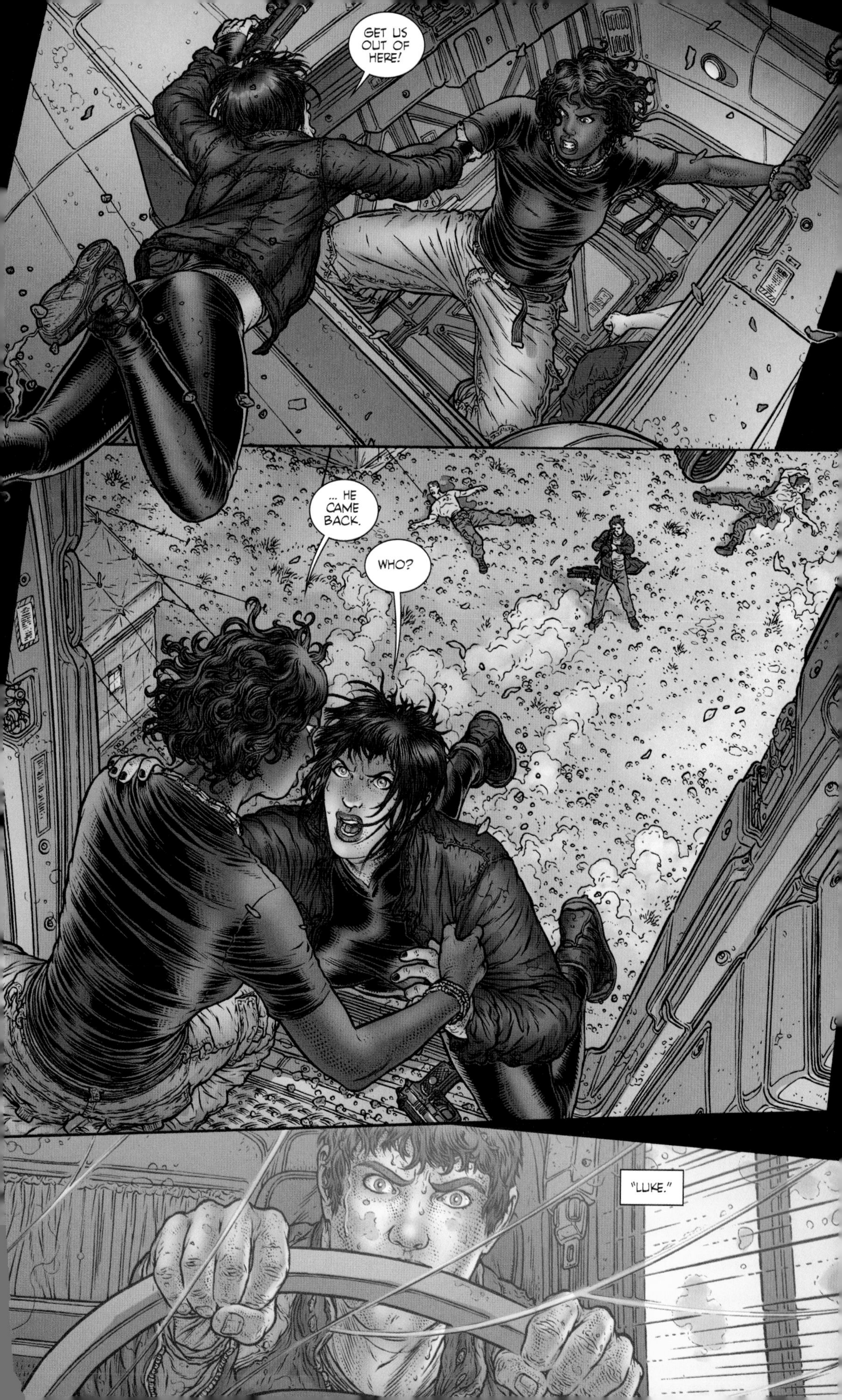
GET US OUT OF HERE!
... HE CAME BACK.
WHO?
"LUKE."

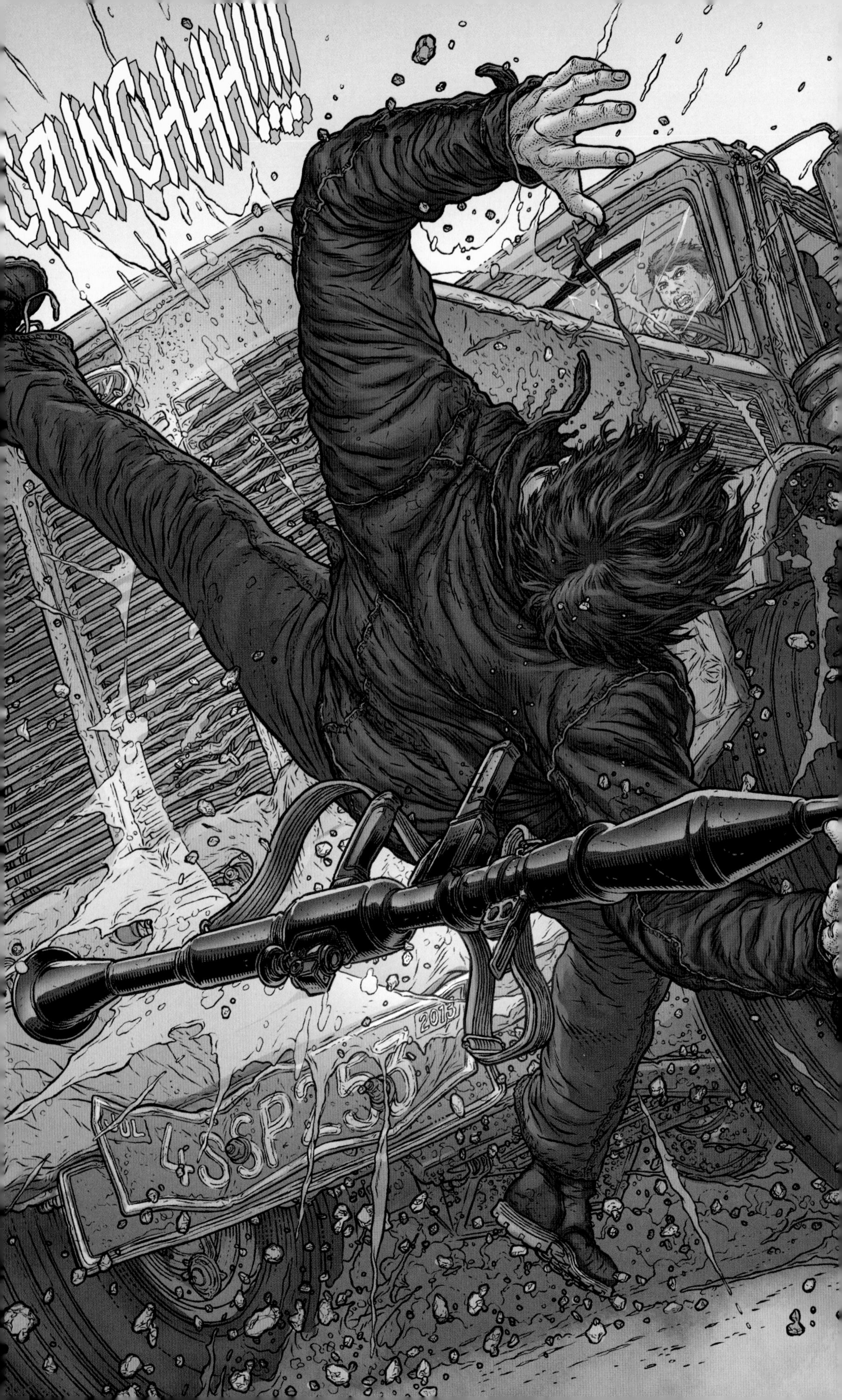
CRUNCHHH!!!...

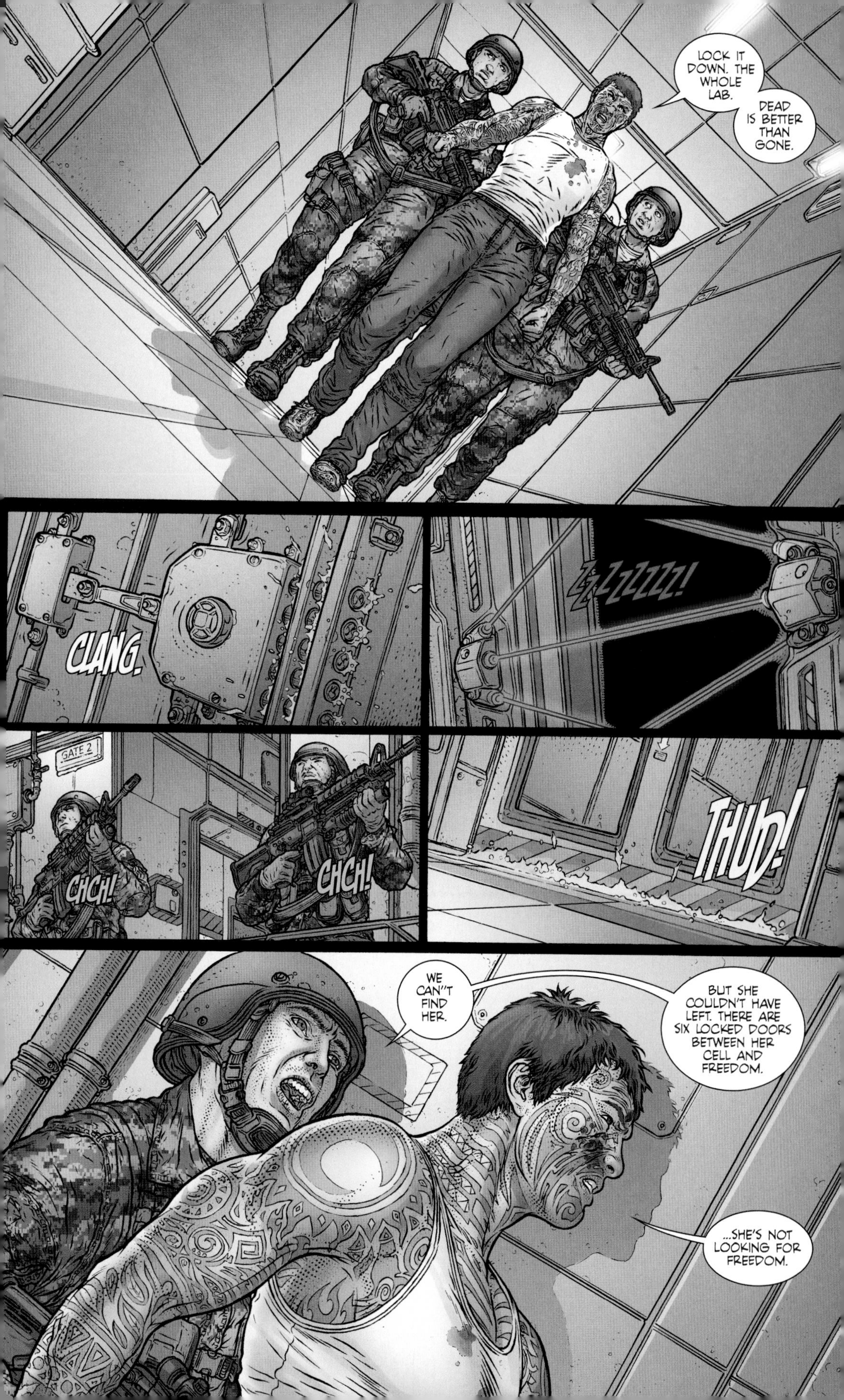
LOCK IT DOWN. THE WHOLE LAB.
DEAD IS BETTER THAN GONE.
CLANG.
ZZZZZZZ!
GATE 2
CHCH!
CHCH!
THUD!
WE CAN''T FIND HER.
BUT SHE COULDN'T HAVE LEFT. THERE ARE SIX LOCKED DOORS BETWEEN HER CELL AND FREEDOM.
...SHE'S NOT LOOKING FOR FREEDOM.

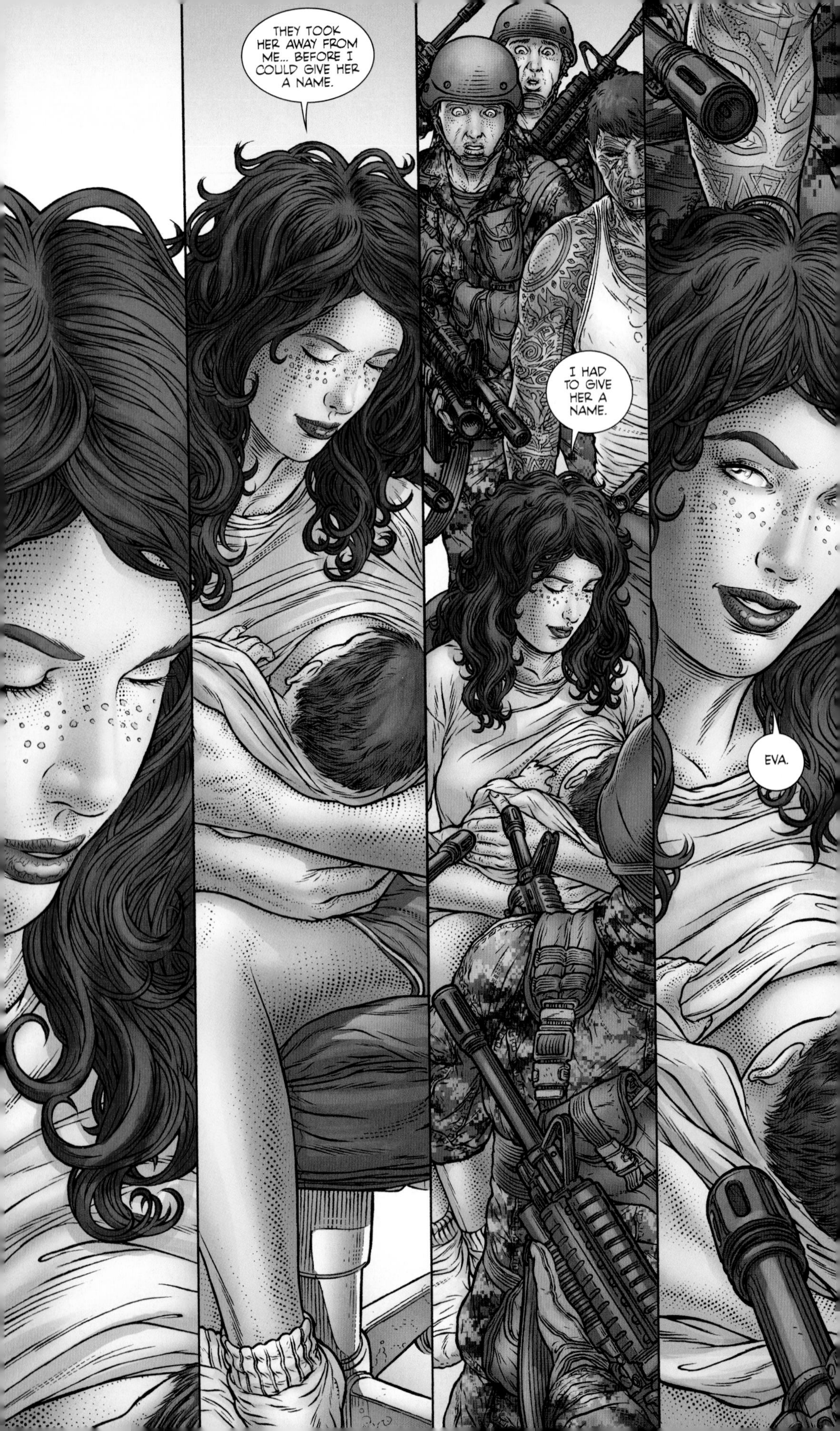
THEY TOOK HER AWAY FROM ME... BEFORE I COULD GIVE HER A NAME.
I HAD TO GIVE HER A NAME.
EVA.

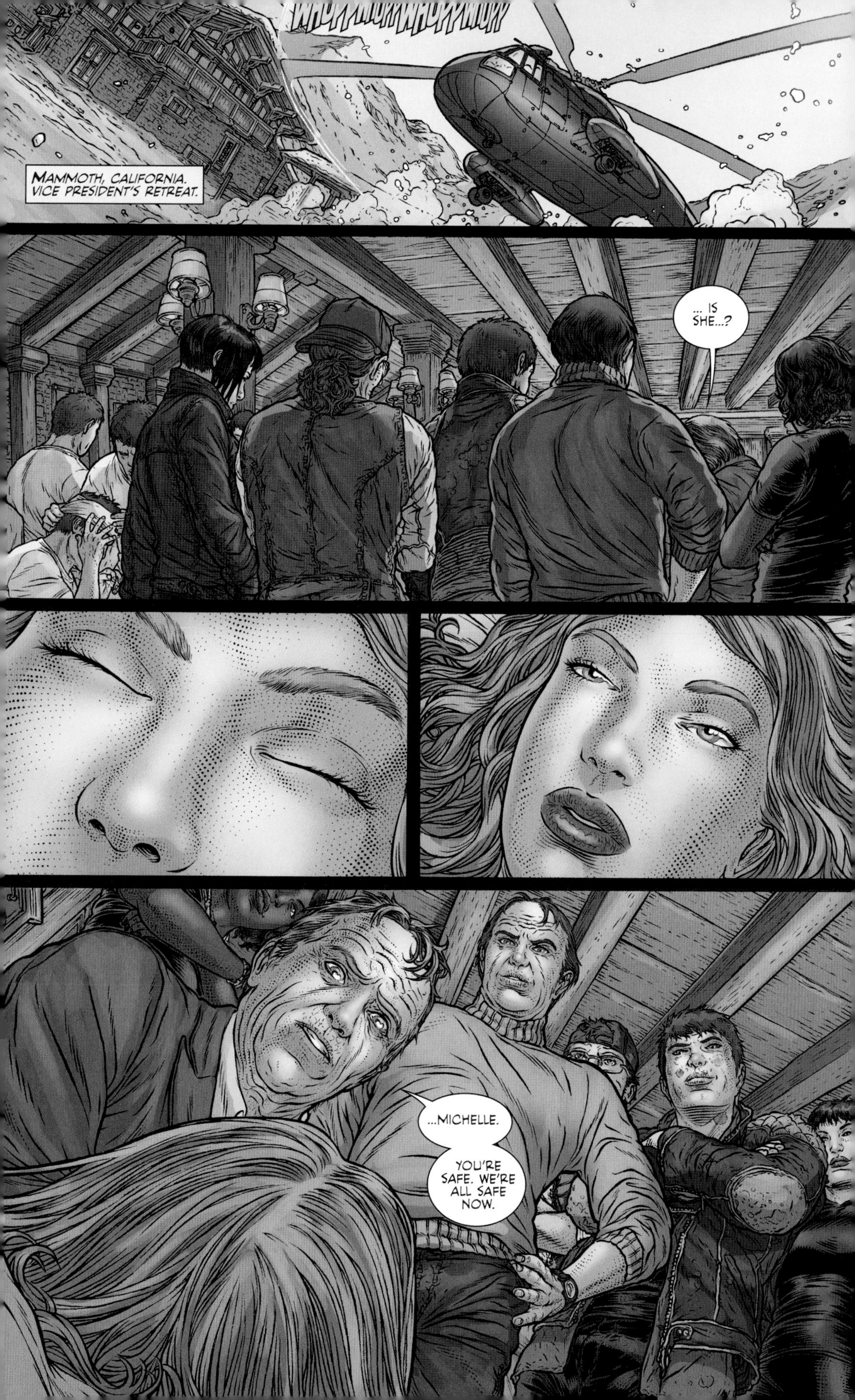
WHUPWHUPWHUPWHUP
MAMMOTH, CALIFORNIA.
VICE PRESIDENT'S RETREAT.
... IS SHE...?
...MICHELLE.
YOU'RE SAFE. WE'RE ALL SAFE NOW.

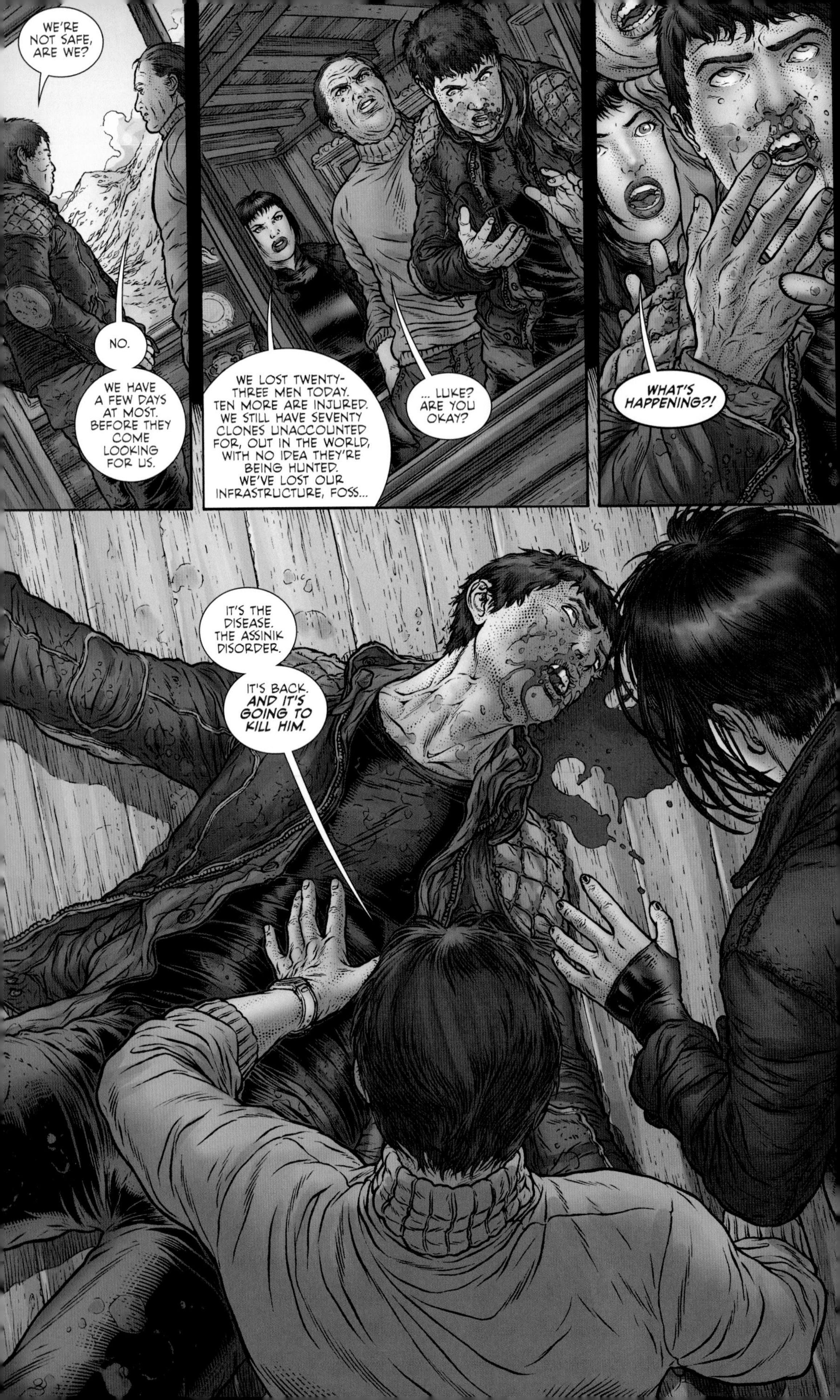
WE'RE NOT SAFE, ARE WE?
NO.
WE HAVE A FEW DAYS AT MOST. BEFORE THEY COME LOOKING FOR US.
WE LOST TWENTY-THREE MEN TODAY. TEN MORE ARE INJURED. WE STILL HAVE SEVENTY CLONES UNACCOUNTED FOR, OUT IN THE WORLD, WITH NO IDEA THEY'RE BEING HUNTED. WE'VE LOST OUR INFRASTRUCTURE, FOSS...
... LUKE? ARE YOU OKAY?
WHAT'S HAPPENING?!
IT'S THE DISEASE. THE ASSINIK DISORDER.
IT'S BACK. AND IT'S GOING TO KILL HIM.

# CHAPTER 8

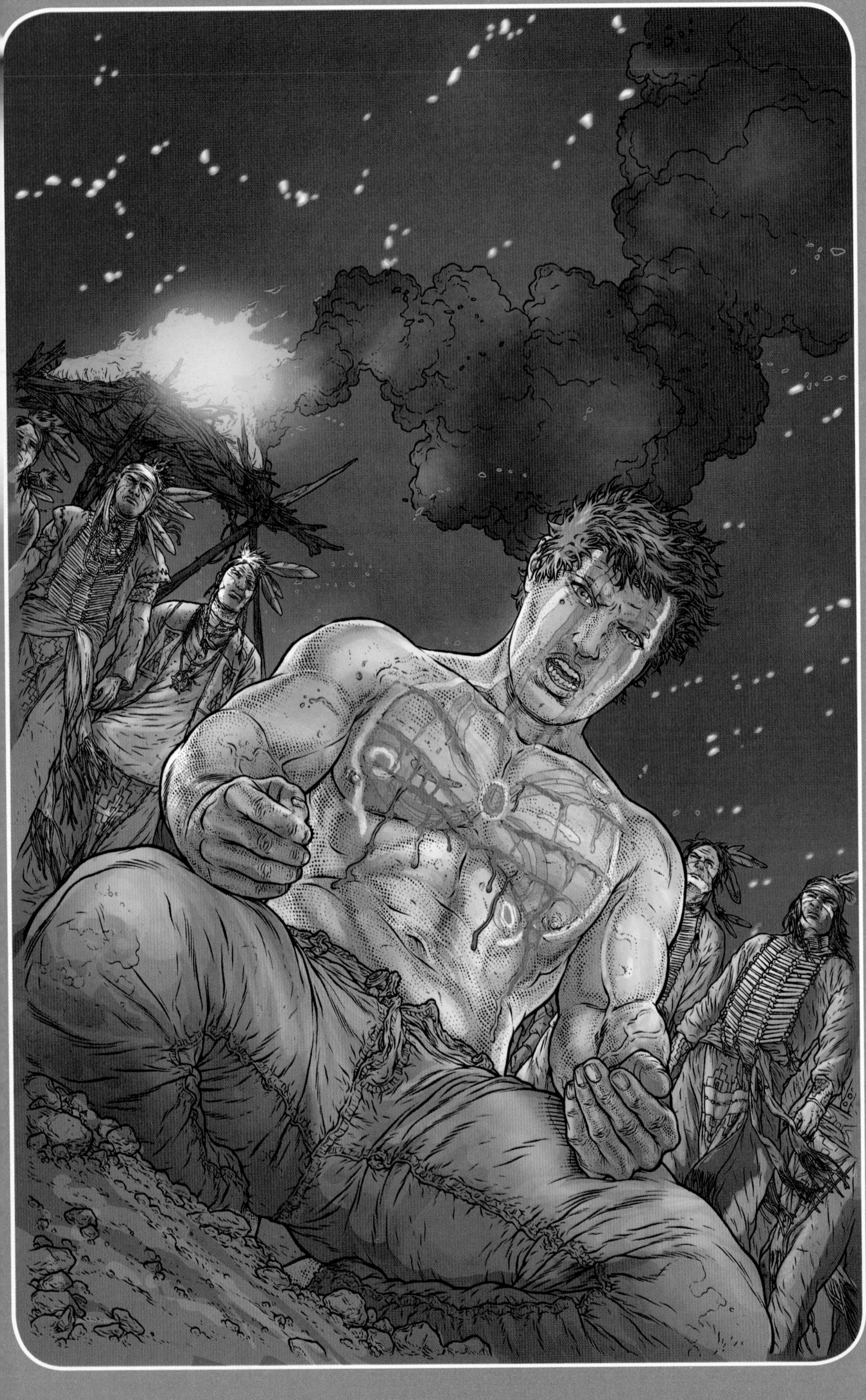

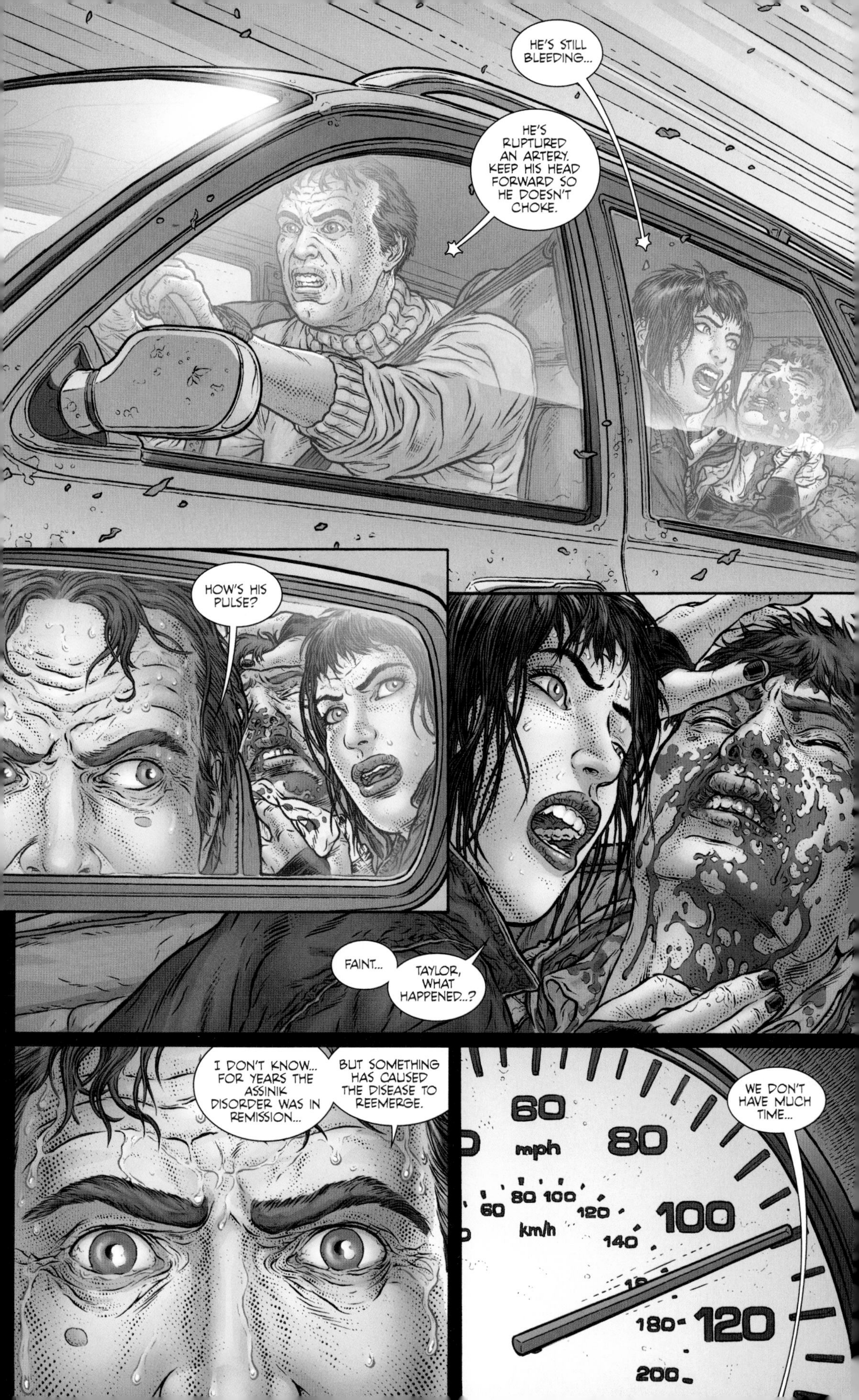
HE'S STILL BLEEDING...
HE'S RUPTURED AN ARTERY. KEEP HIS HEAD FORWARD SO HE DOESN'T CHOKE.
HOW'S HIS PULSE?
FAINT...
TAYLOR, WHAT HAPPENED...?
I DON'T KNOW... FOR YEARS THE ASSINIK DISORDER WAS IN REMISSION...
BUT SOMETHING HAS CAUSED THE DISEASE TO REEMERGE.
WE DON'T HAVE MUCH TIME...

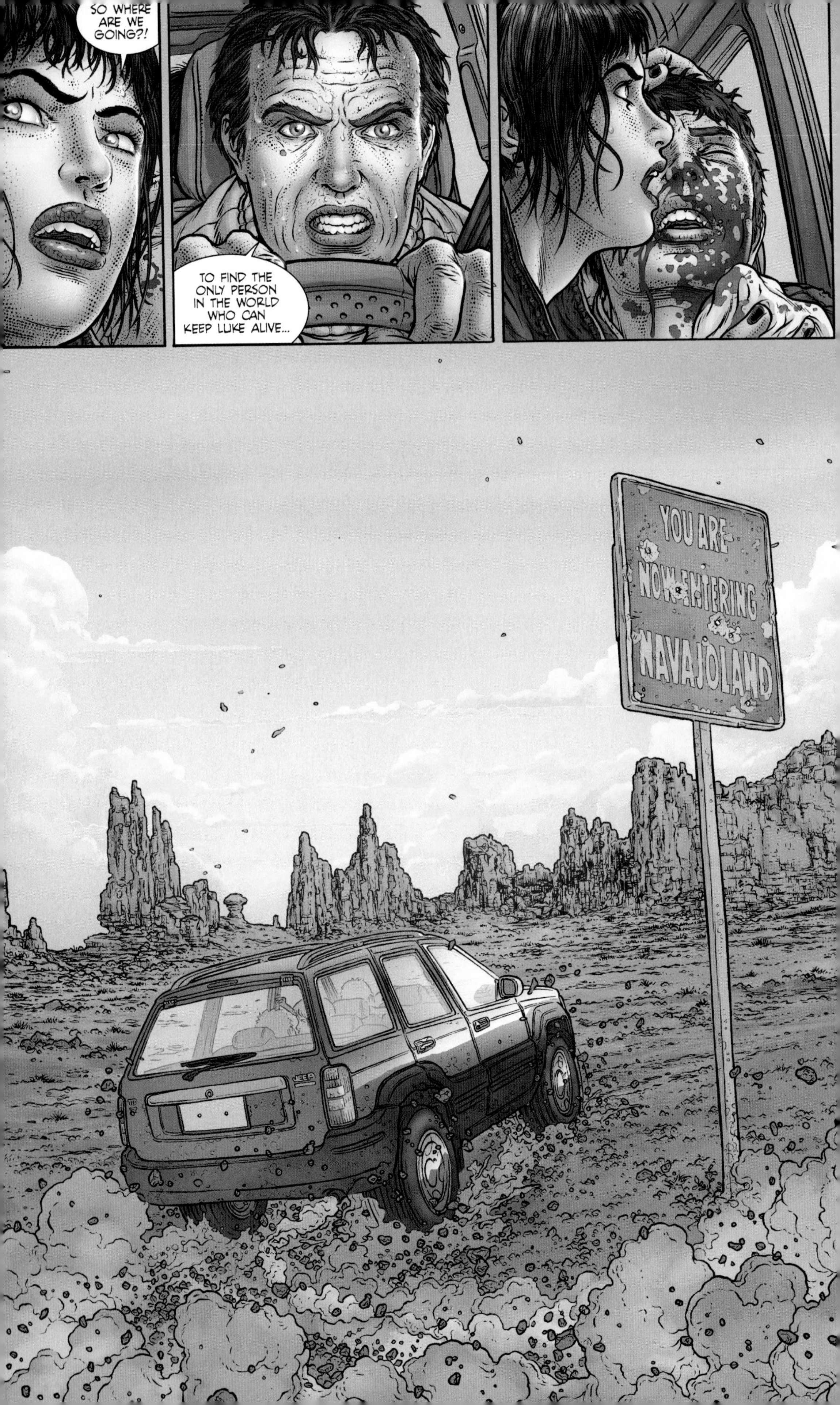
SO WHERE ARE WE GOING?!
TO FIND THE ONLY PERSON IN THE WORLD WHO CAN KEEP LUKE ALIVE...
YOU ARE NOW ENTERING NAVAJOLAND
JEEP

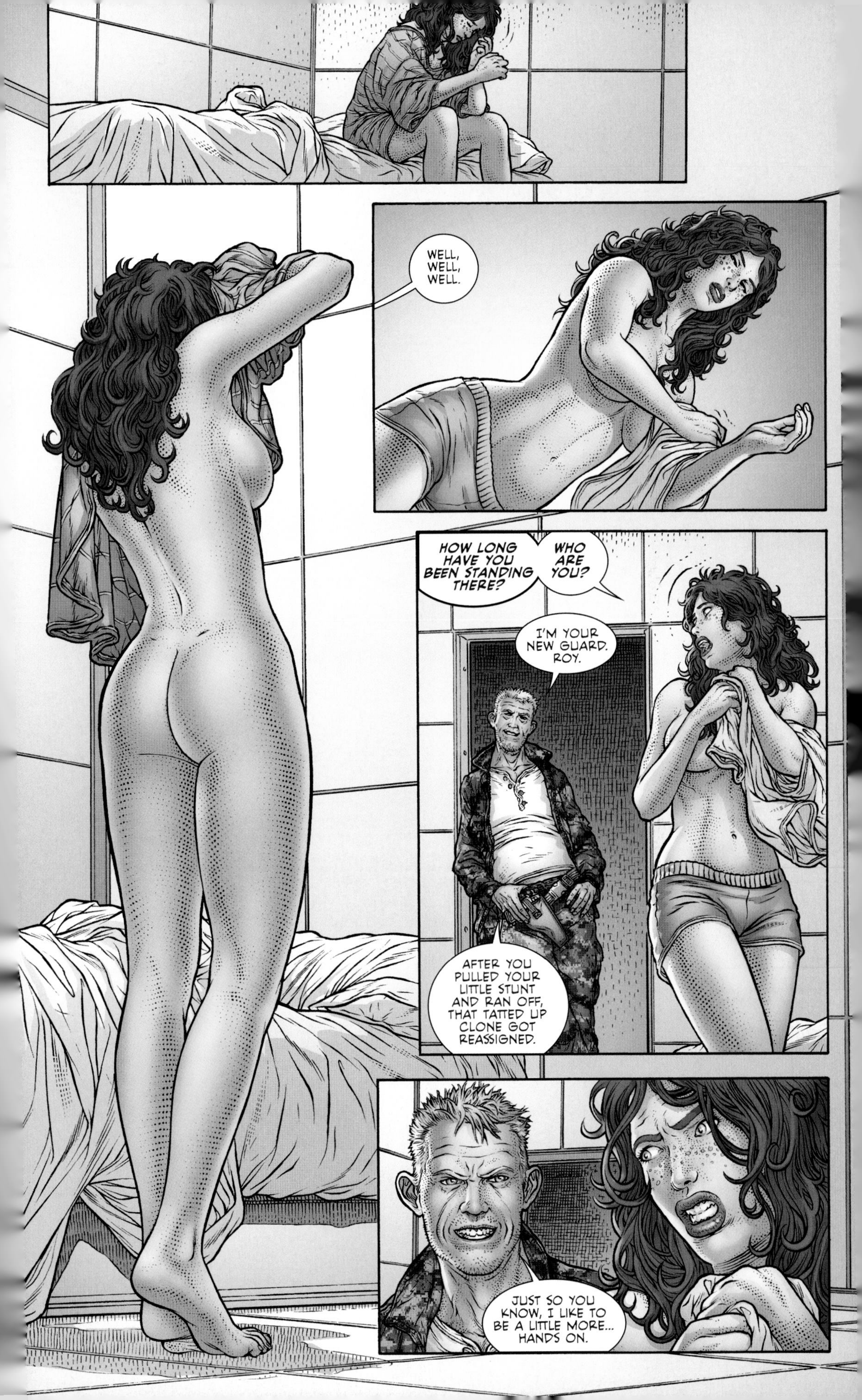
WELL, WELL, WELL.
HOW LONG HAVE YOU BEEN STANDING THERE?
WHO ARE YOU?
I'M YOUR NEW GUARD. ROY.
AFTER YOU PULLED YOUR LITTLE STUNT AND RAN OFF, THAT TATTED UP CLONE GOT REASSIGNED.
JUST SO YOU KNOW, I LIKE TO BE A LITTLE MORE... HANDS ON.

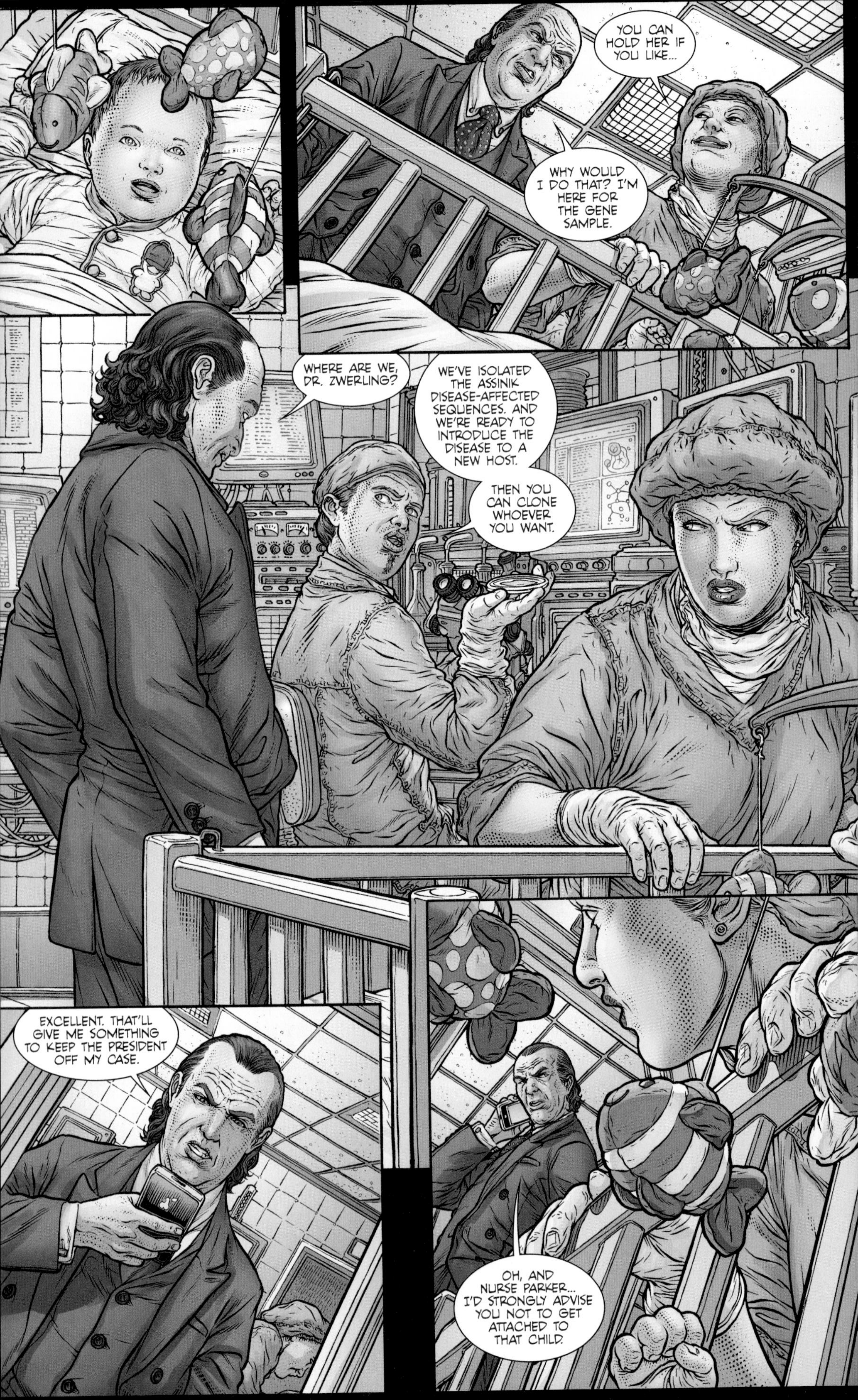
YOU CAN HOLD HER IF YOU LIKE...
WHY WOULD I DO THAT? I'M HERE FOR THE GENE SAMPLE.
WHERE ARE WE, DR. ZWERLING?
WE'VE ISOLATED THE ASSINIK DISEASE-AFFECTED SEQUENCES. AND WE'RE READY TO INTRODUCE THE DISEASE TO A NEW HOST.
THEN YOU CAN CLONE WHOEVER YOU WANT.
EXCELLENT. THAT'LL GIVE ME SOMETHING TO KEEP THE PRESIDENT OFF MY CASE.
OH, AND NURSE PARKER... I'D STRONGLY ADVISE YOU NOT TO GET ATTACHED TO THAT CHILD.

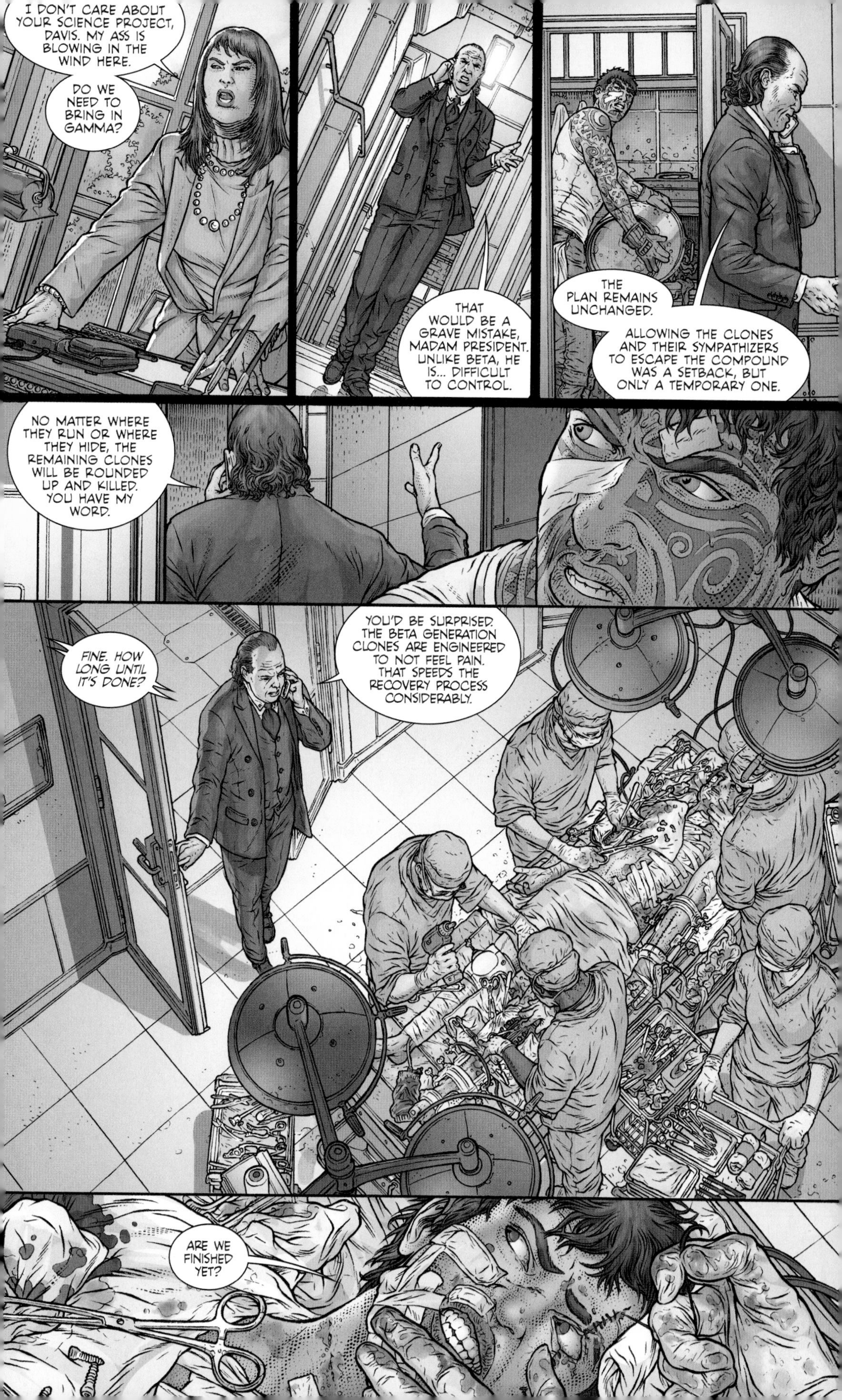

I DON'T CARE ABOUT YOUR SCIENCE PROJECT, DAVIS. MY ASS IS BLOWING IN THE WIND HERE.
DO WE NEED TO BRING IN GAMMA?
THAT WOULD BE A GRAVE MISTAKE, MADAM PRESIDENT. UNLIKE BETA, HE IS... DIFFICULT TO CONTROL.
THE PLAN REMAINS UNCHANGED.
ALLOWING THE CLONES AND THEIR SYMPATHIZERS TO ESCAPE THE COMPOUND WAS A SETBACK, BUT ONLY A TEMPORARY ONE.
NO MATTER WHERE THEY RUN OR WHERE THEY HIDE, THE REMAINING CLONES WILL BE ROUNDED UP AND KILLED. YOU HAVE MY WORD.
*FINE. HOW LONG UNTIL IT'S DONE?*
YOU'D BE SURPRISED. THE BETA GENERATION CLONES ARE ENGINEERED TO NOT FEEL PAIN. THAT SPEEDS THE RECOVERY PROCESS CONSIDERABLY.
ARE WE FINISHED YET?

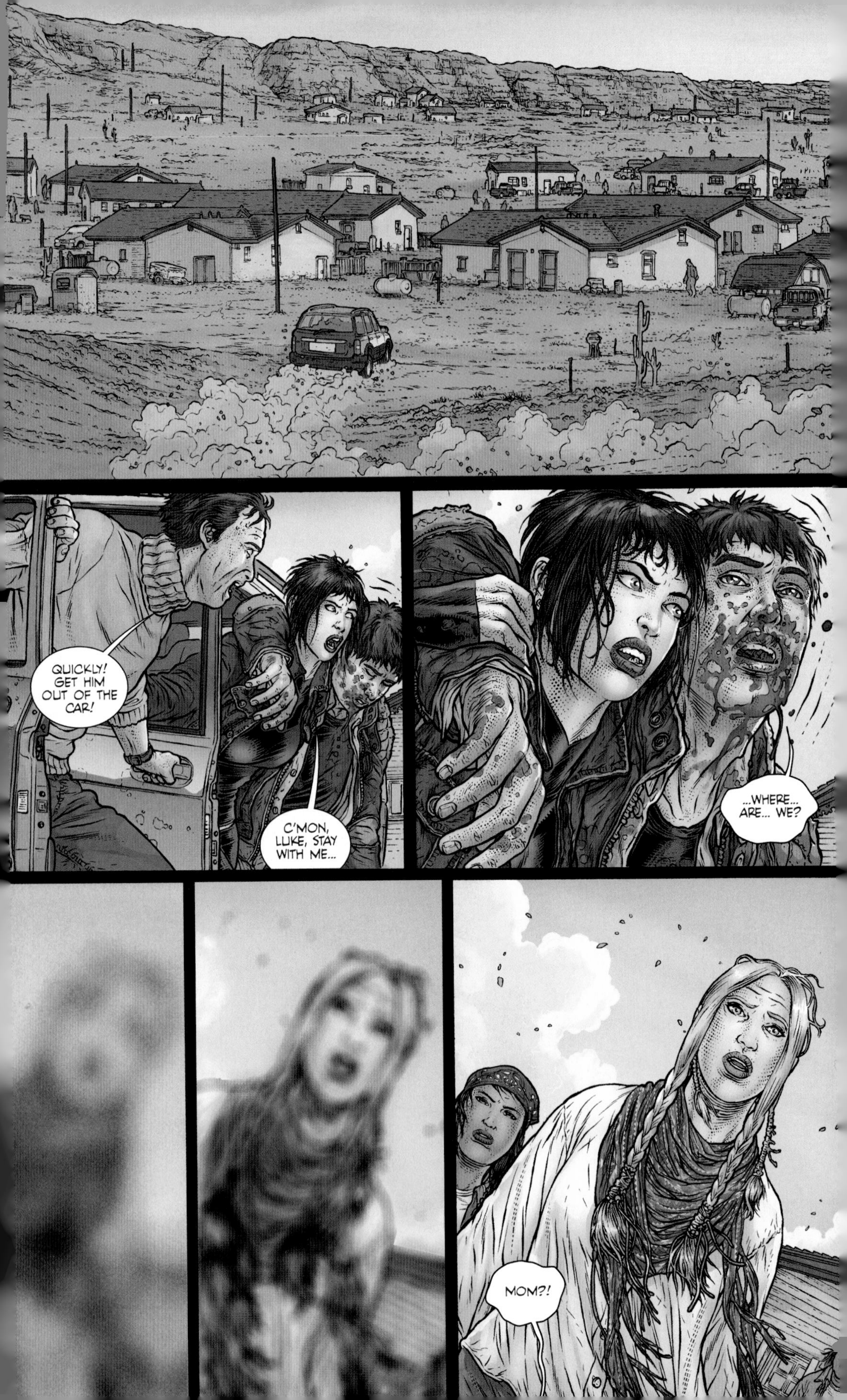
QUICKLY! GET HIM OUT OF THE CAR!
C'MON, LUKE, STAY WITH ME...
...WHERE... ARE... WE?
MOM?!

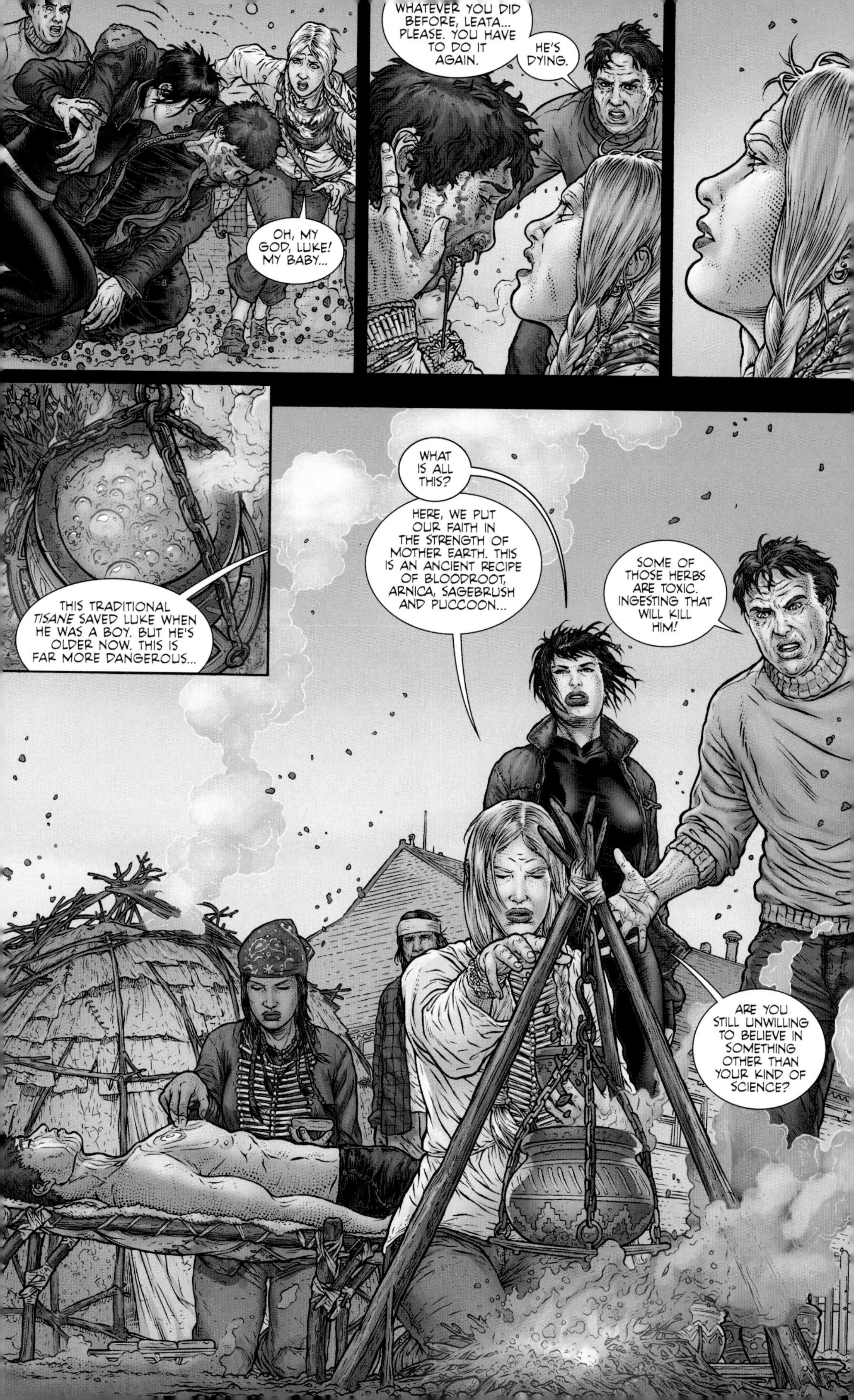
OH, MY GOD, LUKE! MY BABY...
WHATEVER YOU DID BEFORE, LEATA... PLEASE. YOU HAVE TO DO IT AGAIN.
HE'S DYING.
THIS TRADITIONAL *TISANE* SAVED LUKE WHEN HE WAS A BOY. BUT HE'S OLDER NOW. THIS IS FAR MORE DANGEROUS...
WHAT IS ALL THIS?
HERE, WE PUT OUR FAITH IN THE STRENGTH OF MOTHER EARTH. THIS IS AN ANCIENT RECIPE OF BLOODROOT, ARNICA, SAGEBRUSH AND PUCCOON...
SOME OF THOSE HERBS ARE TOXIC. INGESTING THAT WILL KILL HIM!
ARE YOU STILL UNWILLING TO BELIEVE IN SOMETHING OTHER THAN YOUR KIND OF SCIENCE?

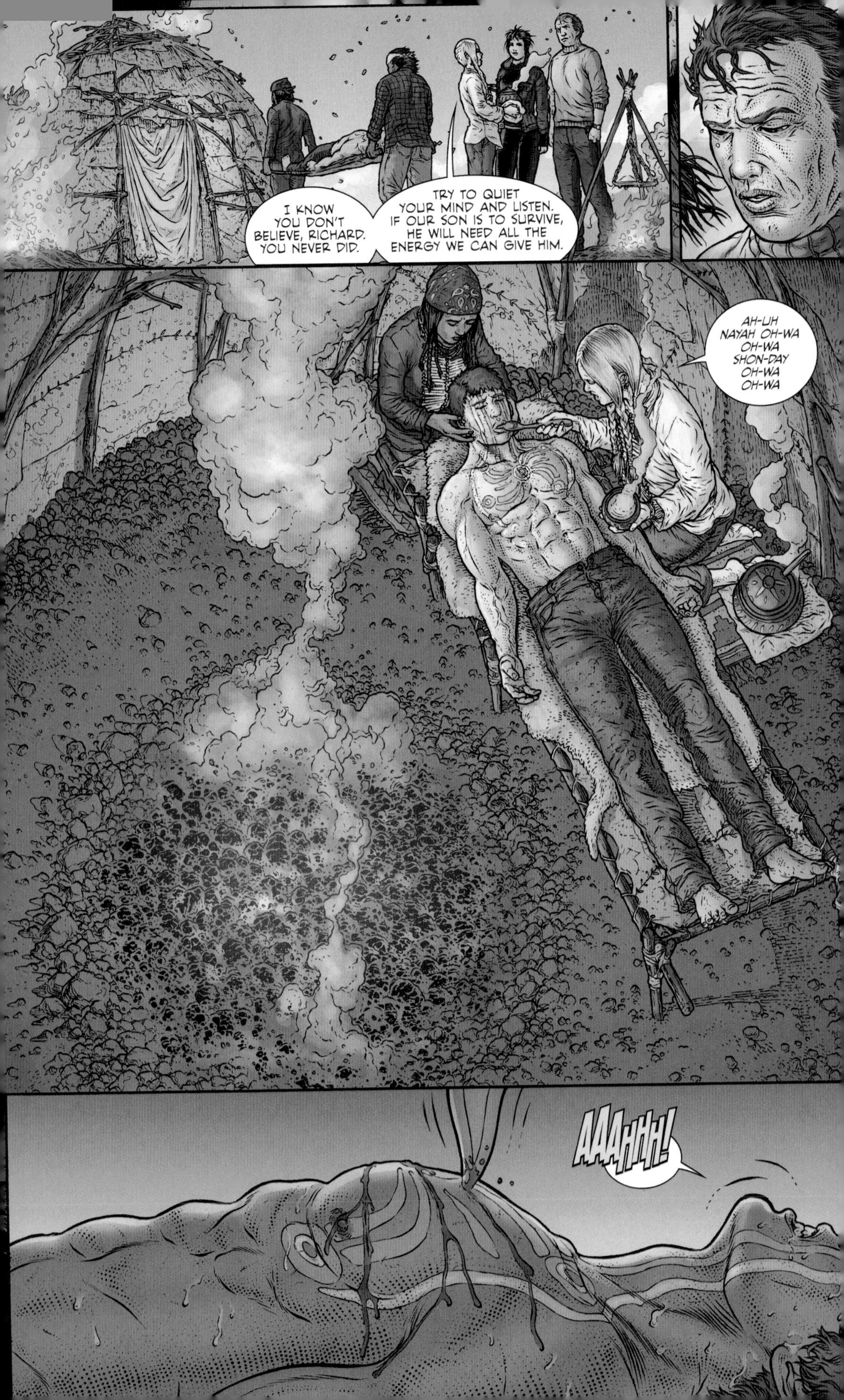
I KNOW YOU DON'T BELIEVE, RICHARD. YOU NEVER DID.
TRY TO QUIET YOUR MIND AND LISTEN. IF OUR SON IS TO SURVIVE, HE WILL NEED ALL THE ENERGY WE CAN GIVE HIM.
AH-UH NAYAH OH-WA OH-WA SHON-DAY OH-WA OH-WA
AAAHHH!

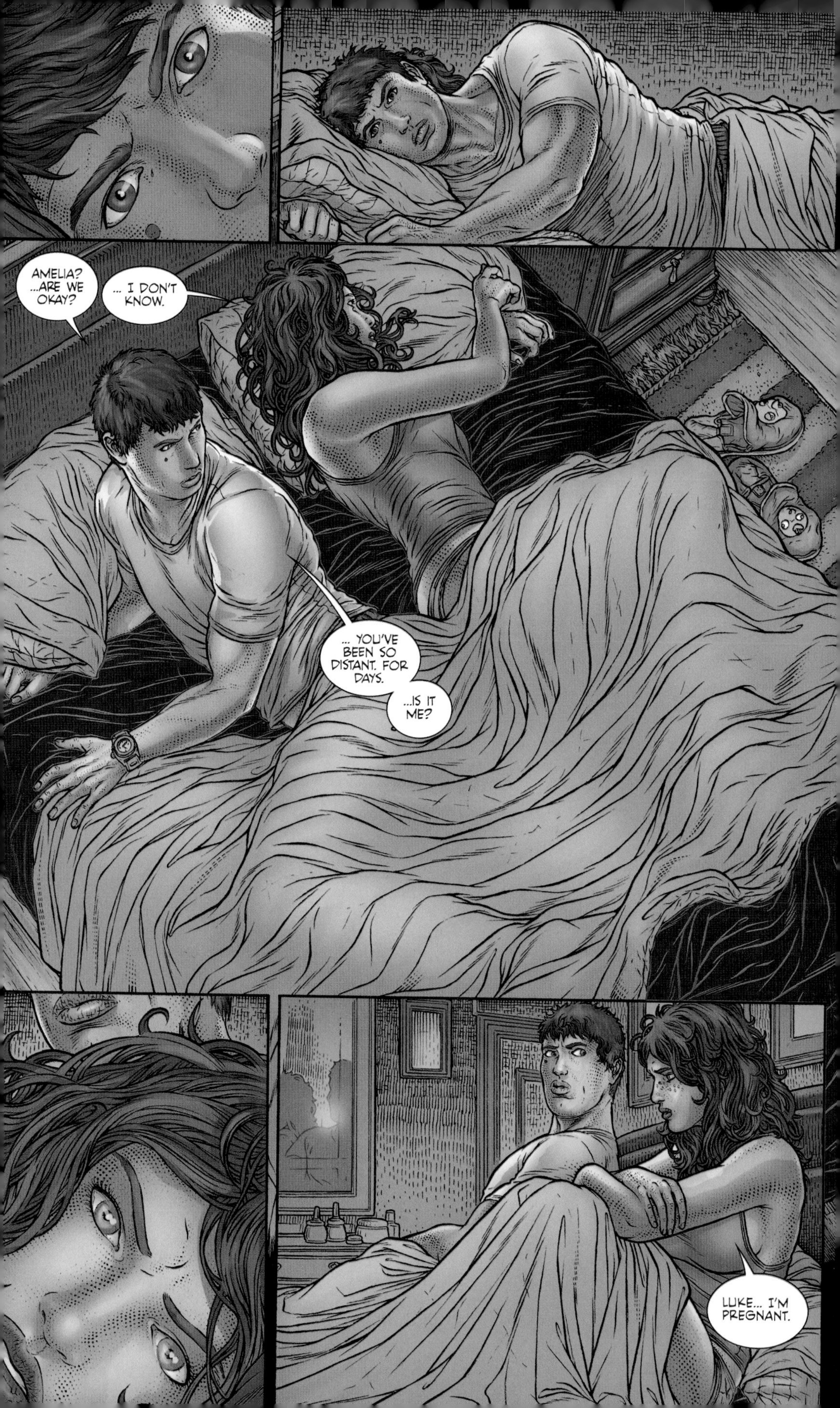
AMELIA? ...ARE WE OKAY?
... I DON'T KNOW.
... YOU'VE BEEN SO DISTANT. FOR DAYS.
...IS IT ME?
LUKE... I'M PREGNANT.

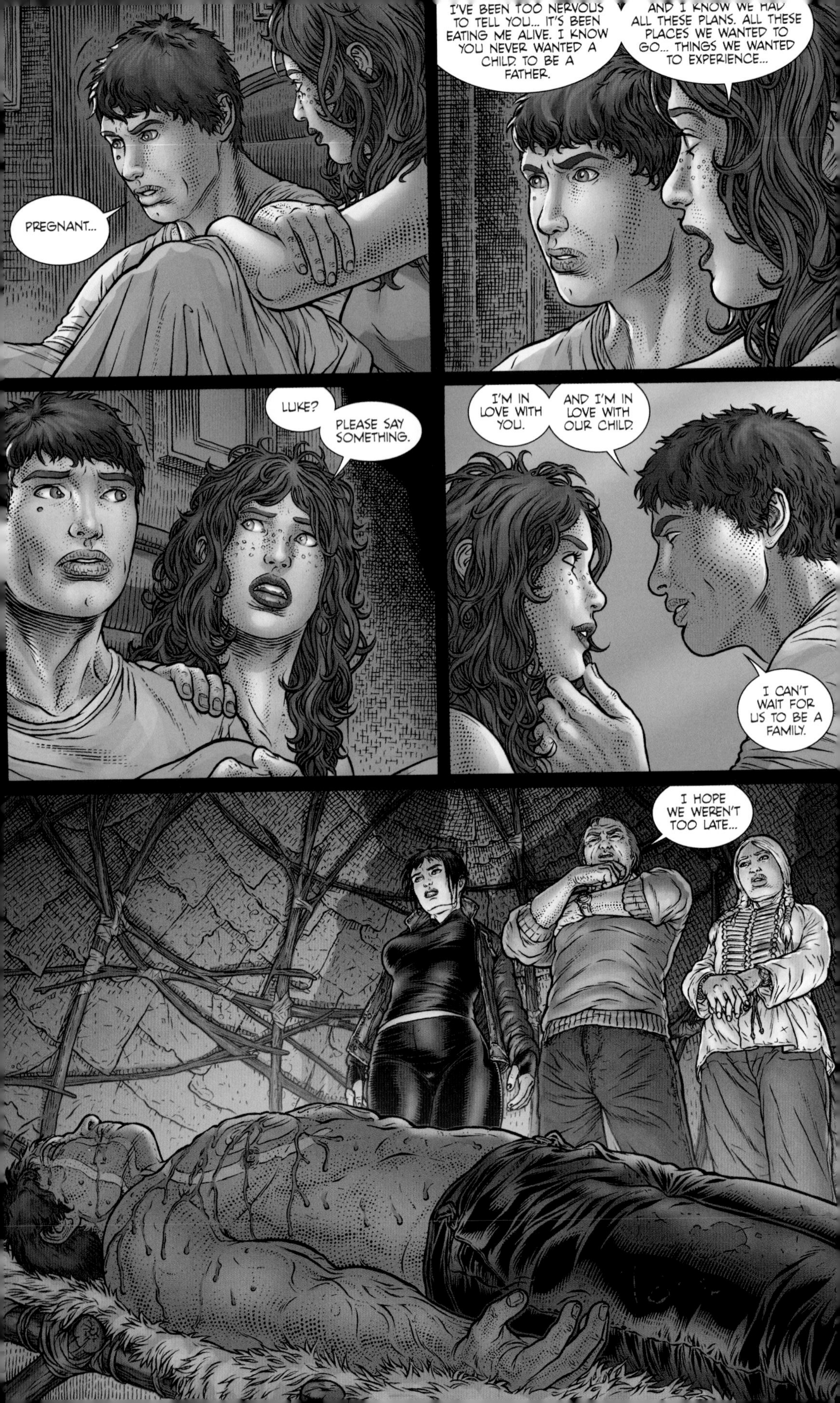
PREGNANT...
I'VE BEEN TOO NERVOUS TO TELL YOU... IT'S BEEN EATING ME ALIVE. I KNOW YOU NEVER WANTED A CHILD. TO BE A FATHER.
AND I KNOW WE HAD ALL THESE PLANS. ALL THESE PLACES WE WANTED TO GO... THINGS WE WANTED TO EXPERIENCE...
LUKE?
PLEASE SAY SOMETHING.
I'M IN LOVE WITH YOU.
AND I'M IN LOVE WITH OUR CHILD.
I CAN'T WAIT FOR US TO BE A FAMILY.
I HOPE WE WEREN'T TOO LATE...

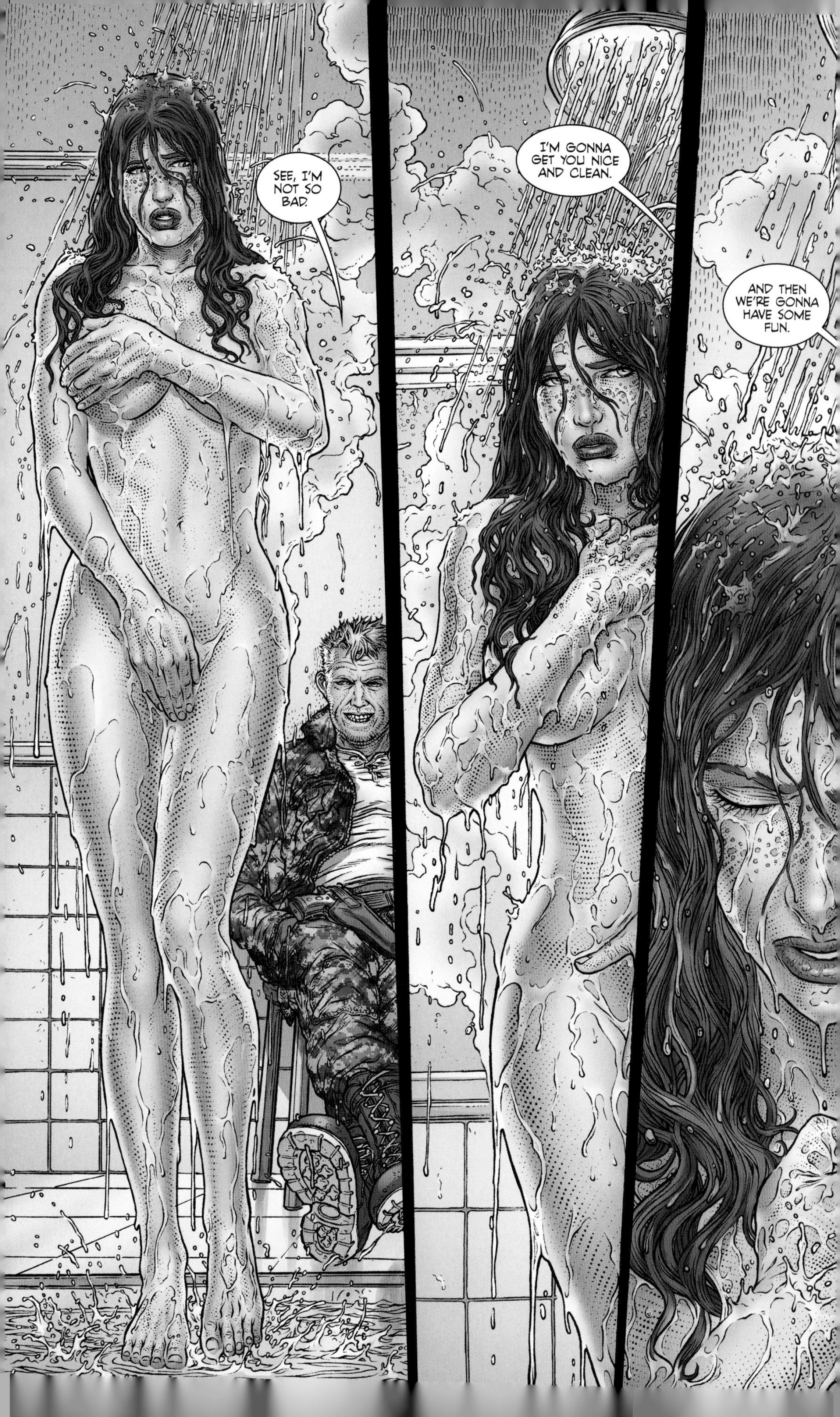
SEE, I'M NOT SO BAD.
I'M GONNA GET YOU NICE AND CLEAN.
AND THEN WE'RE GONNA HAVE SOME FUN.

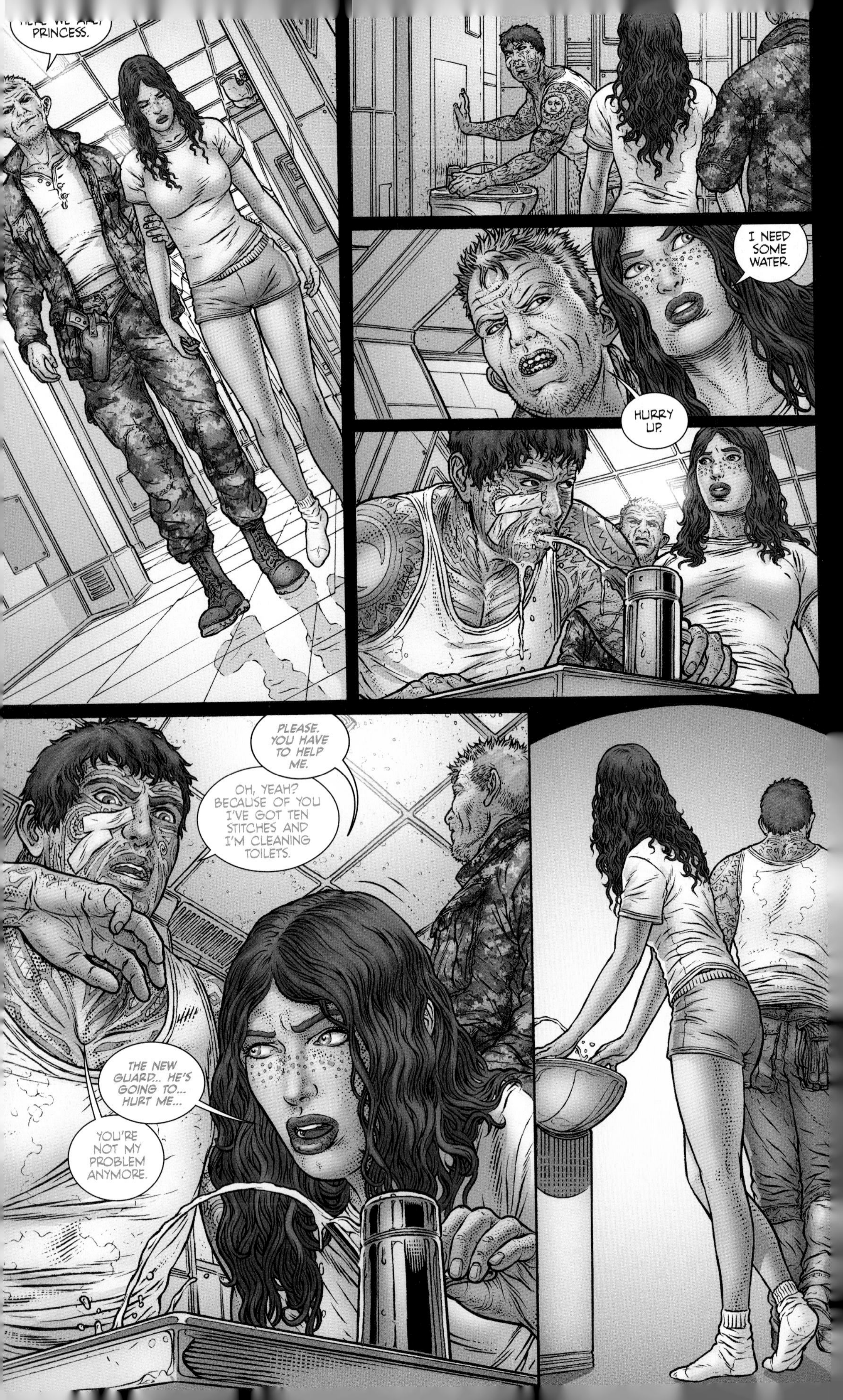
PRINCESS.
I NEED SOME WATER.
HURRY UP.
PLEASE. YOU HAVE TO HELP ME.
OH, YEAH? BECAUSE OF YOU I'VE GOT TEN STITCHES AND I'M CLEANING TOILETS.
THE NEW GUARD.. HE'S GOING TO... HURT ME...
YOU'RE NOT MY PROBLEM ANYMORE.

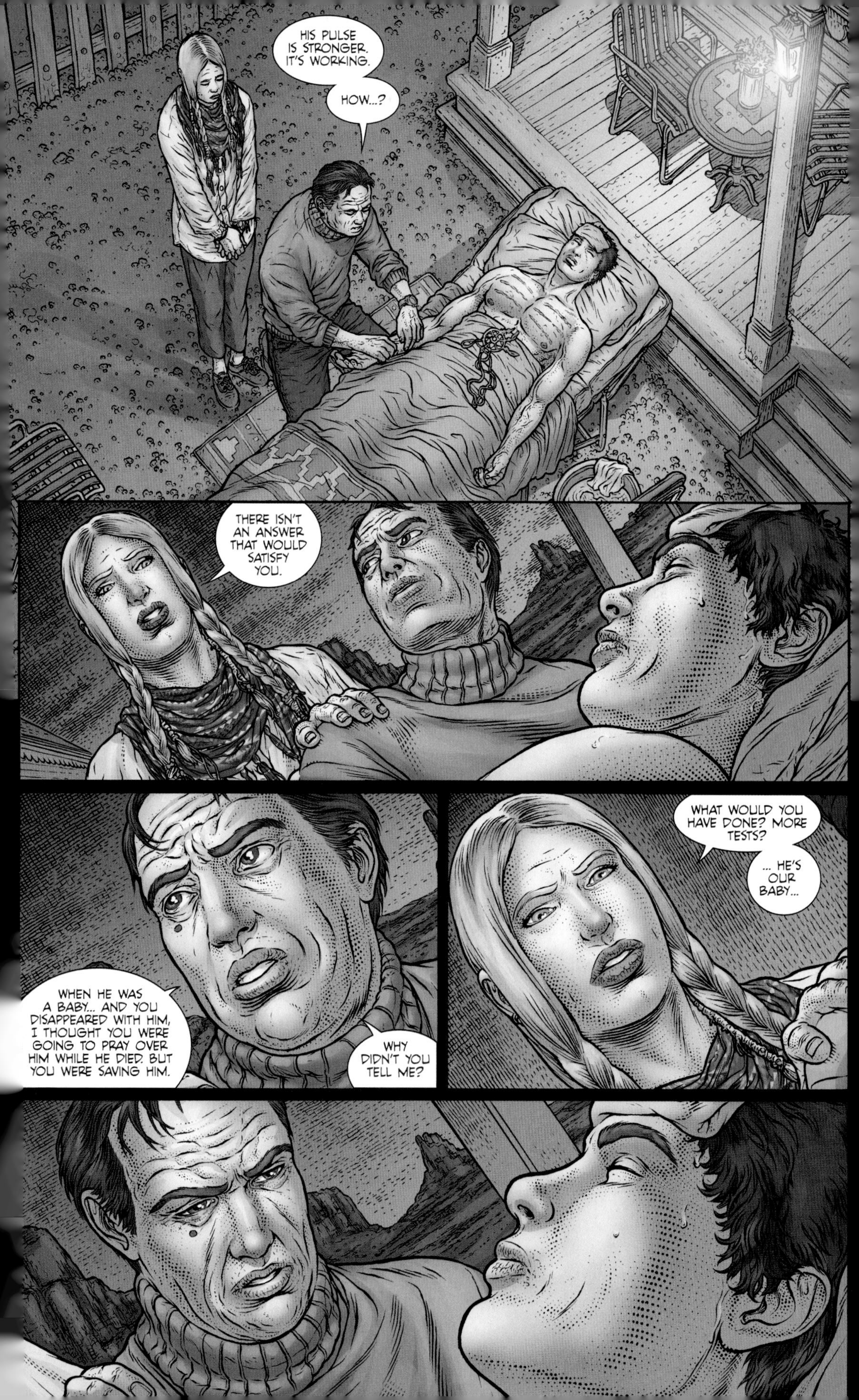
HIS PULSE IS STRONGER. IT'S WORKING.
HOW...?
THERE ISN'T AN ANSWER THAT WOULD SATISFY YOU.
WHEN HE WAS A BABY... AND YOU DISAPPEARED WITH HIM, I THOUGHT YOU WERE GOING TO PRAY OVER HIM WHILE HE DIED. BUT YOU WERE SAVING HIM.
WHY DIDN'T YOU TELL ME?
WHAT WOULD YOU HAVE DONE? MORE TESTS?
... HE'S OUR BABY...

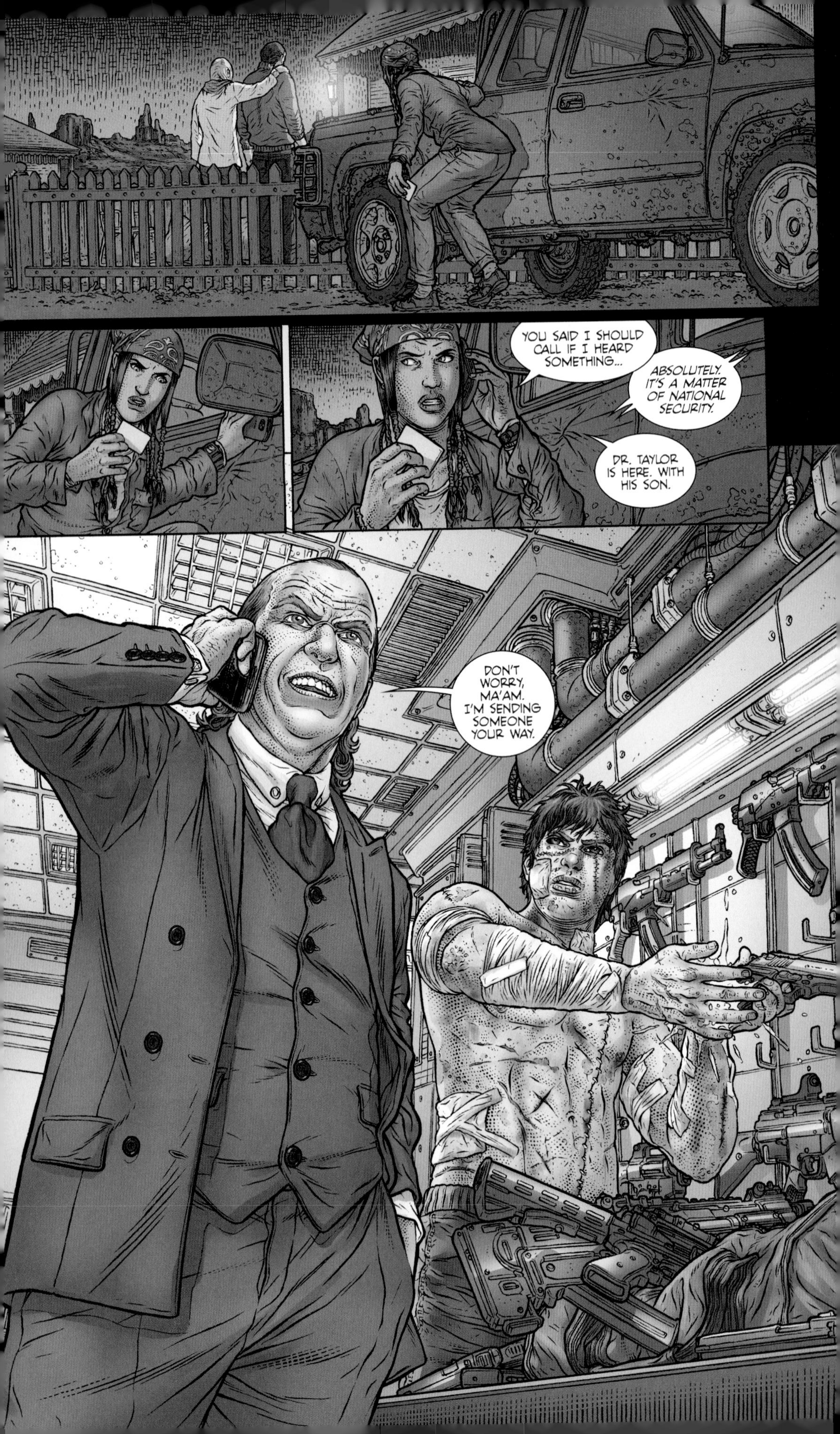
YOU SAID I SHOULD CALL IF I HEARD SOMETHING...
ABSOLUTELY. IT'S A MATTER OF NATIONAL SECURITY.
DR. TAYLOR IS HERE. WITH HIS SON.
DON'T WORRY, MA'AM. I'M SENDING SOMEONE YOUR WAY.

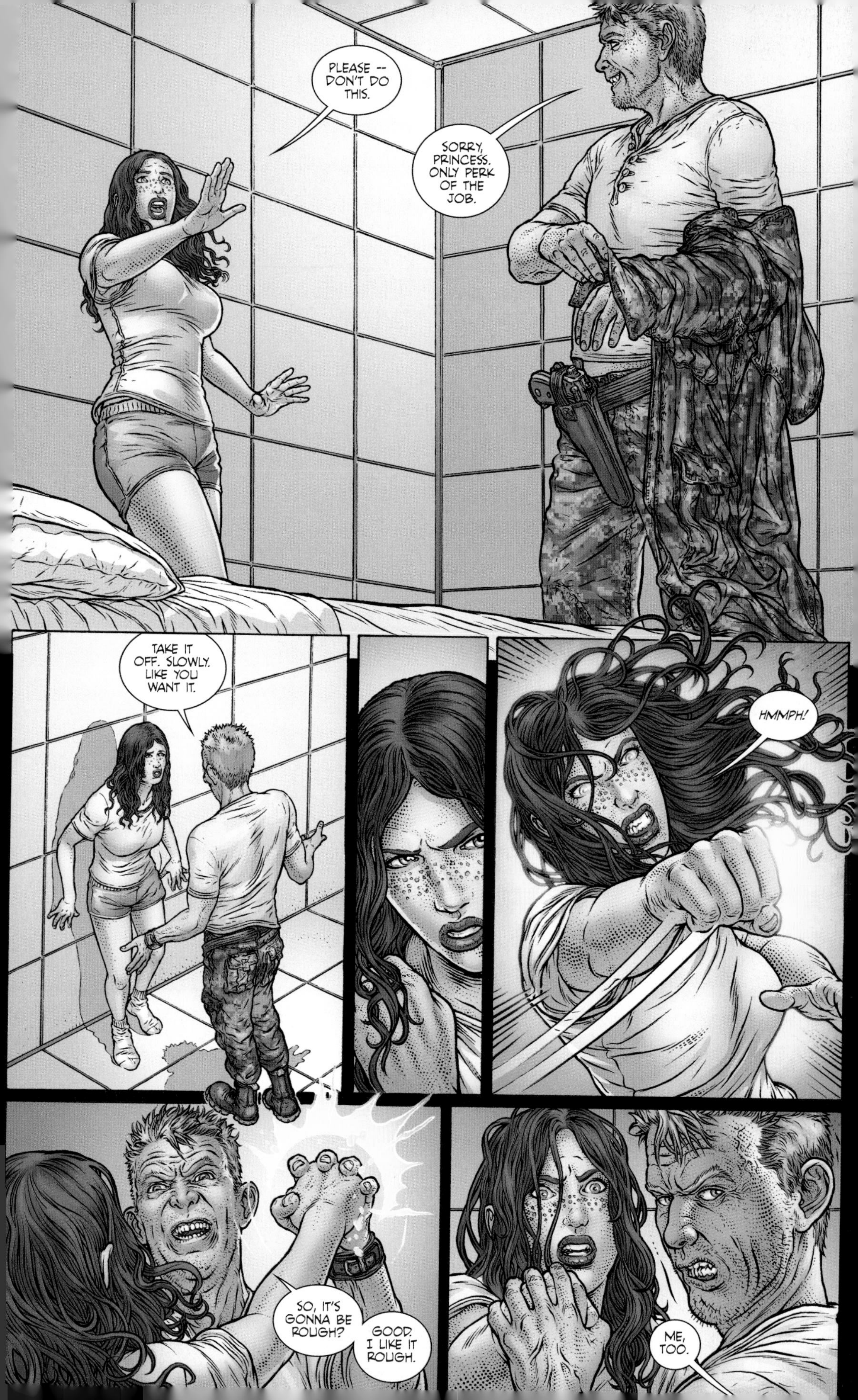
PLEASE -- DON'T DO THIS.
SORRY, PRINCESS. ONLY PERK OF THE JOB.
TAKE IT OFF. SLOWLY. LIKE YOU WANT IT.
HMMPH!
SO, IT'S GONNA BE ROUGH?
GOOD. I LIKE IT ROUGH.
ME, TOO.

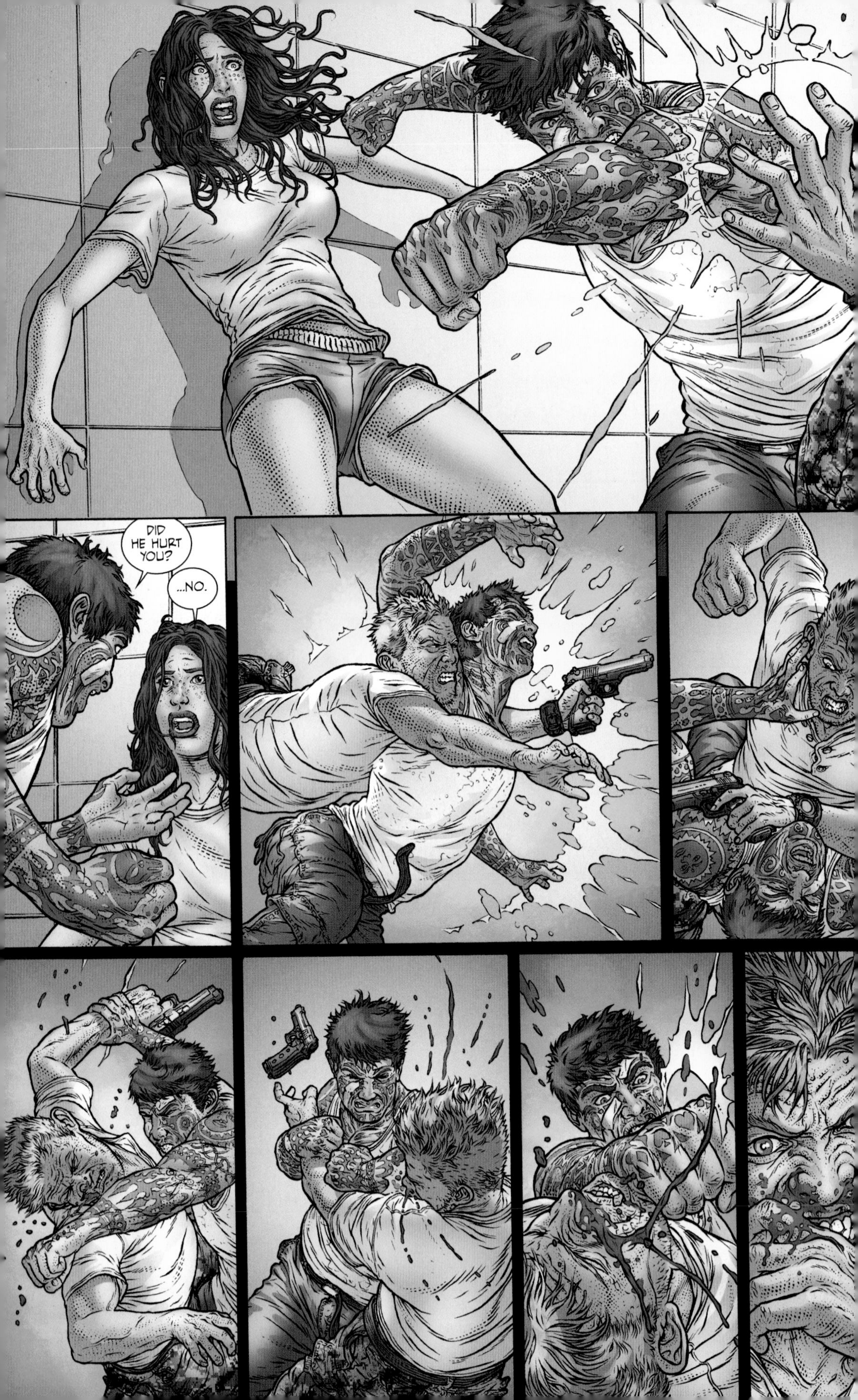
DID HE HURT YOU?
...NO.

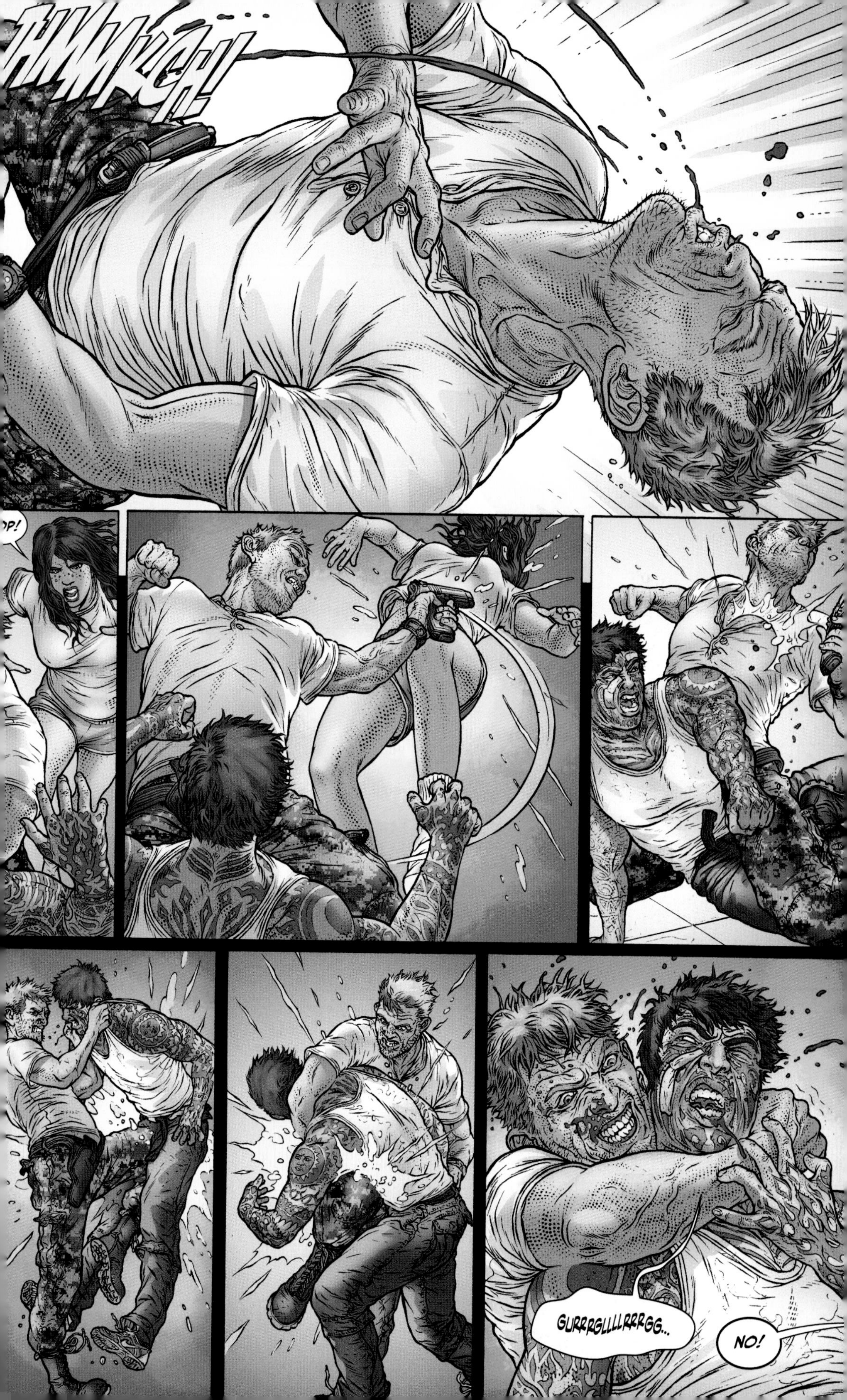
THWUKCH!
GURRRGLLLLRRRGG...
NO!

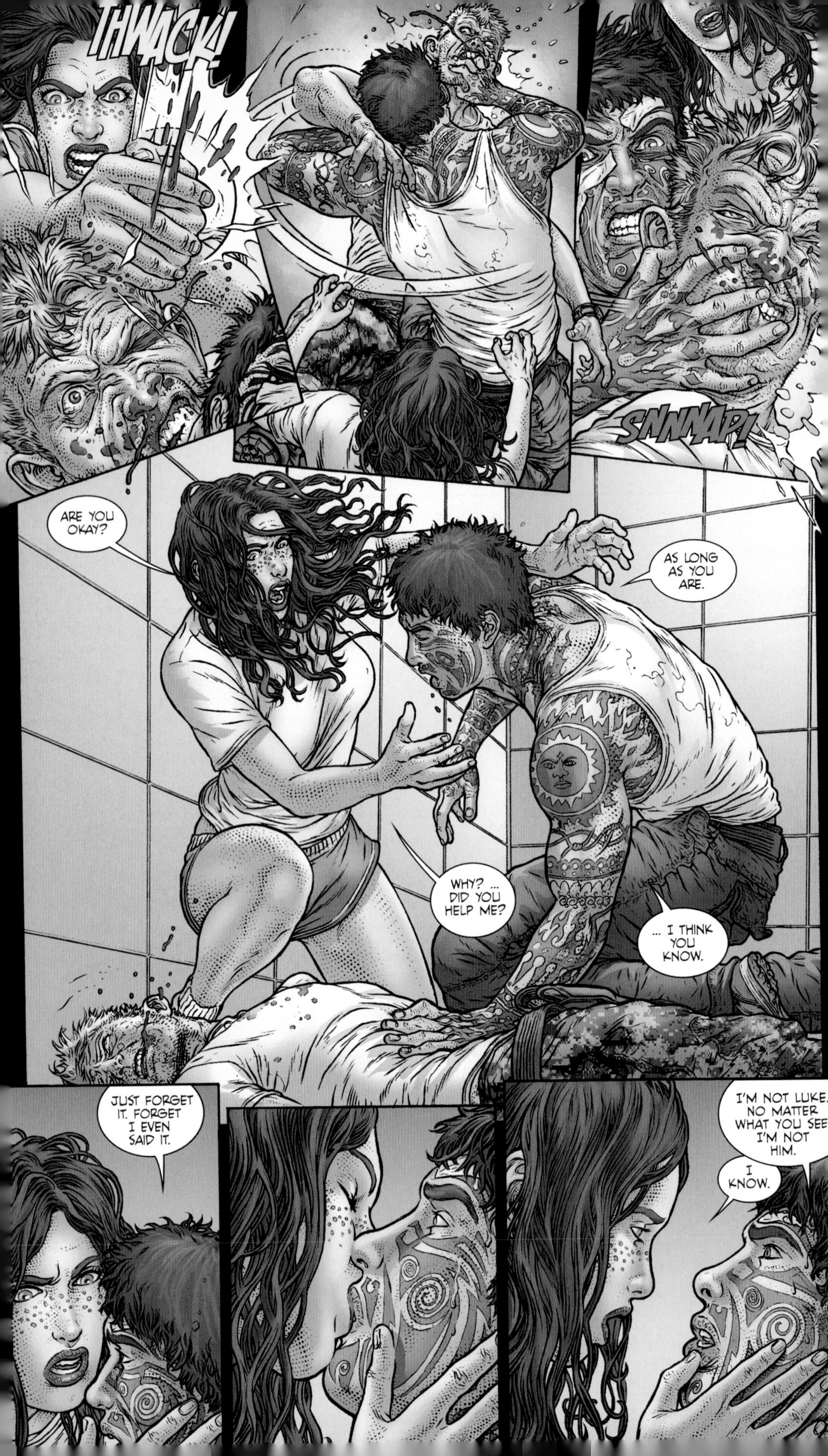
THWACK!
SNNNAP!
ARE YOU OKAY?
AS LONG AS YOU ARE.
WHY? ... DID YOU HELP ME?
... I THINK YOU KNOW.
JUST FORGET IT. FORGET I EVEN SAID IT.
I'M NOT LUKE. NO MATTER WHAT YOU SEE, I'M NOT HIM.
I KNOW.

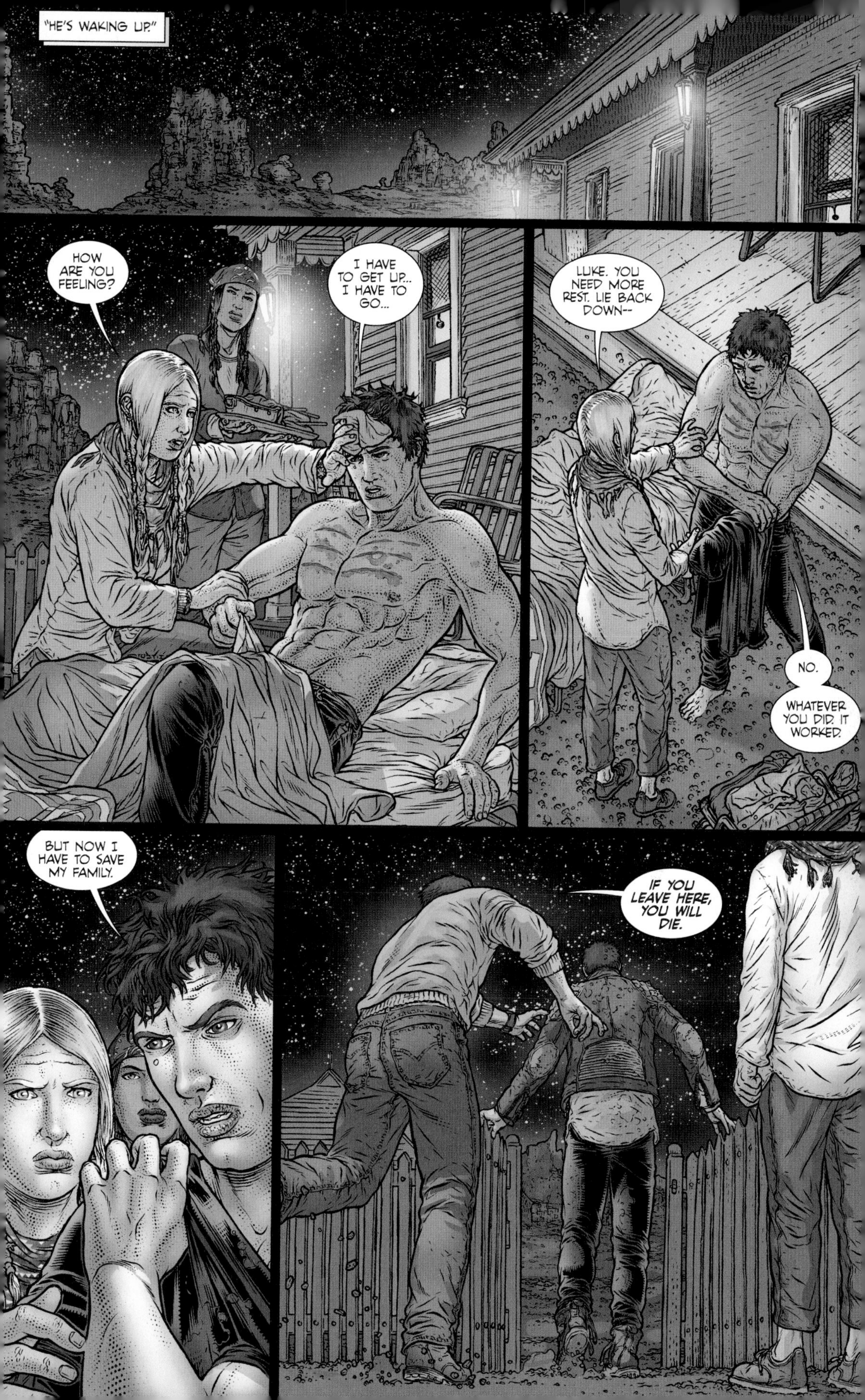
"HE'S WAKING UP."
HOW ARE YOU FEELING?
I HAVE TO GET UP... I HAVE TO GO...
LUKE. YOU NEED MORE REST. LIE BACK DOWN--
NO.
WHATEVER YOU DID, IT WORKED.
BUT NOW I HAVE TO SAVE MY FAMILY.
IF YOU LEAVE HERE, YOU WILL DIE.

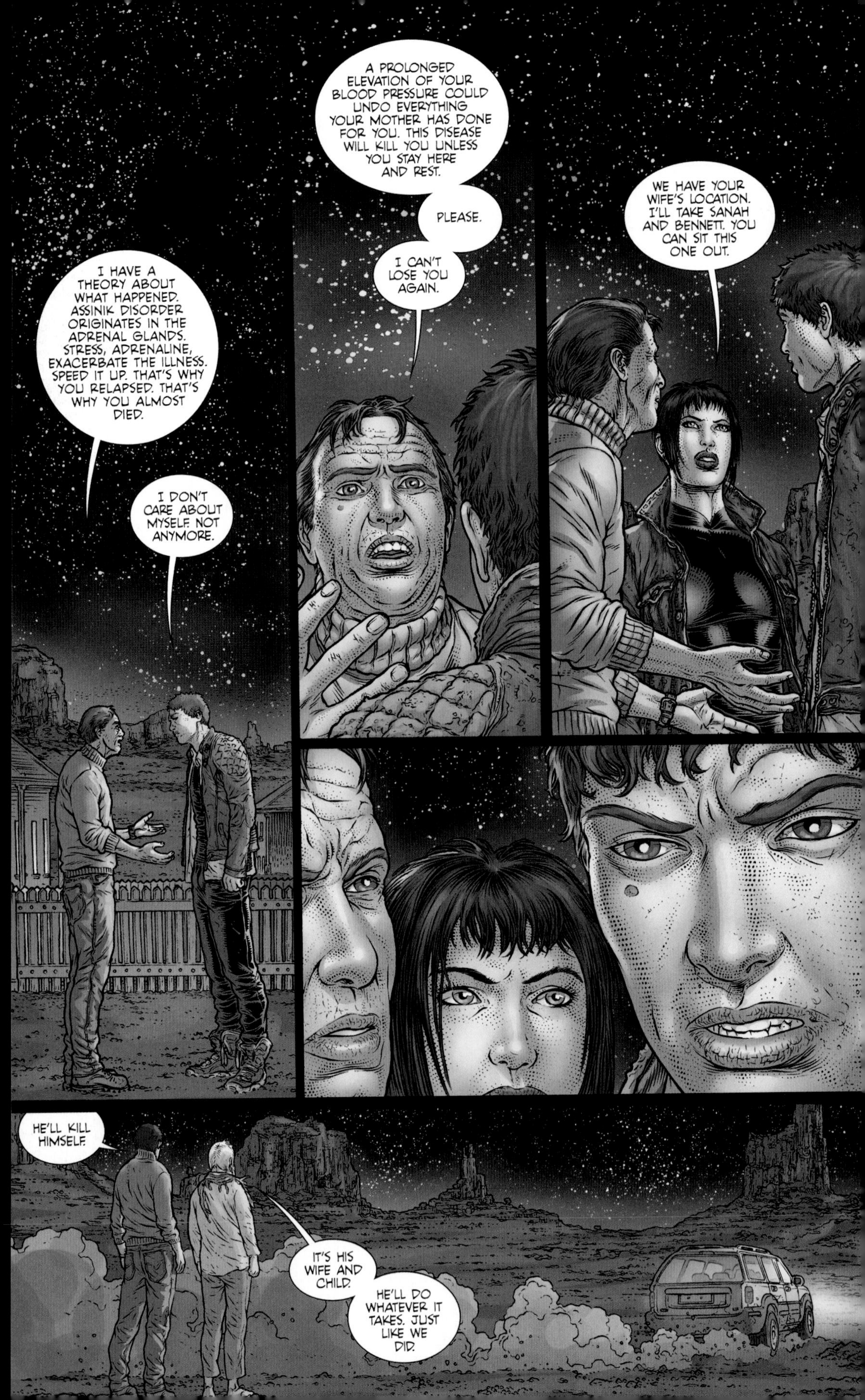
I HAVE A THEORY ABOUT WHAT HAPPENED. ASSINIK DISORDER ORIGINATES IN THE ADRENAL GLANDS. STRESS, ADRENALINE, EXACERBATE THE ILLNESS. SPEED IT UP. THAT'S WHY YOU RELAPSED. THAT'S WHY YOU ALMOST DIED.
I DON'T CARE ABOUT MYSELF. NOT ANYMORE.
A PROLONGED ELEVATION OF YOUR BLOOD PRESSURE COULD UNDO EVERYTHING YOUR MOTHER HAS DONE FOR YOU. THIS DISEASE WILL KILL YOU UNLESS YOU STAY HERE AND REST.
PLEASE.
I CAN'T LOSE YOU AGAIN.
WE HAVE YOUR WIFE'S LOCATION. I'LL TAKE SANAH AND BENNETT. YOU CAN SIT THIS ONE OUT.
HE'LL KILL HIMSELF.
IT'S HIS WIFE AND CHILD.
HE'LL DO WHATEVER IT TAKES. JUST LIKE WE DID.

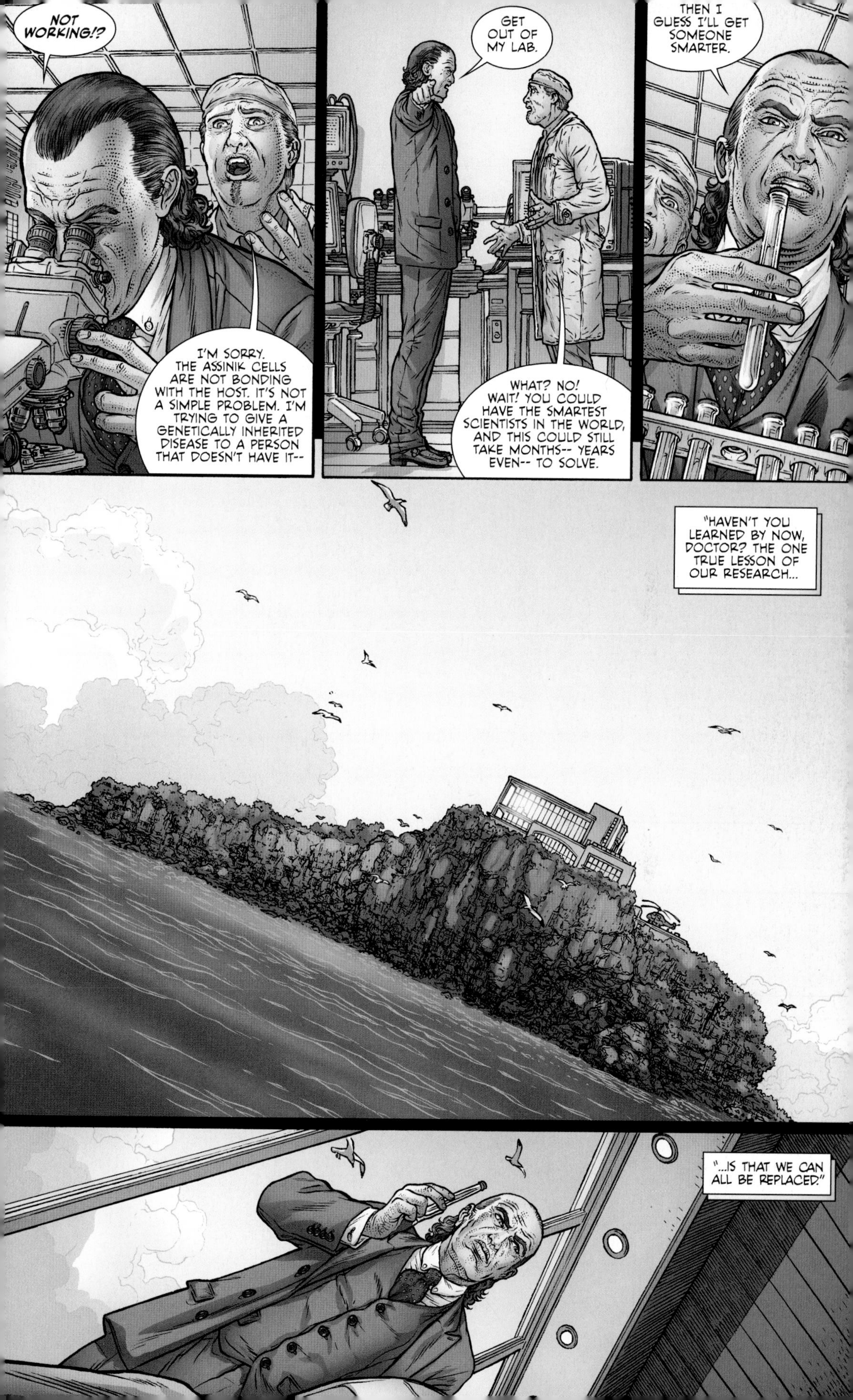
NOT WORKING!?
I'M SORRY. THE ASSINIK CELLS ARE NOT BONDING WITH THE HOST. IT'S NOT A SIMPLE PROBLEM. I'M TRYING TO GIVE A GENETICALLY INHERITED DISEASE TO A PERSON THAT DOESN'T HAVE IT--
GET OUT OF MY LAB.
WHAT? NO! WAIT! YOU COULD HAVE THE SMARTEST SCIENTISTS IN THE WORLD, AND THIS COULD STILL TAKE MONTHS-- YEARS EVEN-- TO SOLVE.
THEN I GUESS I'LL GET SOMEONE SMARTER.
"HAVEN'T YOU LEARNED BY NOW, DOCTOR? THE ONE TRUE LESSON OF OUR RESEARCH...
"...IS THAT WE CAN ALL BE REPLACED."

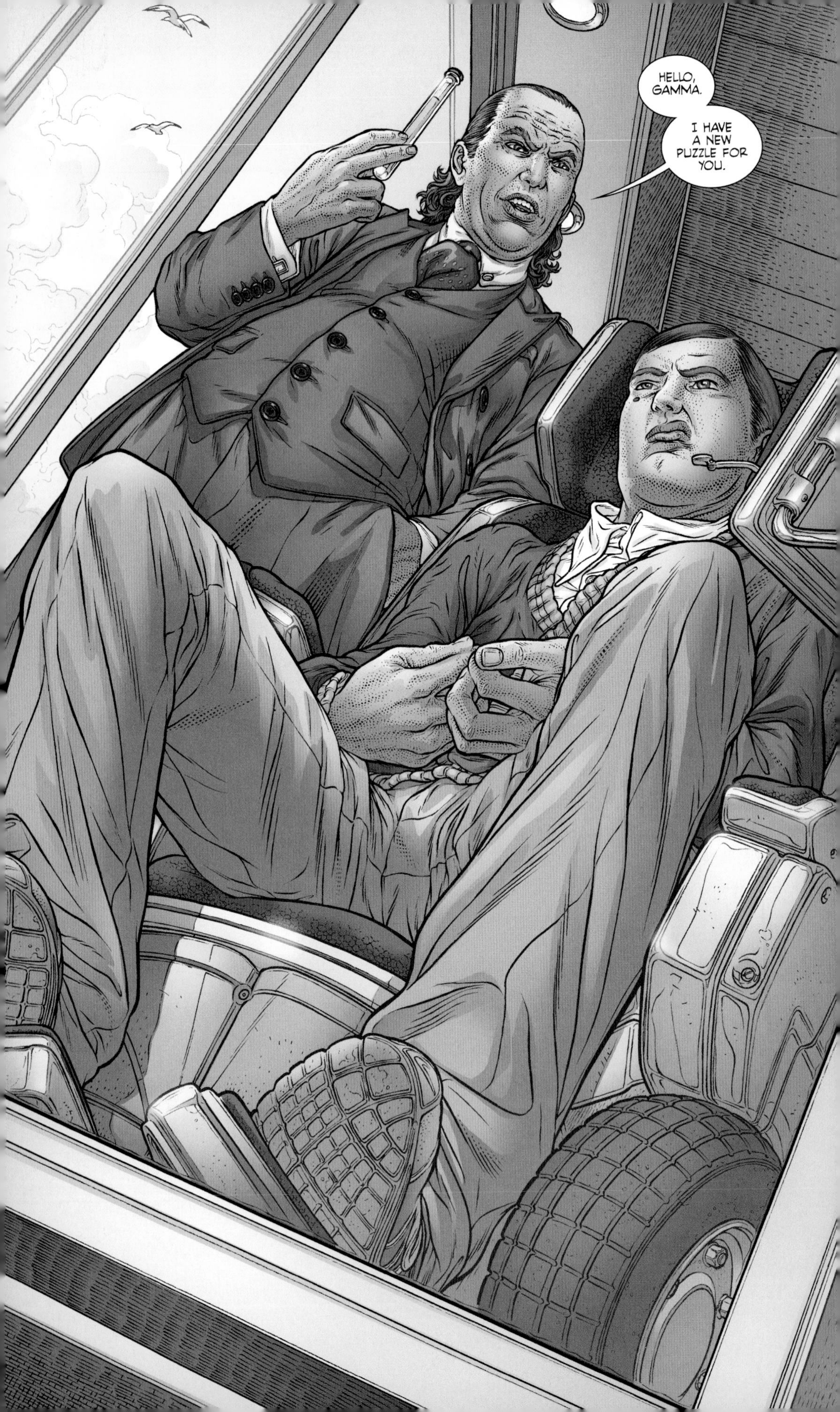
HELLO, GAMMA.
I HAVE A NEW PUZZLE FOR YOU.

# CHAPTER 9

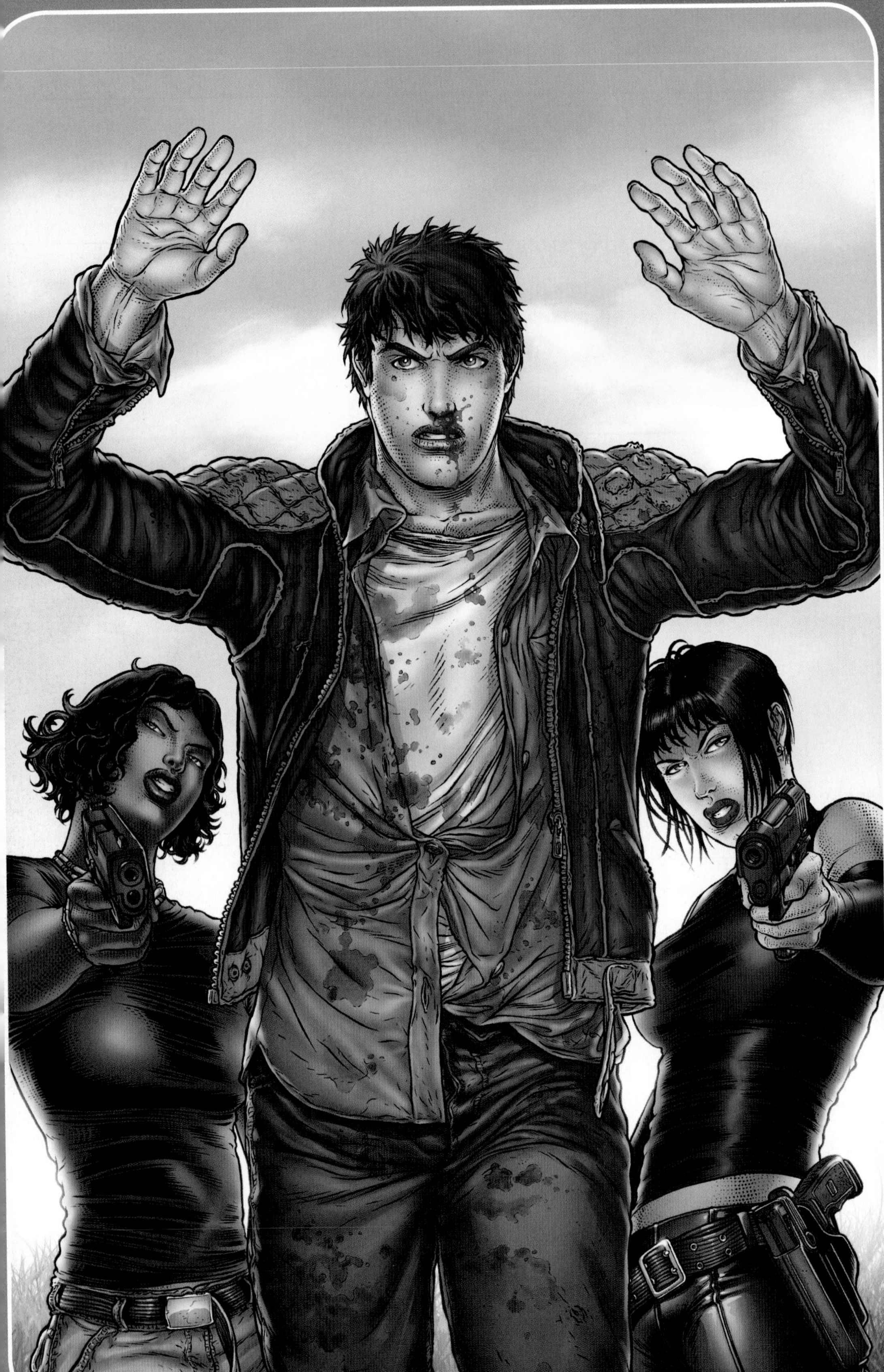

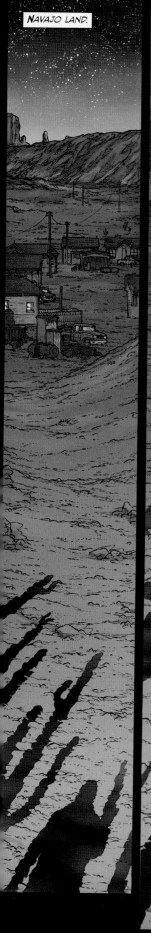

NAVAJO LAND.

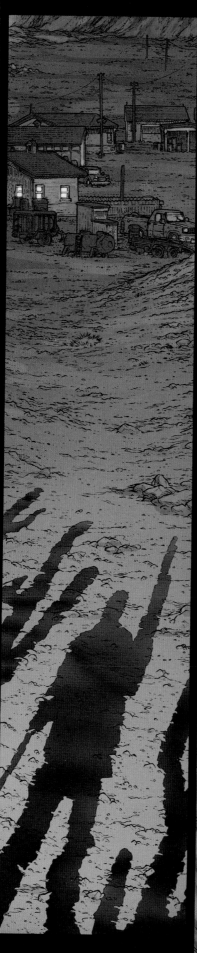

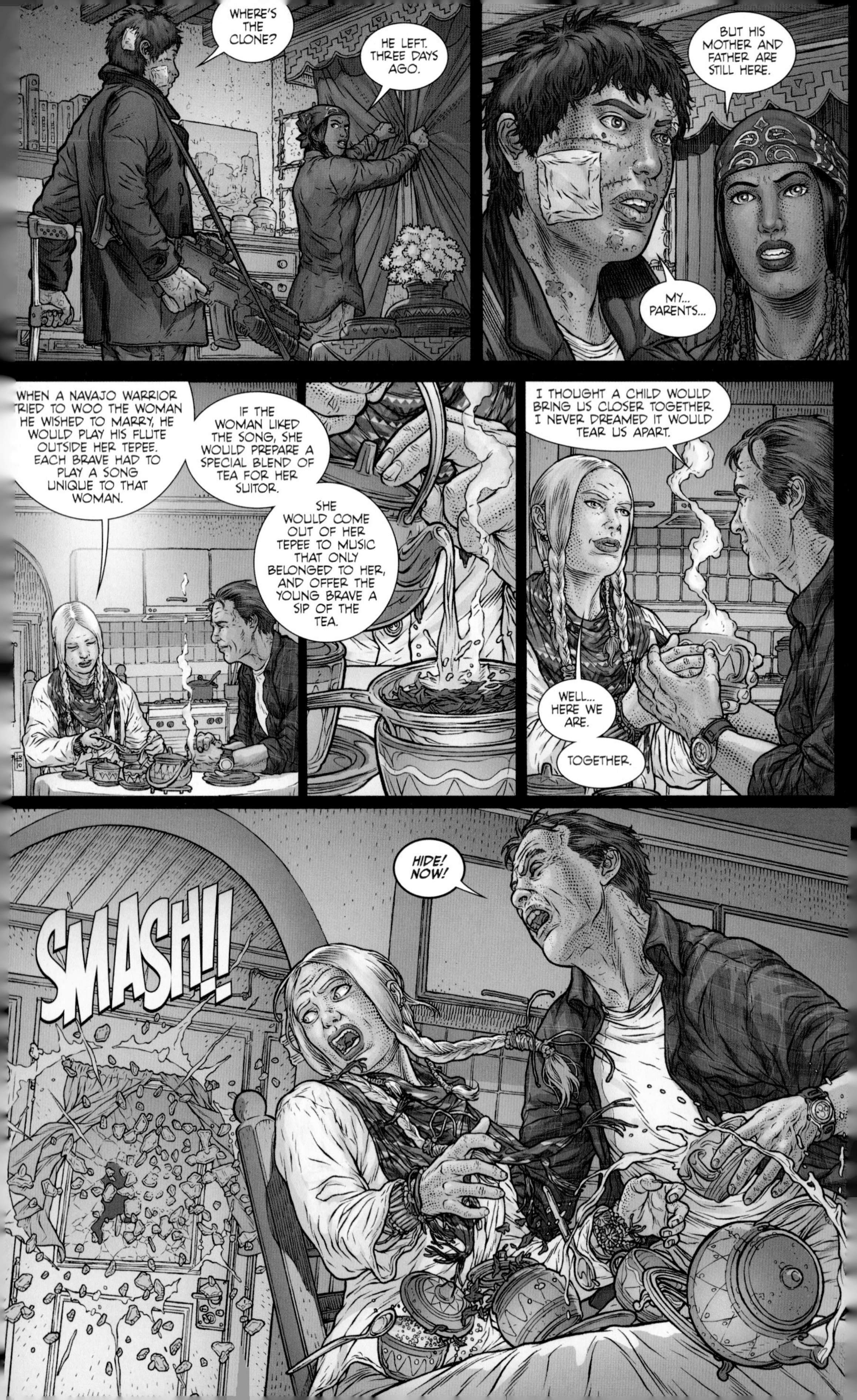
WHERE'S THE CLONE?
HE LEFT. THREE DAYS AGO.
BUT HIS MOTHER AND FATHER ARE STILL HERE.
MY... PARENTS...
WHEN A NAVAJO WARRIOR TRIED TO WOO THE WOMAN HE WISHED TO MARRY, HE WOULD PLAY HIS FLUTE OUTSIDE HER TEPEE. EACH BRAVE HAD TO PLAY A SONG UNIQUE TO THAT WOMAN.
IF THE WOMAN LIKED THE SONG, SHE WOULD PREPARE A SPECIAL BLEND OF TEA FOR HER SUITOR.
SHE WOULD COME OUT OF HER TEPEE TO MUSIC THAT ONLY BELONGED TO HER, AND OFFER THE YOUNG BRAVE A SIP OF THE TEA.
I THOUGHT A CHILD WOULD BRING US CLOSER TOGETHER. I NEVER DREAMED IT WOULD TEAR US APART.
WELL... HERE WE ARE.
TOGETHER.
SMASH!!!
HIDE! NOW!

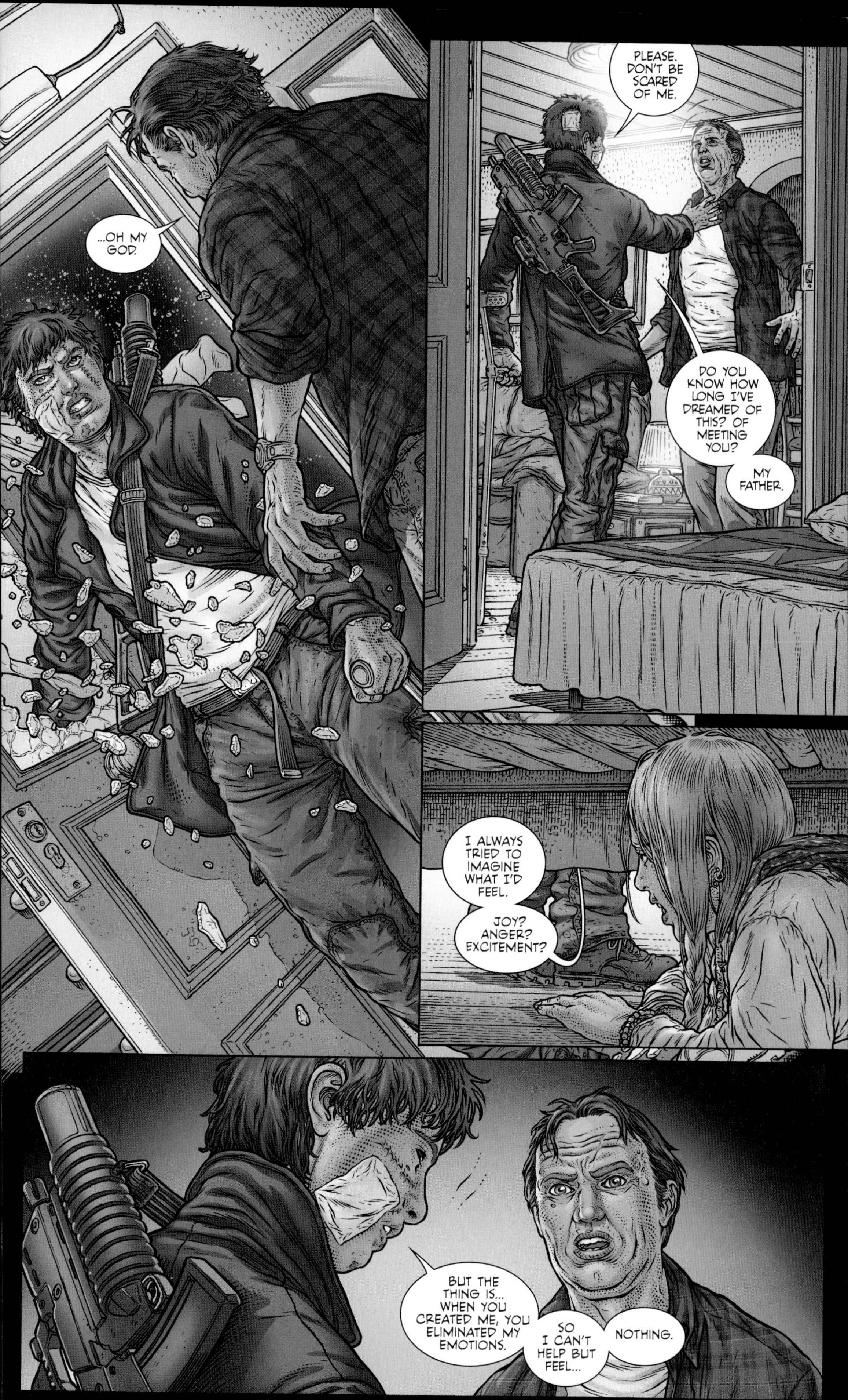
...OH MY GOD.
PLEASE. DON'T BE SCARED OF ME.
DO YOU KNOW HOW LONG I'VE DREAMED OF THIS? OF MEETING YOU?
MY FATHER.
I ALWAYS TRIED TO IMAGINE WHAT I'D FEEL.
JOY? ANGER? EXCITEMENT?
BUT THE THING IS... WHEN YOU CREATED ME, YOU ELIMINATED MY EMOTIONS.
SO I CAN'T HELP BUT FEEL...
NOTHING.

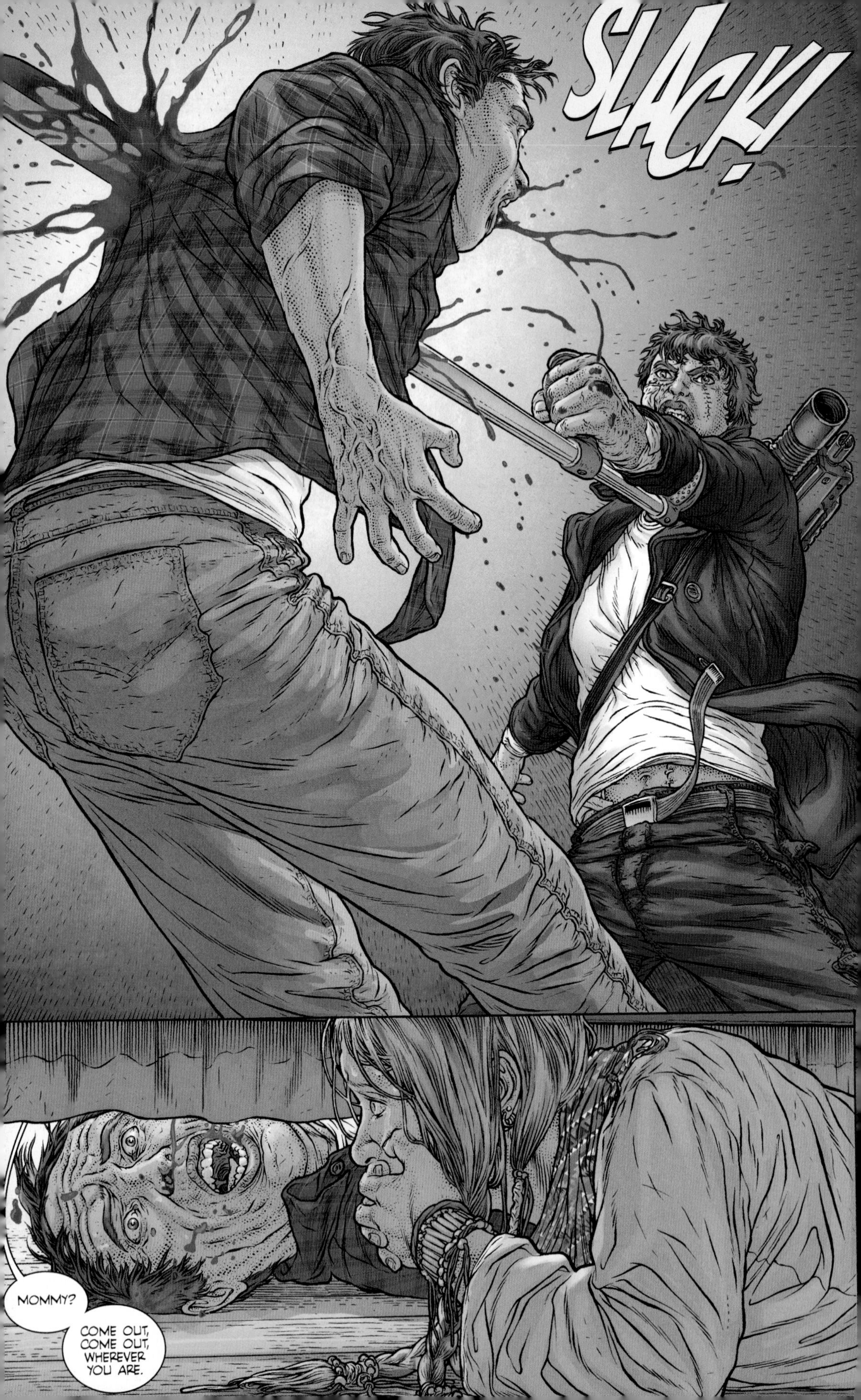
SLACK!
MOMMY?
COME OUT, COME OUT, WHEREVER YOU ARE.

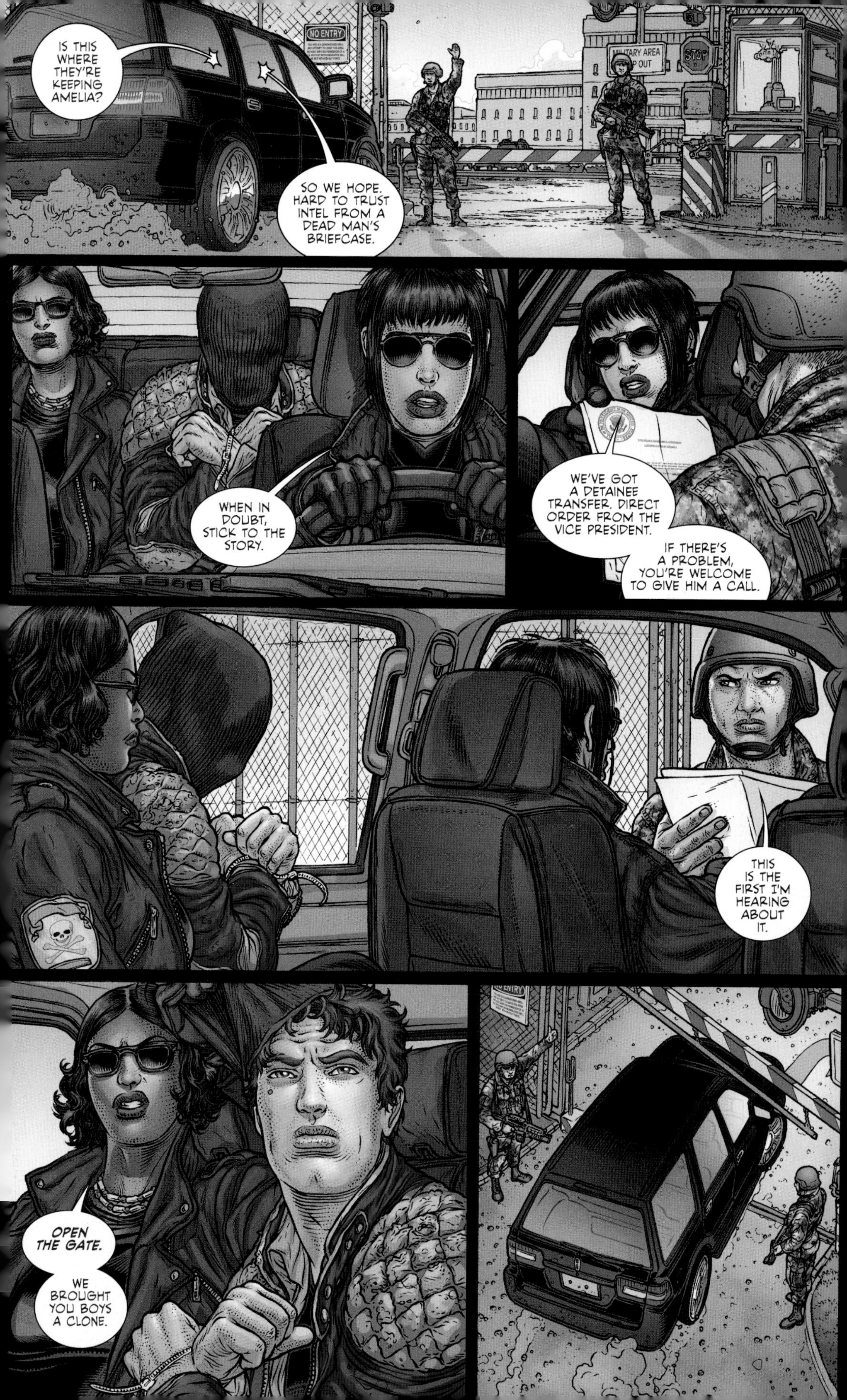
NO ENTRY
MILITARY AREA
STOP
IS THIS WHERE THEY'RE KEEPING AMELIA?
SO WE HOPE. HARD TO TRUST INTEL FROM A DEAD MAN'S BRIEFCASE.
WHEN IN DOUBT, STICK TO THE STORY.
WE'VE GOT A DETAINEE TRANSFER. DIRECT ORDER FROM THE VICE PRESIDENT.
IF THERE'S A PROBLEM, YOU'RE WELCOME TO GIVE HIM A CALL.
THIS IS THE FIRST I'M HEARING ABOUT IT.
*OPEN THE GATE.*
WE BROUGHT YOU BOYS A CLONE.
NO ENTRY

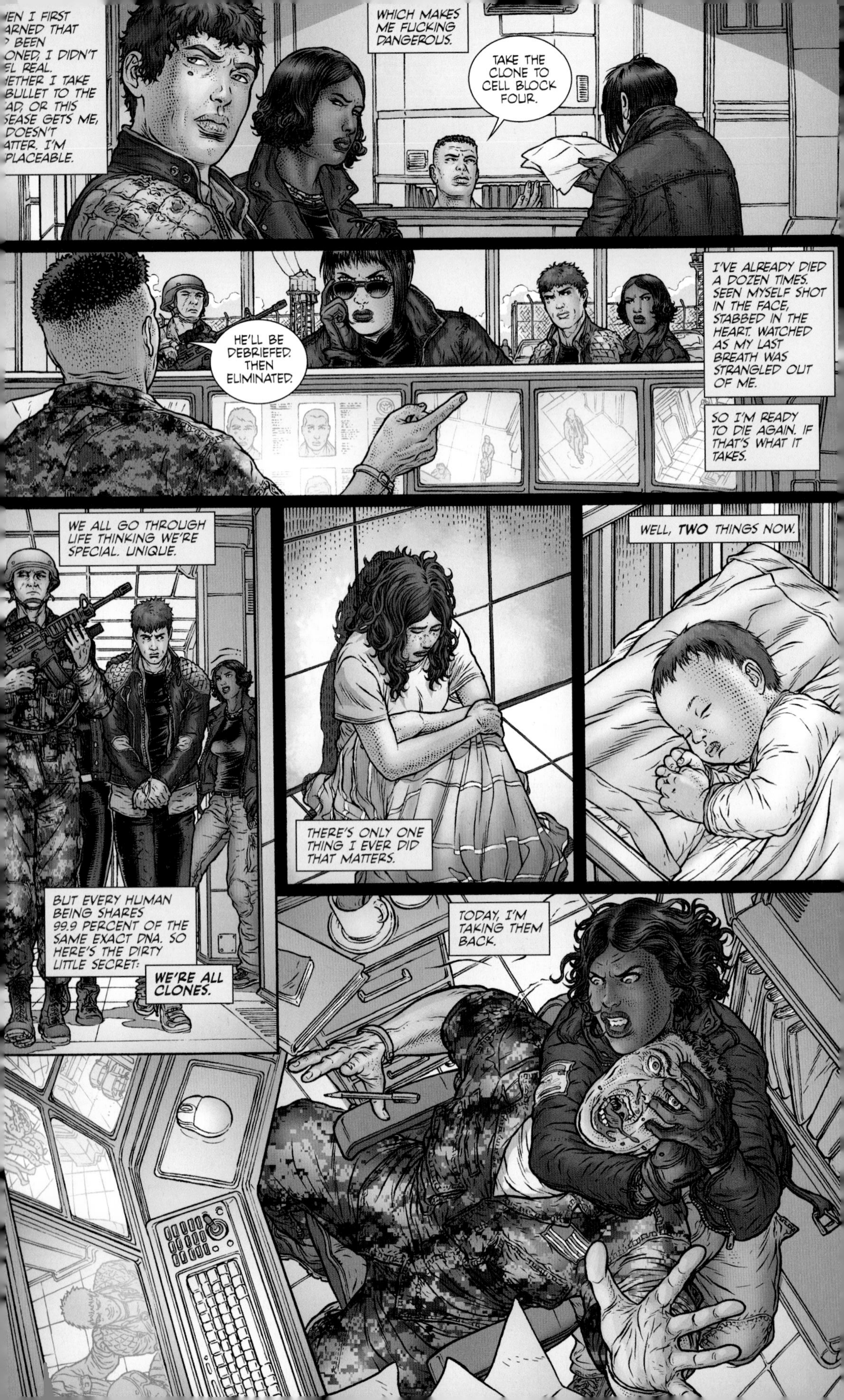

IEN I FIRST ARNED THAT D BEEN ONED, I DIDN'T EL REAL. IETHER I TAKE BULLET TO THE AD, OR THIS SEASE GETS ME, DOESN'T ATTER. I'M PLACEABLE.
WHICH MAKES ME FUCKING DANGEROUS.
TAKE THE CLONE TO CELL BLOCK FOUR.
HE'LL BE DEBRIEFED. THEN ELIMINATED.
I'VE ALREADY DIED A DOZEN TIMES. SEEN MYSELF SHOT IN THE FACE, STABBED IN THE HEART. WATCHED AS MY LAST BREATH WAS STRANGLED OUT OF ME.
SO I'M READY TO DIE AGAIN. IF THAT'S WHAT IT TAKES.
WE ALL GO THROUGH LIFE THINKING WE'RE SPECIAL. UNIQUE.
BUT EVERY HUMAN BEING SHARES 99.9 PERCENT OF THE SAME EXACT DNA. SO HERE'S THE DIRTY LITTLE SECRET:
WE'RE ALL CLONES.
THERE'S ONLY ONE THING I EVER DID THAT MATTERS.
WELL, TWO THINGS NOW.
TODAY, I'M TAKING THEM BACK.

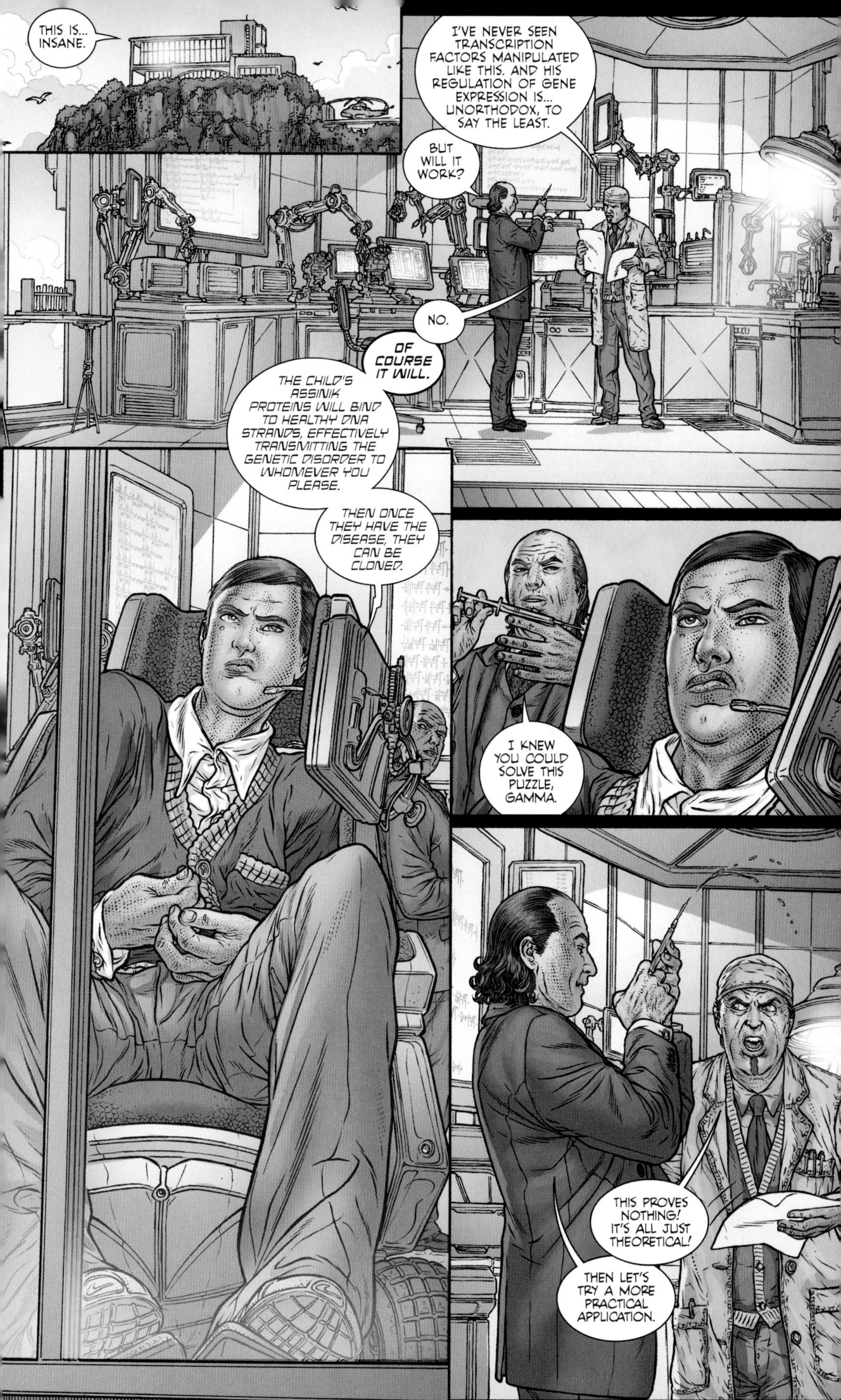
THIS IS... INSANE.
I'VE NEVER SEEN TRANSCRIPTION FACTORS MANIPULATED LIKE THIS. AND HIS REGULATION OF GENE EXPRESSION IS... UNORTHODOX, TO SAY THE LEAST.
BUT WILL IT WORK?
NO.
OF COURSE IT WILL.
THE CHILD'S ASSINIK PROTEINS WILL BIND TO HEALTHY DNA STRANDS, EFFECTIVELY TRANSMITTING THE GENETIC DISORDER TO WHOMEVER YOU PLEASE.
THEN ONCE THEY HAVE THE DISEASE, THEY CAN BE CLONED.
I KNEW YOU COULD SOLVE THIS PUZZLE, GAMMA.
THIS PROVES NOTHING! IT'S ALL JUST THEORETICAL!
THEN LET'S TRY A MORE PRACTICAL APPLICATION.

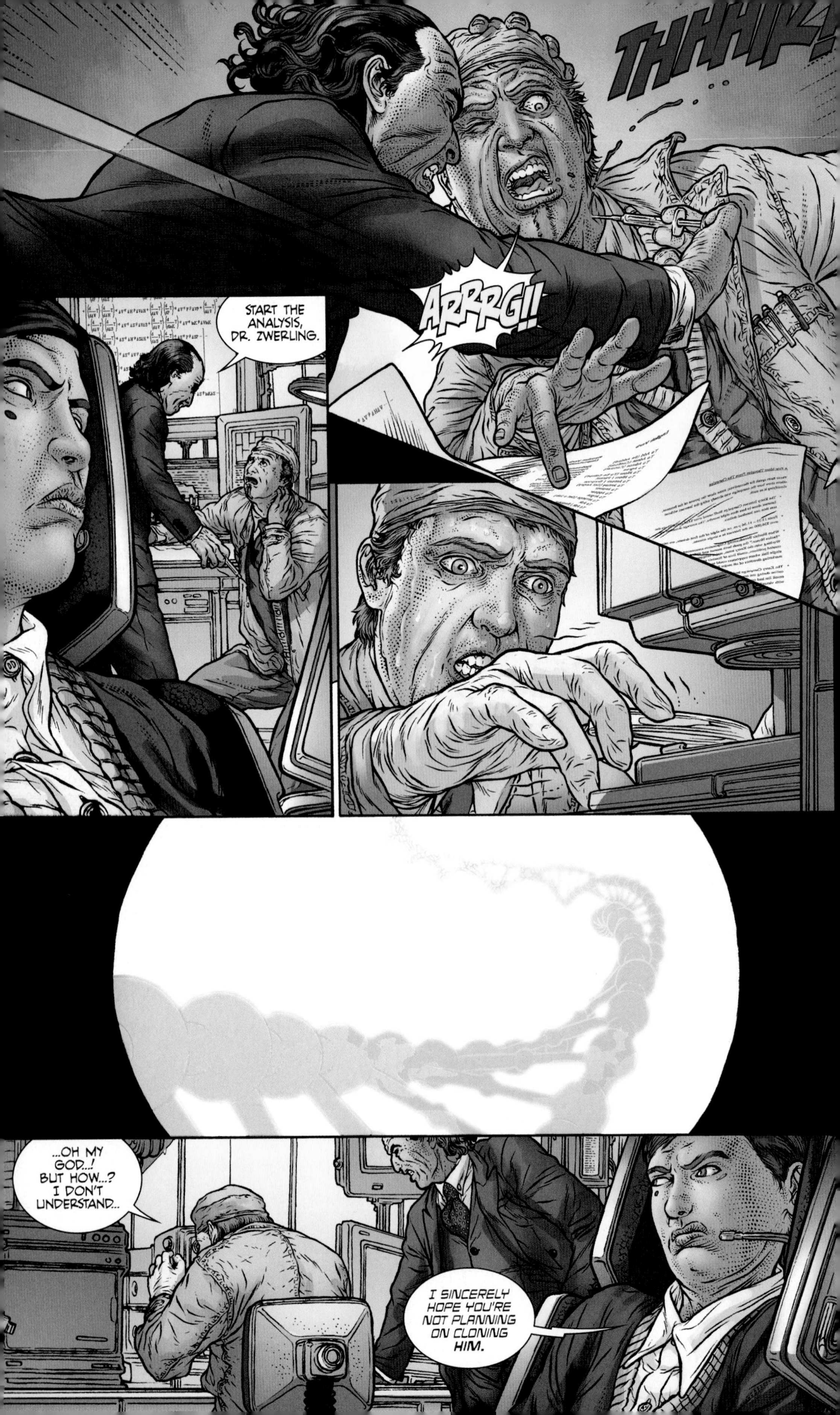
THHHK!
ARRRG!!
START THE ANALYSIS, DR. ZWERLING.
...OH MY GOD...! BUT HOW...? I DON'T UNDERSTAND...
I SINCERELY HOPE YOU'RE NOT PLANNING ON CLONING HIM.

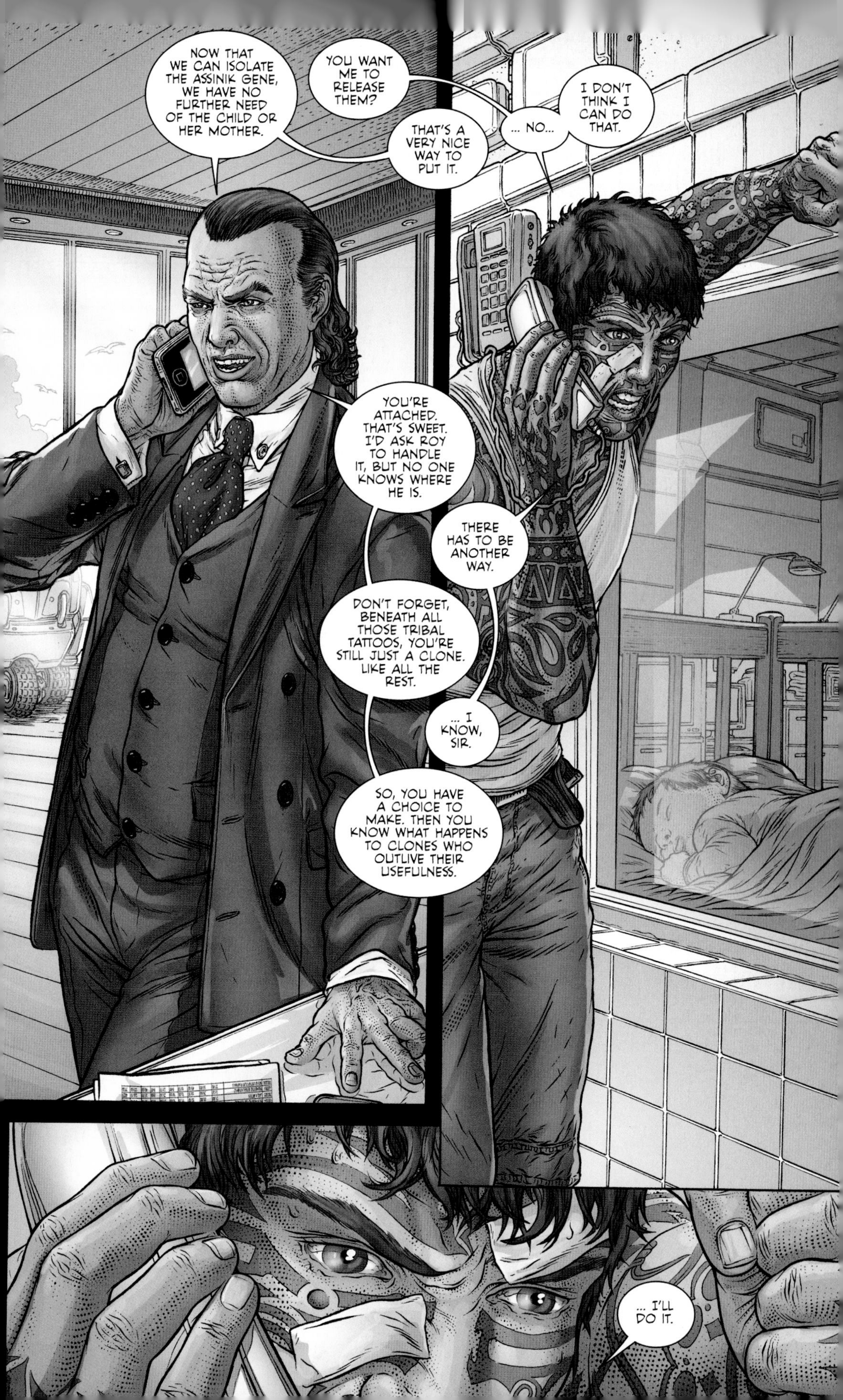
NOW THAT WE CAN ISOLATE THE ASSINIK GENE, WE HAVE NO FURTHER NEED OF THE CHILD OR HER MOTHER.
YOU WANT ME TO RELEASE THEM?
THAT'S A VERY NICE WAY TO PUT IT.
... NO...
I DON'T THINK I CAN DO THAT.
YOU'RE ATTACHED. THAT'S SWEET. I'D ASK ROY TO HANDLE IT, BUT NO ONE KNOWS WHERE HE IS.
THERE HAS TO BE ANOTHER WAY.
DON'T FORGET, BENEATH ALL THOSE TRIBAL TATTOOS, YOU'RE STILL JUST A CLONE. LIKE ALL THE REST.
... I KNOW, SIR.
SO, YOU HAVE A CHOICE TO MAKE. THEN YOU KNOW WHAT HAPPENS TO CLONES WHO OUTLIVE THEIR USEFULNESS.
... I'LL DO IT.

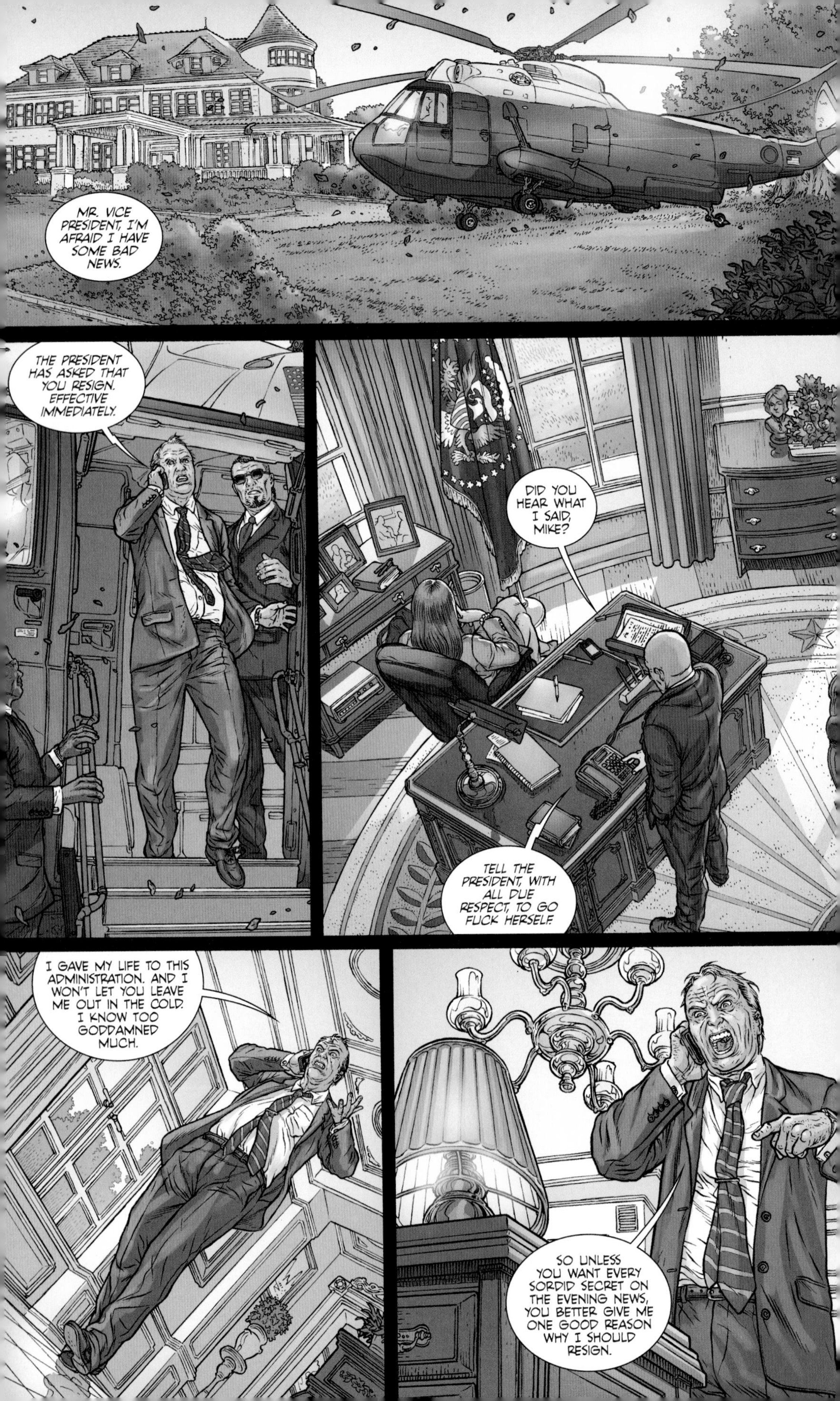
MR. VICE PRESIDENT, I'M AFRAID I HAVE SOME BAD NEWS.
THE PRESIDENT HAS ASKED THAT YOU RESIGN. EFFECTIVE IMMEDIATELY.
DID YOU HEAR WHAT I SAID, MIKE?
TELL THE PRESIDENT, WITH ALL DUE RESPECT, TO GO FUCK HERSELF.
I GAVE MY LIFE TO THIS ADMINISTRATION. AND I WON'T LET YOU LEAVE ME OUT IN THE COLD. I KNOW TOO GODDAMNED MUCH.
SO UNLESS YOU WANT EVERY SORDID SECRET ON THE EVENING NEWS, YOU BETTER GIVE ME ONE GOOD REASON WHY I SHOULD RESIGN.

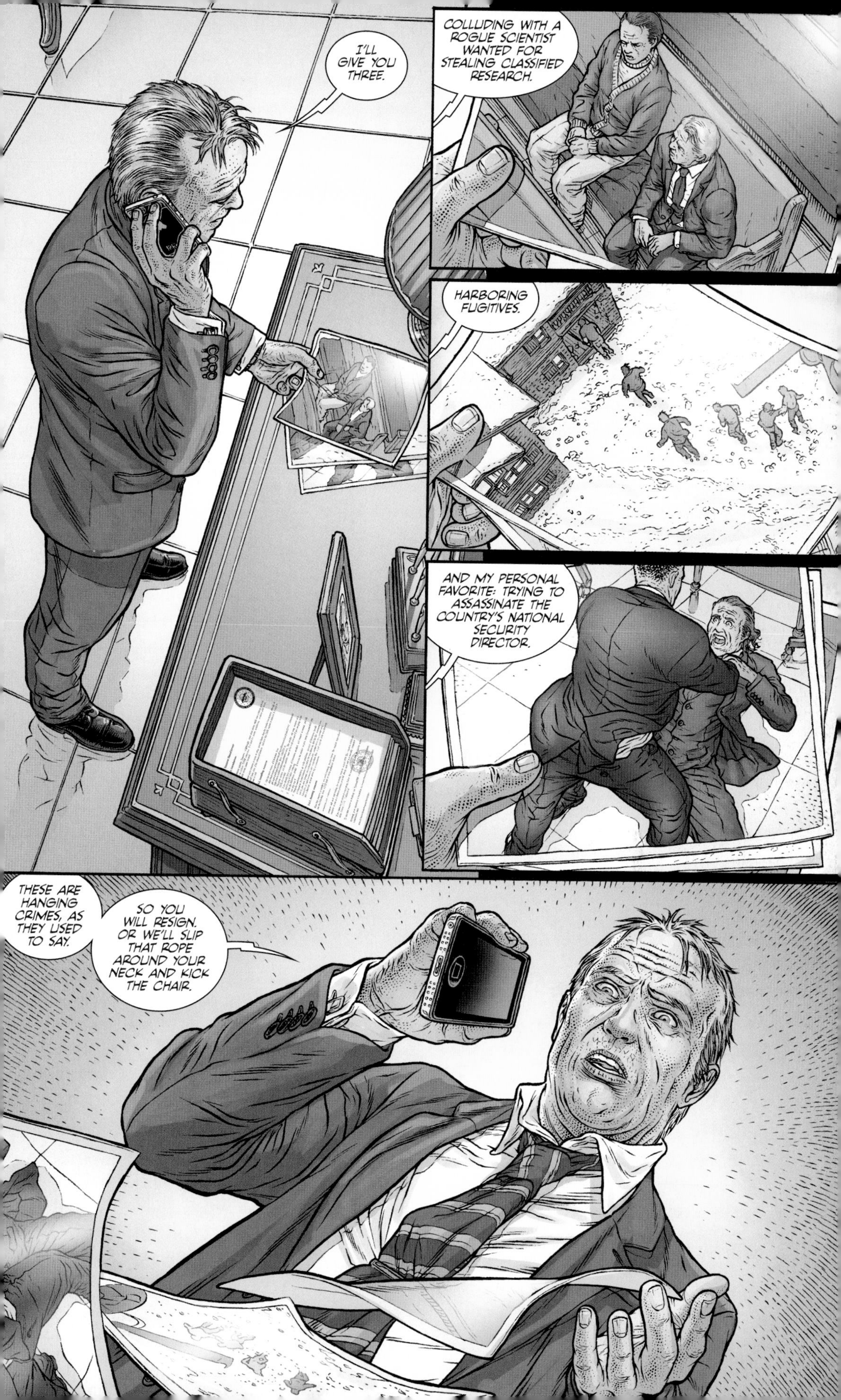
I'LL GIVE YOU THREE.
COLLUDING WITH A ROGUE SCIENTIST WANTED FOR STEALING CLASSIFIED RESEARCH.
HARBORING FUGITIVES.
AND MY PERSONAL FAVORITE: TRYING TO ASSASSINATE THE COUNTRY'S NATIONAL SECURITY DIRECTOR.
THESE ARE HANGING CRIMES, AS THEY USED TO SAY.
SO YOU WILL RESIGN. OR WE'LL SLIP THAT ROPE AROUND YOUR NECK AND KICK THE CHAIR.

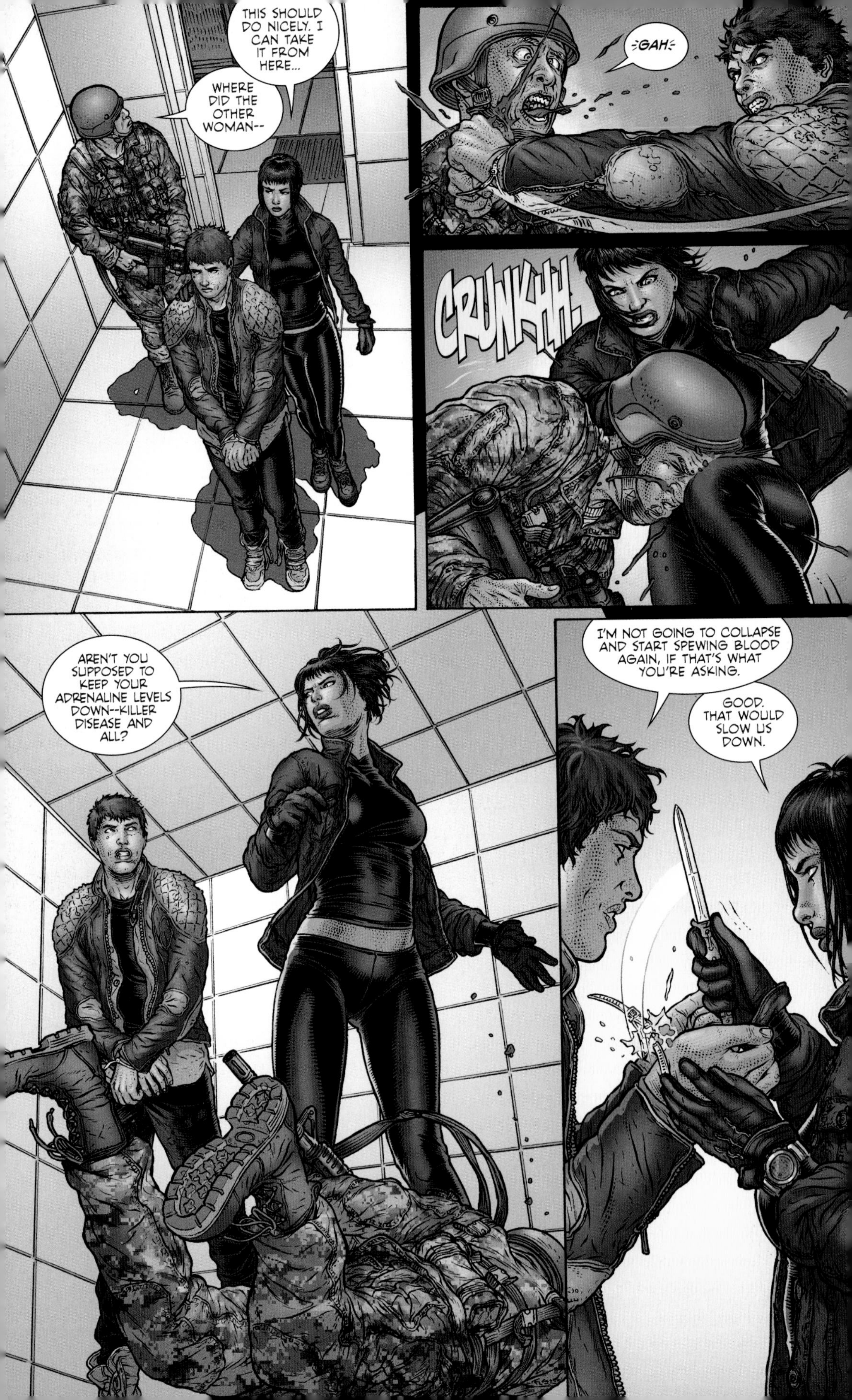
WHERE DID THE OTHER WOMAN--
THIS SHOULD DO NICELY. I CAN TAKE IT FROM HERE...
GAH
CRUNKHH
AREN'T YOU SUPPOSED TO KEEP YOUR ADRENALINE LEVELS DOWN--KILLER DISEASE AND ALL?
I'M NOT GOING TO COLLAPSE AND START SPEWING BLOOD AGAIN, IF THAT'S WHAT YOU'RE ASKING.
GOOD. THAT WOULD SLOW US DOWN.

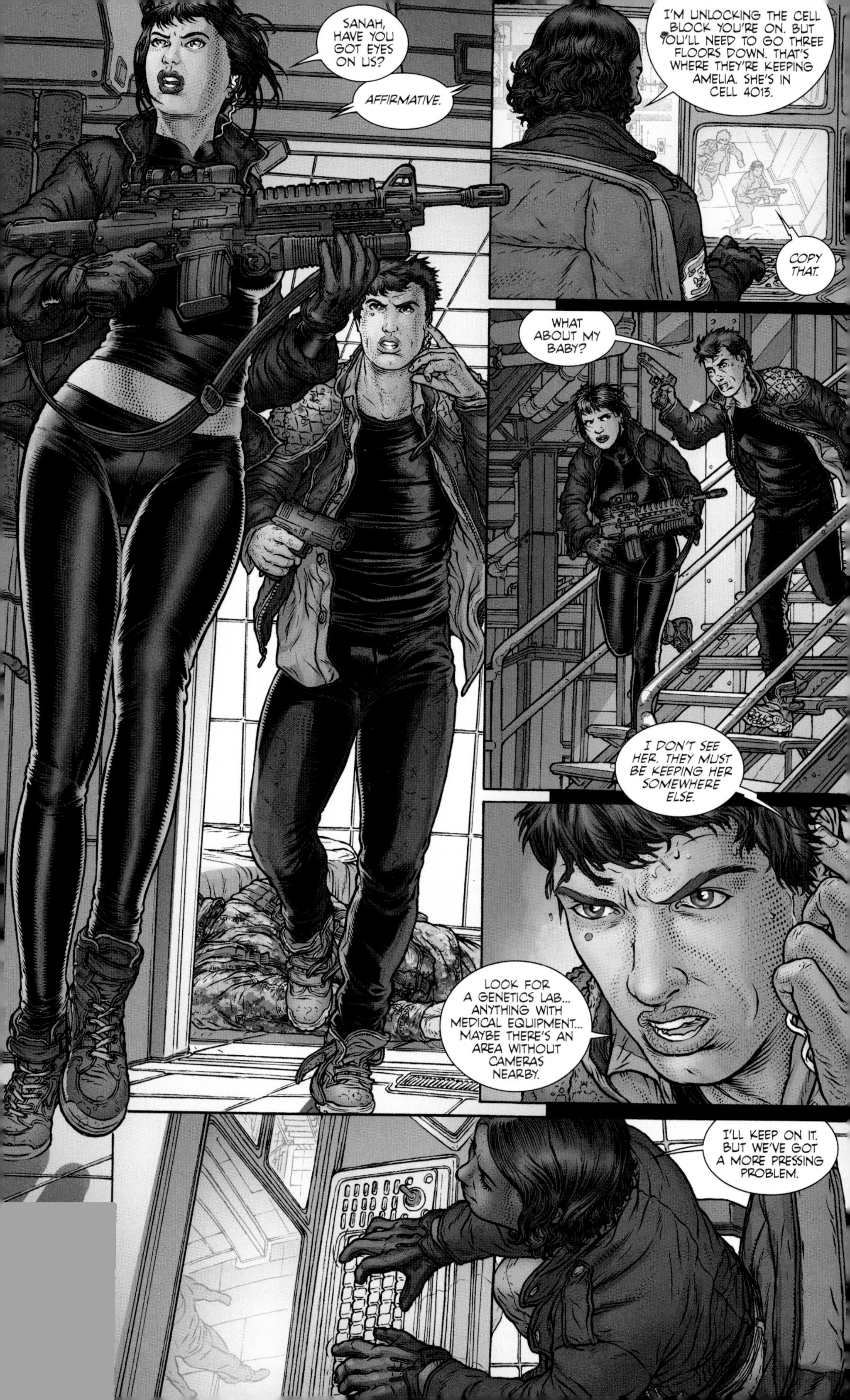

SANAH, HAVE YOU GOT EYES ON US?
AFFIRMATIVE.
I'M UNLOCKING THE CELL BLOCK YOU'RE ON. BUT YOU'LL NEED TO GO THREE FLOORS DOWN. THAT'S WHERE THEY'RE KEEPING AMELIA. SHE'S IN CELL 4013.
COPY THAT.
WHAT ABOUT MY BABY?
I DON'T SEE HER. THEY MUST BE KEEPING HER SOMEWHERE ELSE.
LOOK FOR A GENETICS LAB... ANYTHING WITH MEDICAL EQUIPMENT... MAYBE THERE'S AN AREA WITHOUT CAMERAS NEARBY.
I'LL KEEP ON IT. BUT WE'VE GOT A MORE PRESSING PROBLEM.

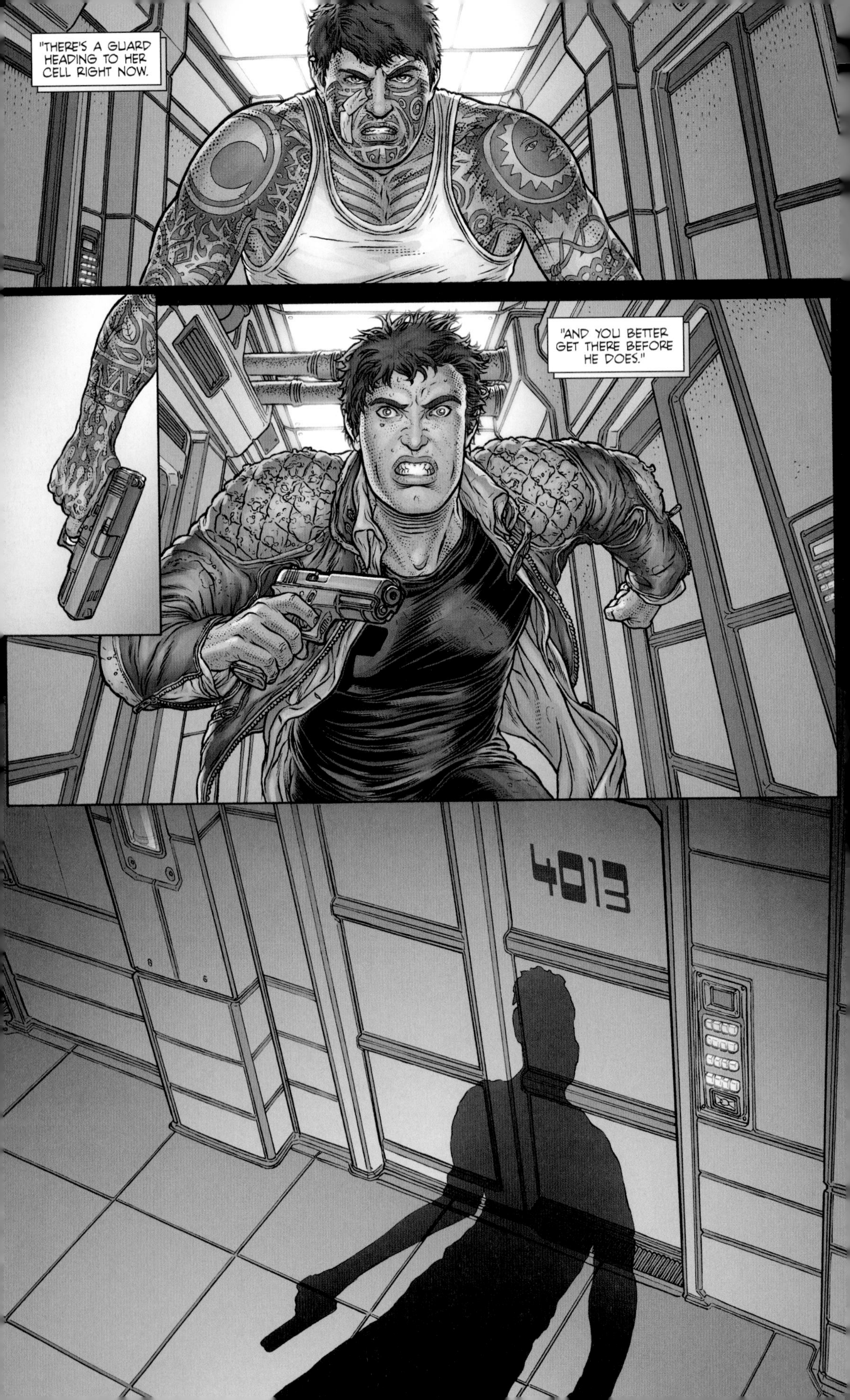
"THERE'S A GUARD HEADING TO HER CELL RIGHT NOW.
"AND YOU BETTER GET THERE BEFORE HE DOES."
4013

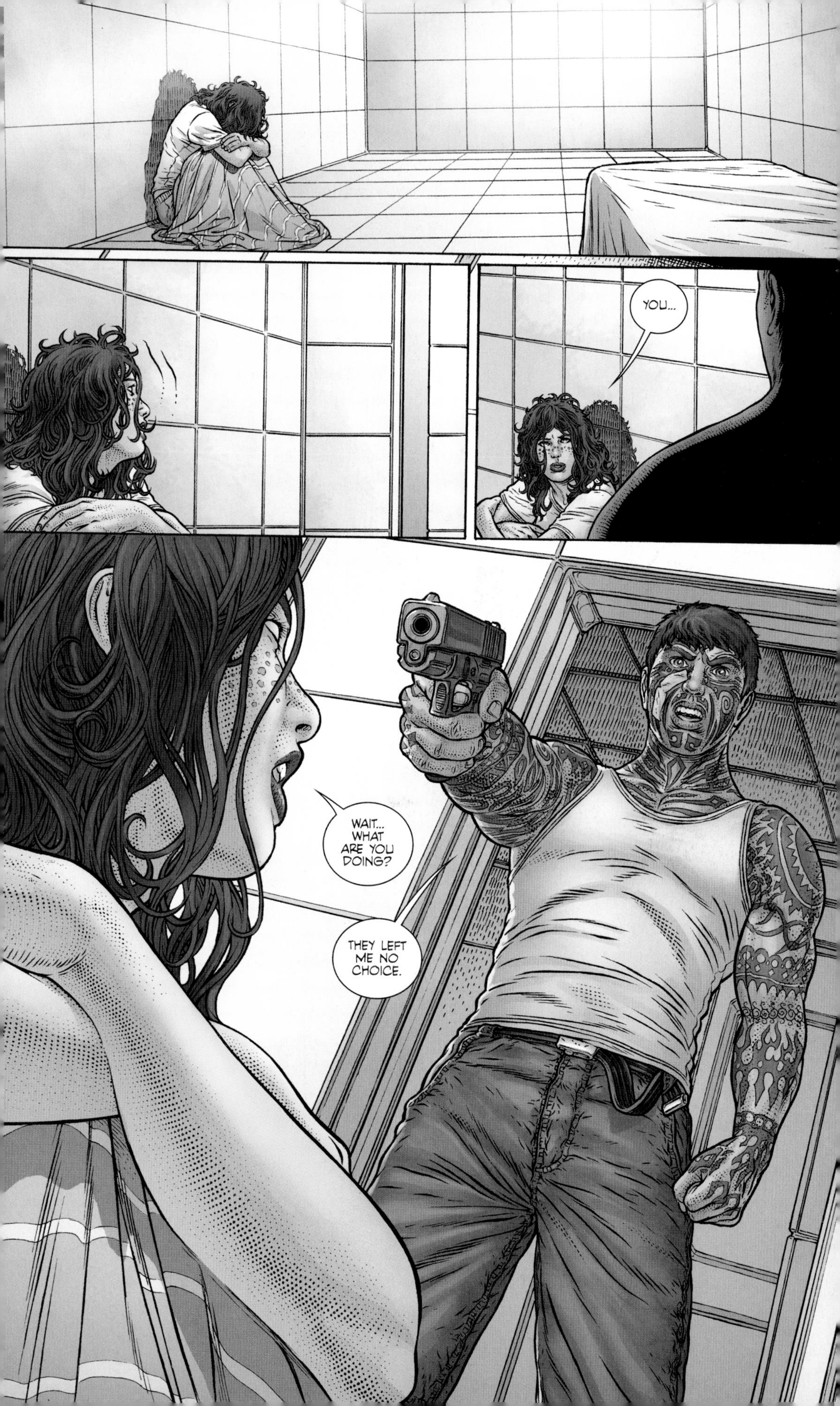
YOU...
WAIT... WHAT ARE YOU DOING?
THEY LEFT ME NO CHOICE.

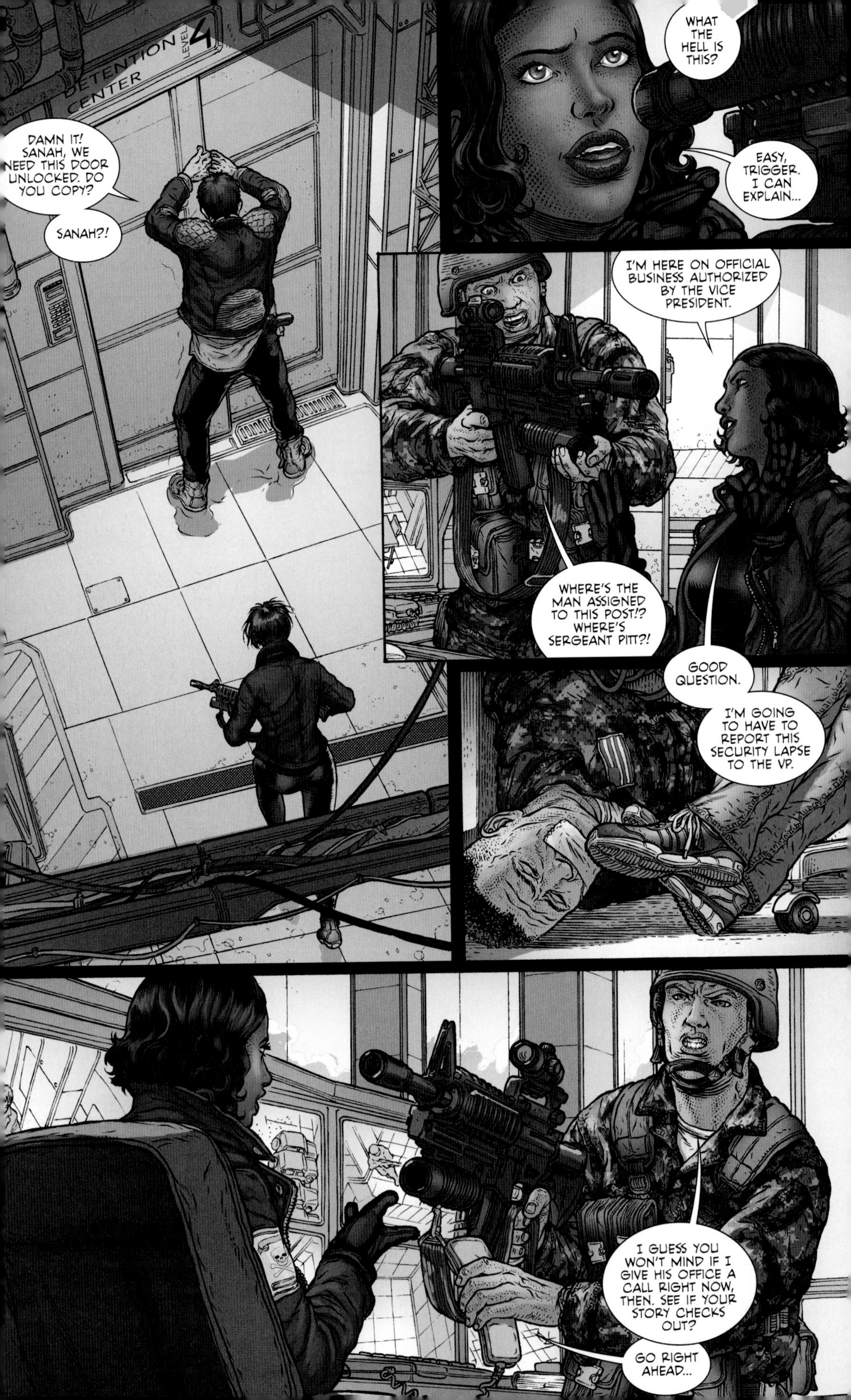
DETENTION CENTER
LEVEL 4
DAMN IT! SANAH, WE NEED THIS DOOR UNLOCKED. DO YOU COPY?
SANAH?!
WHAT THE HELL IS THIS?
EASY, TRIGGER. I CAN EXPLAIN...
I'M HERE ON OFFICIAL BUSINESS AUTHORIZED BY THE VICE PRESIDENT.
WHERE'S THE MAN ASSIGNED TO THIS POST!? WHERE'S SERGEANT PITT?!
GOOD QUESTION.
I'M GOING TO HAVE TO REPORT THIS SECURITY LAPSE TO THE VP.
I GUESS YOU WON'T MIND IF I GIVE HIS OFFICE A CALL RIGHT NOW, THEN. SEE IF YOUR STORY CHECKS OUT?
GO RIGHT AHEAD...

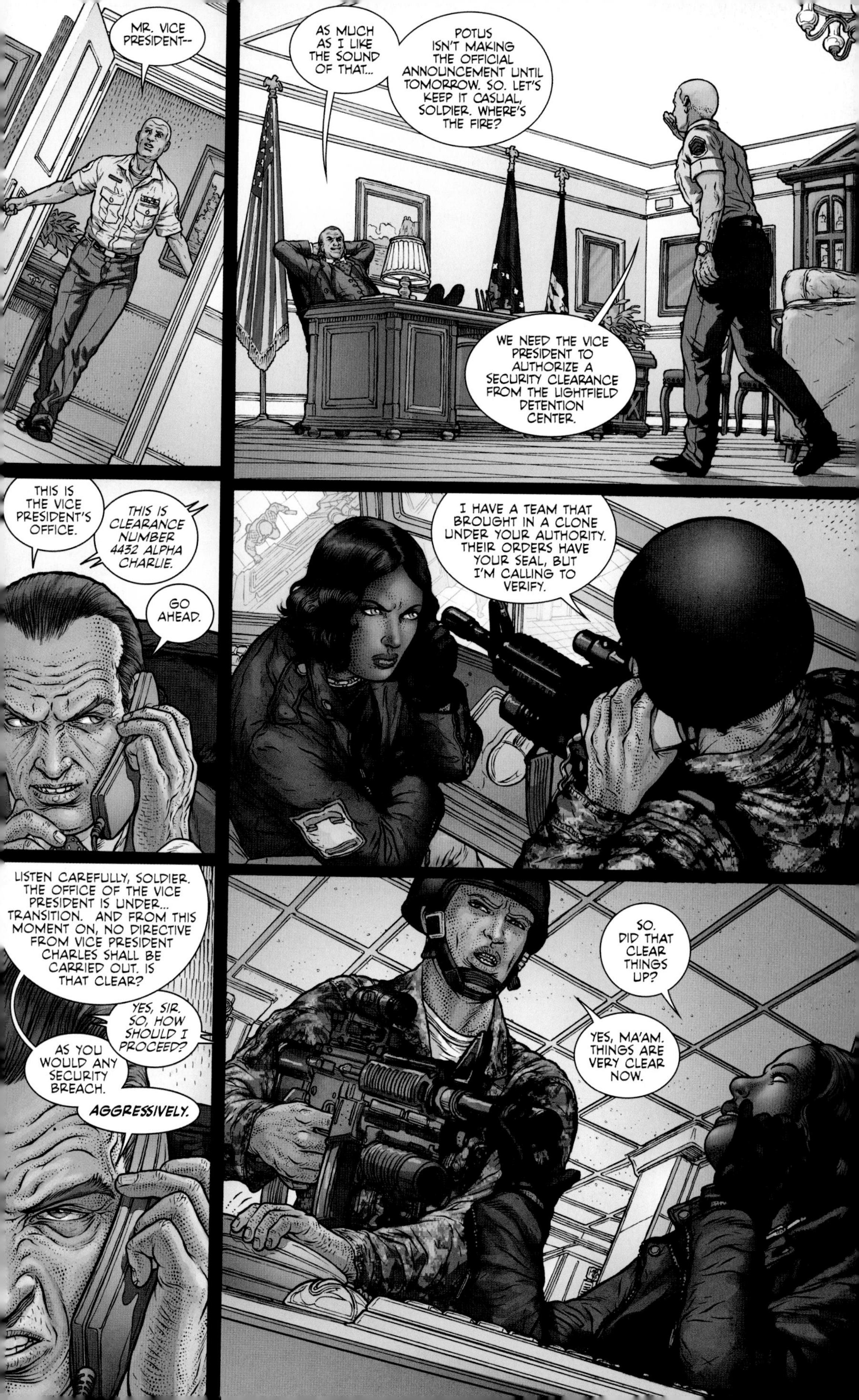
MR. VICE PRESIDENT--
AS MUCH AS I LIKE THE SOUND OF THAT...
POTUS ISN'T MAKING THE OFFICIAL ANNOUNCEMENT UNTIL TOMORROW. SO. LET'S KEEP IT CASUAL, SOLDIER. WHERE'S THE FIRE?
WE NEED THE VICE PRESIDENT TO AUTHORIZE A SECURITY CLEARANCE FROM THE LIGHTFIELD DETENTION CENTER.
THIS IS THE VICE PRESIDENT'S OFFICE.
THIS IS CLEARANCE NUMBER 4432 ALPHA CHARLIE.
GO AHEAD.
I HAVE A TEAM THAT BROUGHT IN A CLONE UNDER YOUR AUTHORITY. THEIR ORDERS HAVE YOUR SEAL, BUT I'M CALLING TO VERIFY.
LISTEN CAREFULLY, SOLDIER. THE OFFICE OF THE VICE PRESIDENT IS UNDER... TRANSITION. AND FROM THIS MOMENT ON, NO DIRECTIVE FROM VICE PRESIDENT CHARLES SHALL BE CARRIED OUT. IS THAT CLEAR?
YES, SIR. SO, HOW SHOULD I PROCEED?
AS YOU WOULD ANY SECURITY BREACH.
AGGRESSIVELY.
SO. DID THAT CLEAR THINGS UP?
YES, MA'AM. THINGS ARE VERY CLEAR NOW.

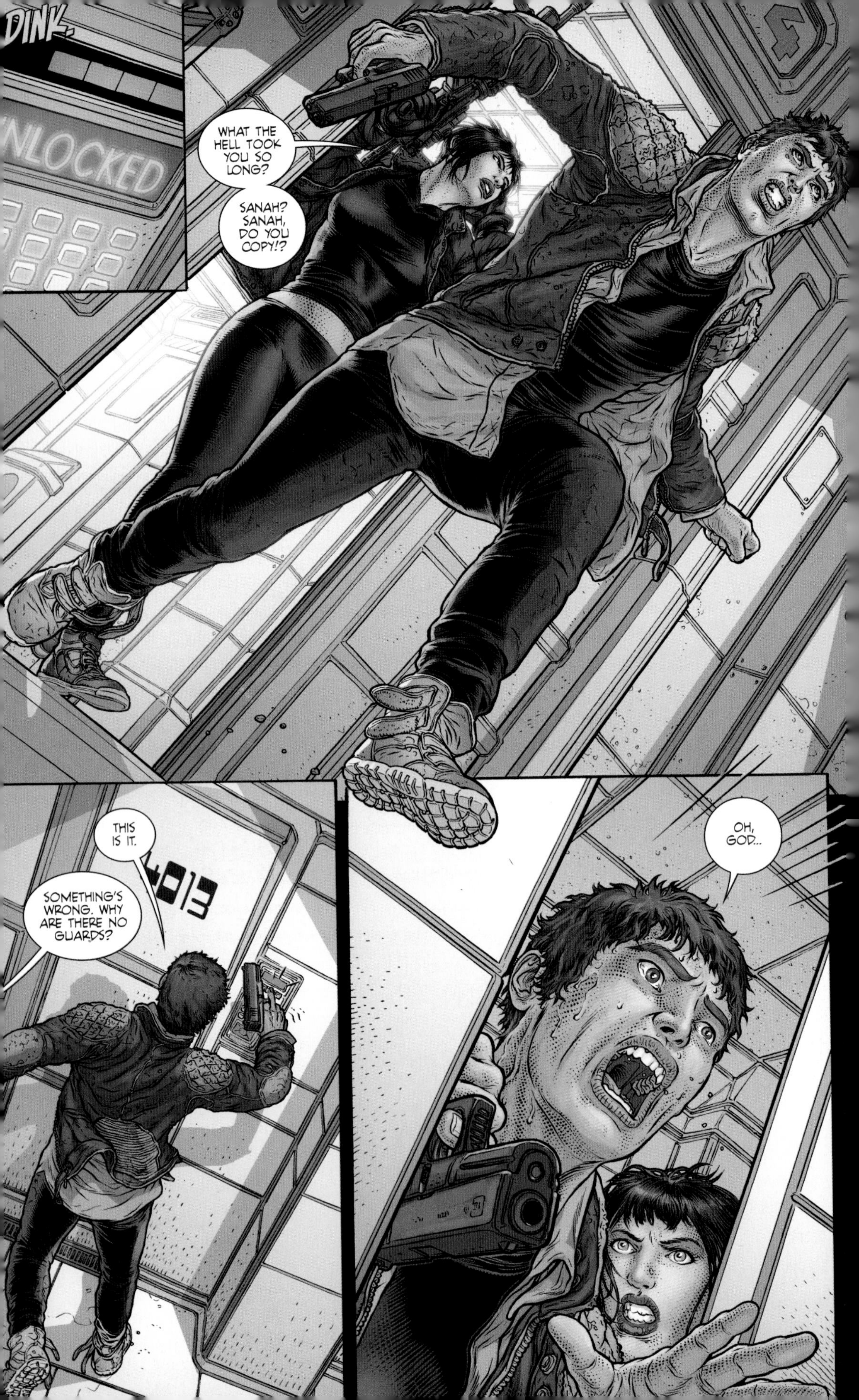
DINK.
UNLOCKED
WHAT THE HELL TOOK YOU SO LONG?
SANAH? SANAH, DO YOU COPY!?
THIS IS IT.
4013
SOMETHING'S WRONG. WHY ARE THERE NO GUARDS?
OH, GOD...

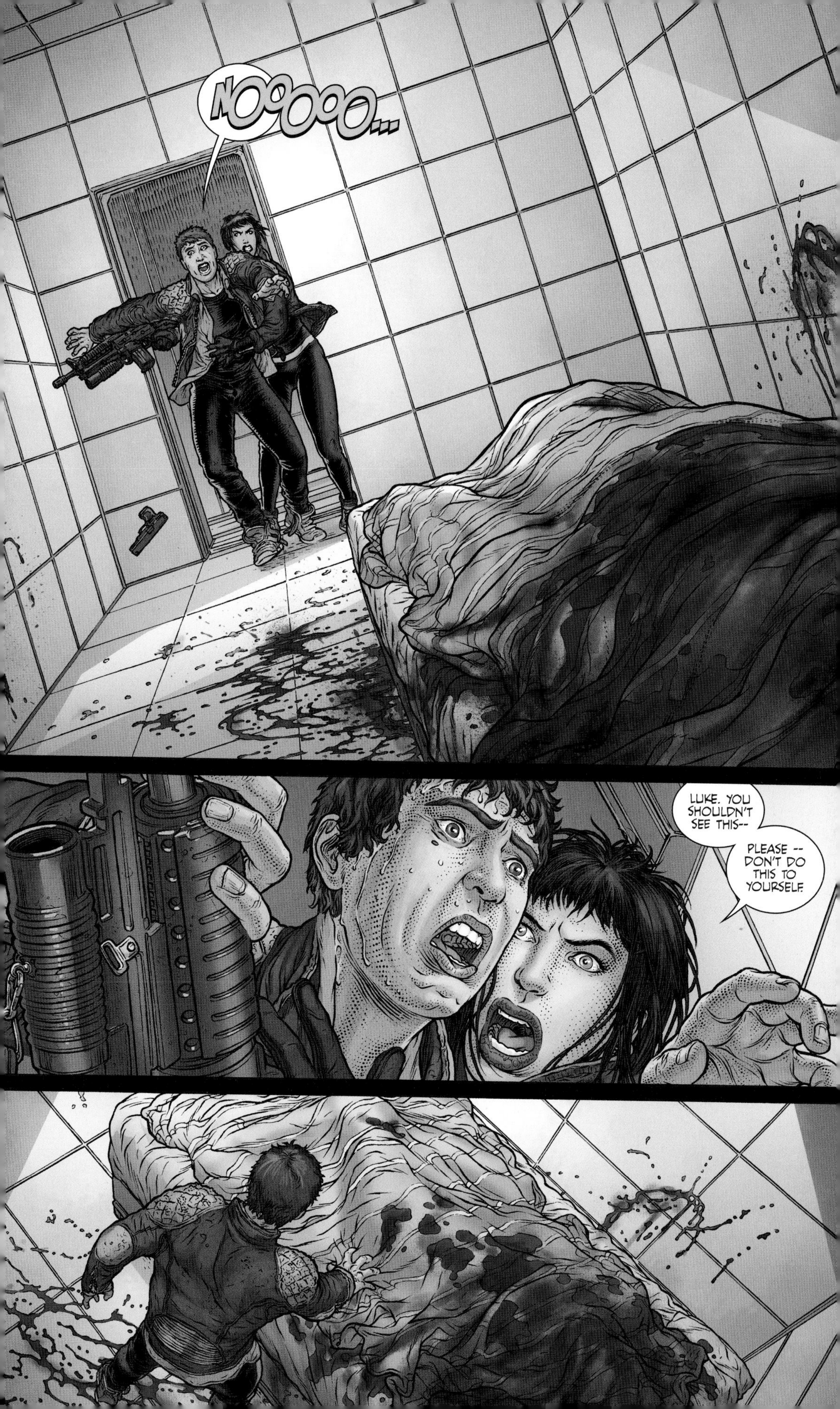
NOOOOO...
LUKE. YOU SHOULDN'T SEE THIS--
PLEASE -- DON'T DO THIS TO YOURSELF.

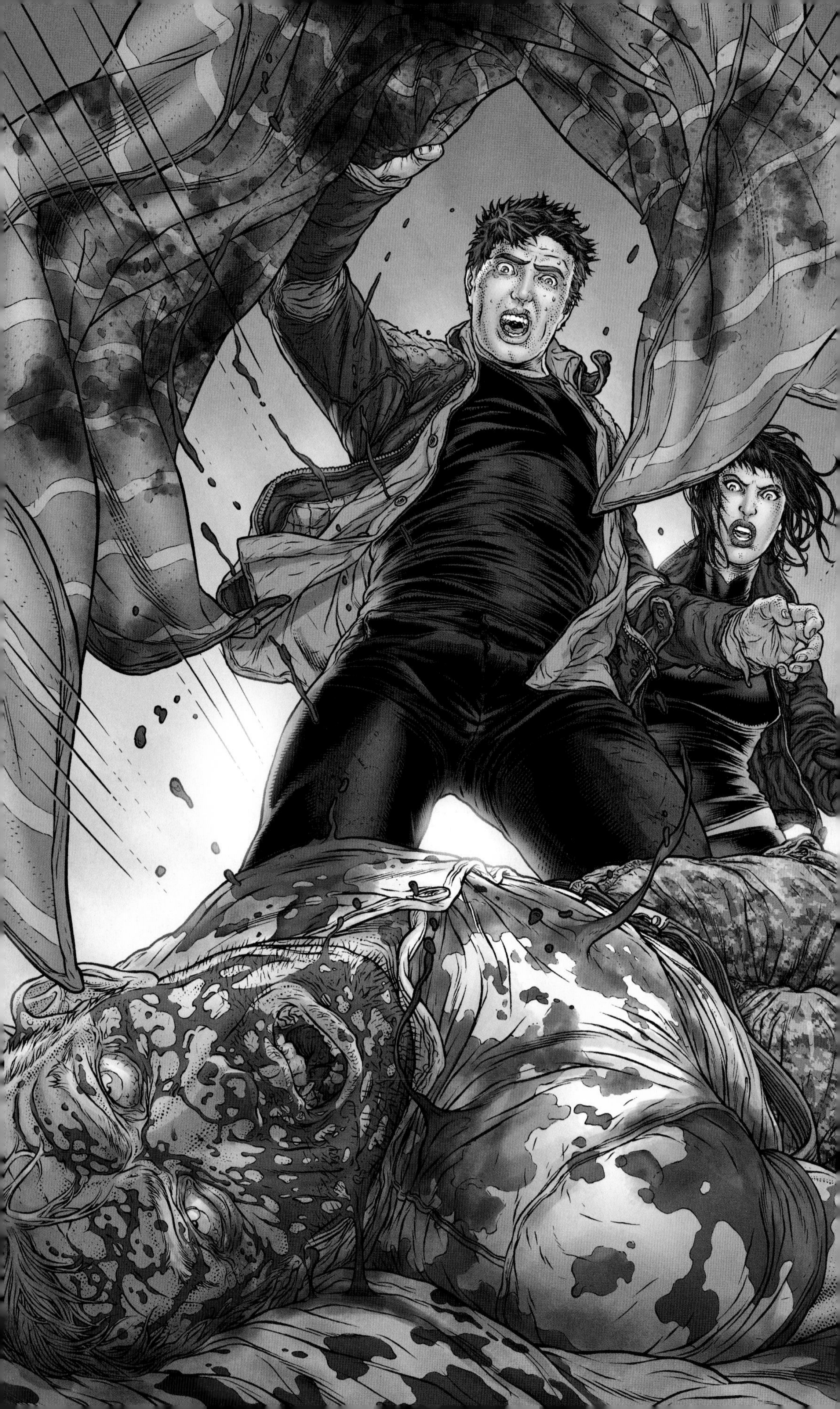

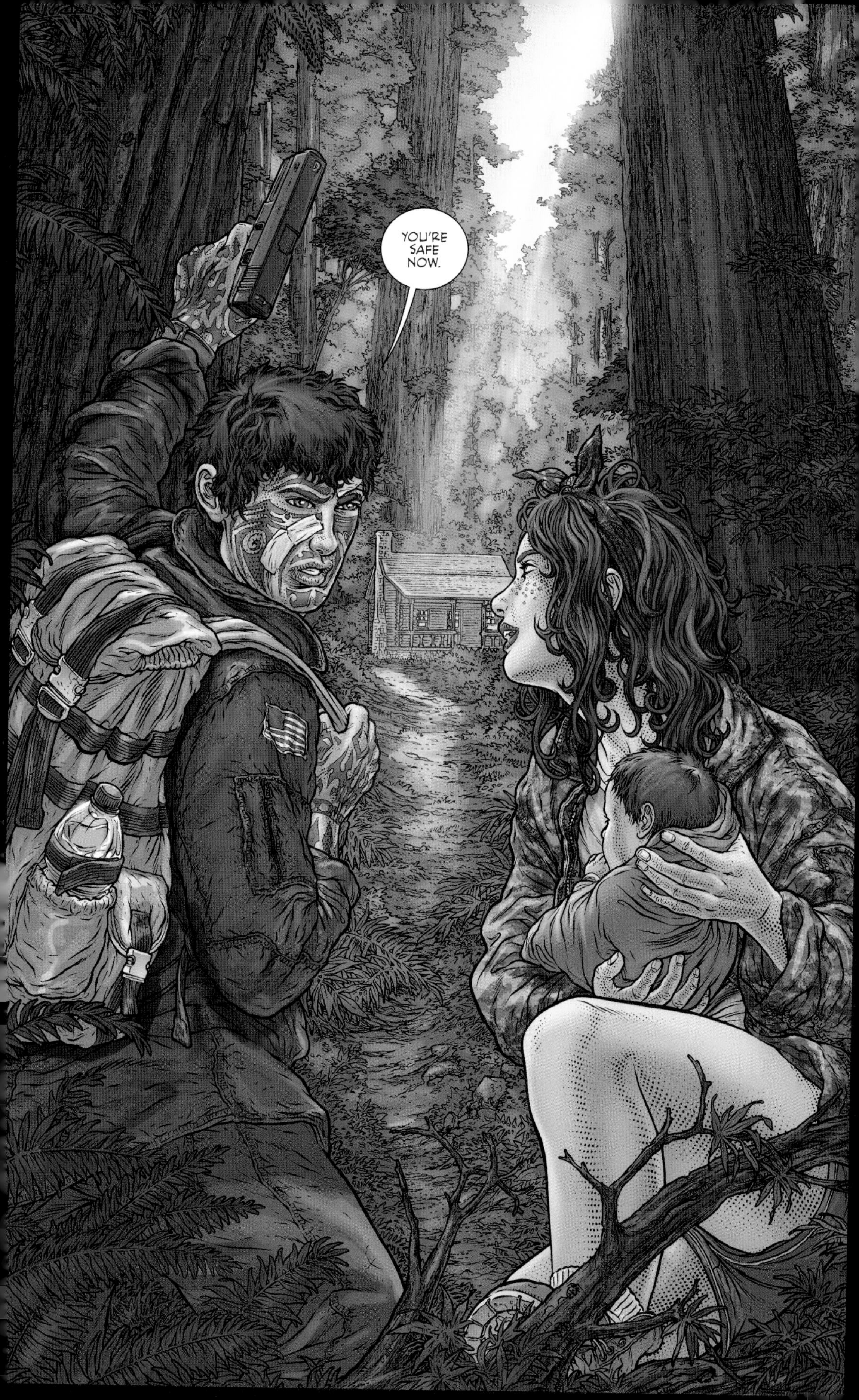
YOU'RE SAFE NOW.

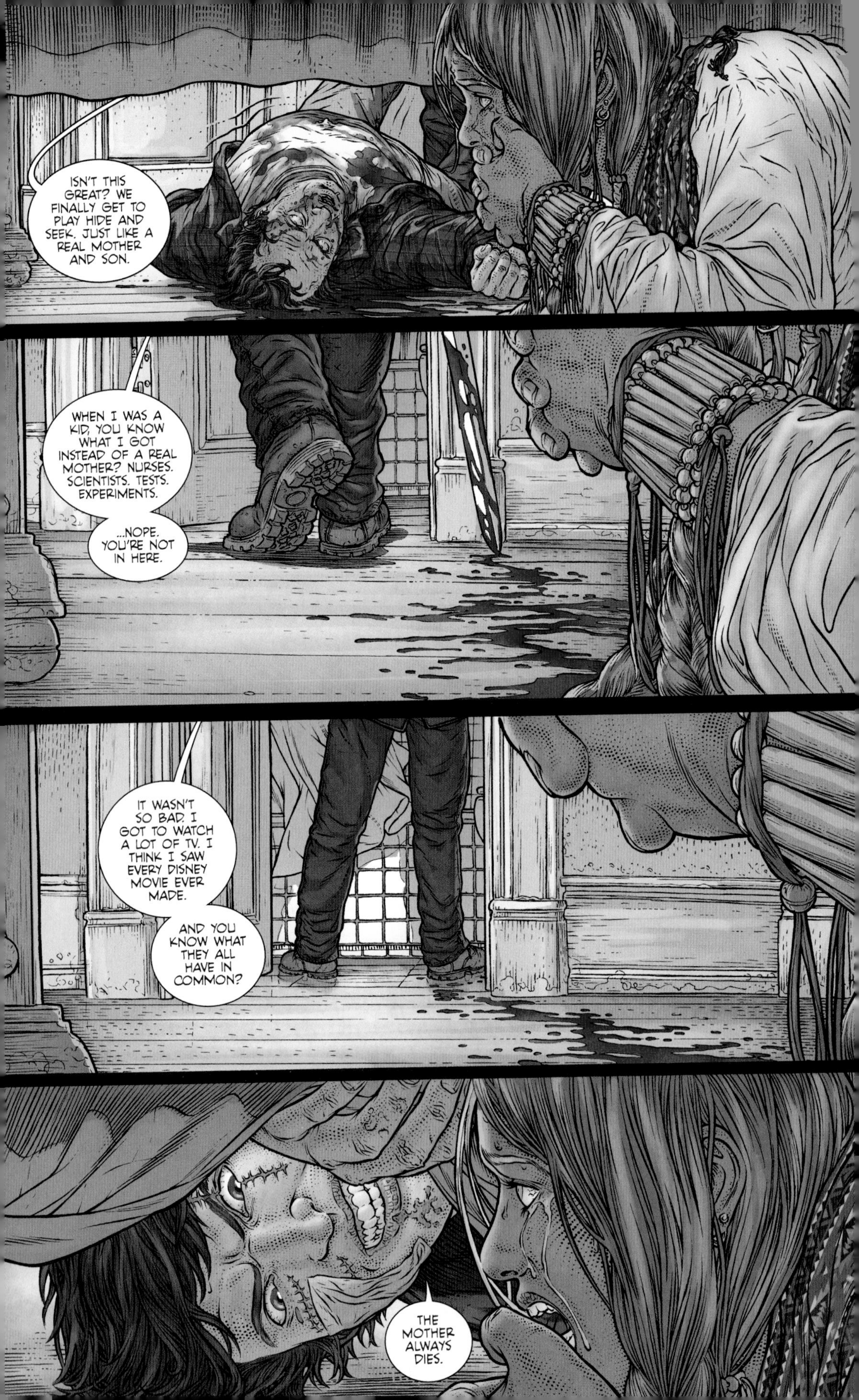
ISN'T THIS GREAT? WE FINALLY GET TO PLAY HIDE AND SEEK. JUST LIKE A REAL MOTHER AND SON.
WHEN I WAS A KID, YOU KNOW WHAT I GOT INSTEAD OF A REAL MOTHER? NURSES. SCIENTISTS. TESTS. EXPERIMENTS.
...NOPE. YOU'RE NOT IN HERE.
IT WASN'T SO BAD. I GOT TO WATCH A LOT OF TV. I THINK I SAW EVERY DISNEY MOVIE EVER MADE.
AND YOU KNOW WHAT THEY ALL HAVE IN COMMON?
THE MOTHER ALWAYS DIES.

# CHAPTER 10

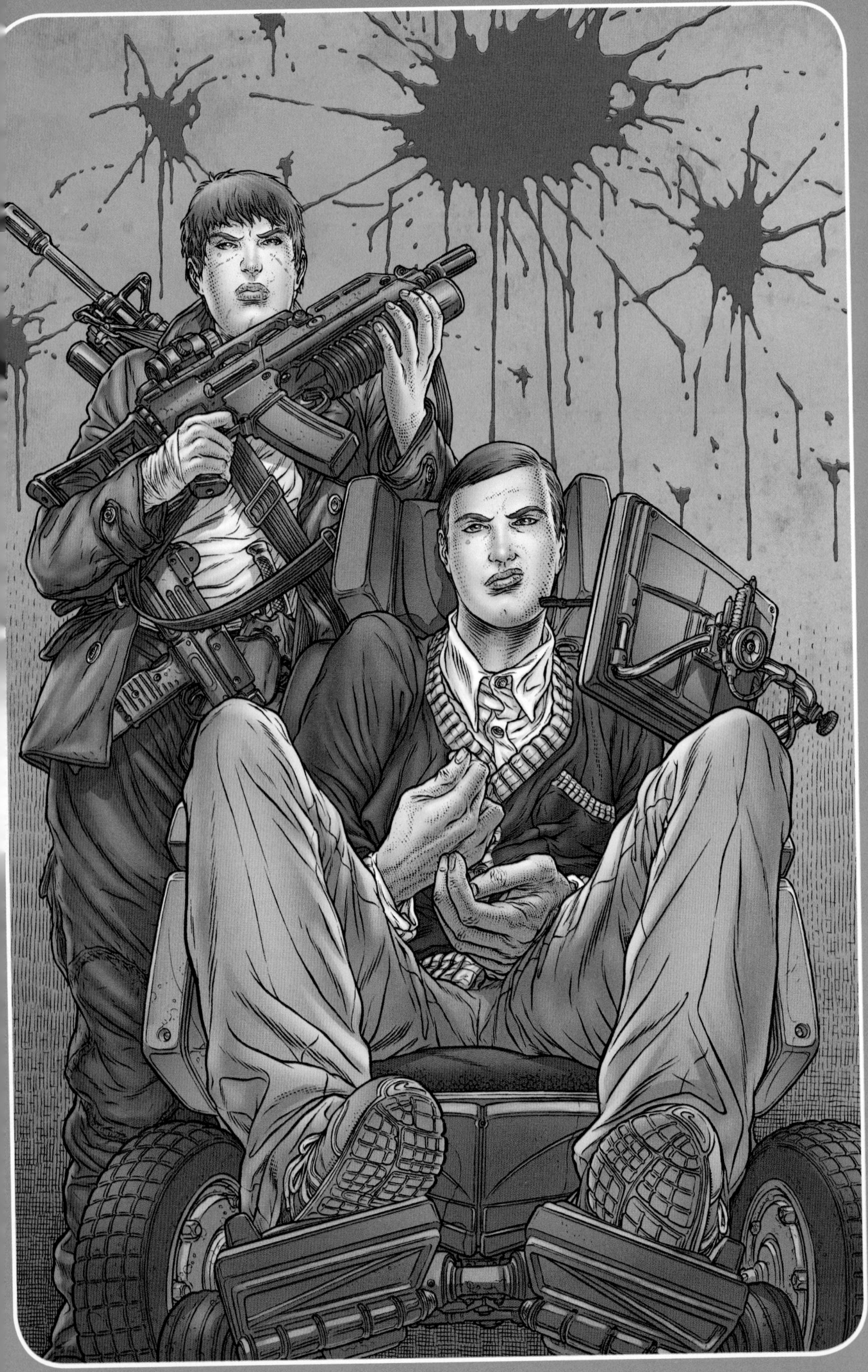

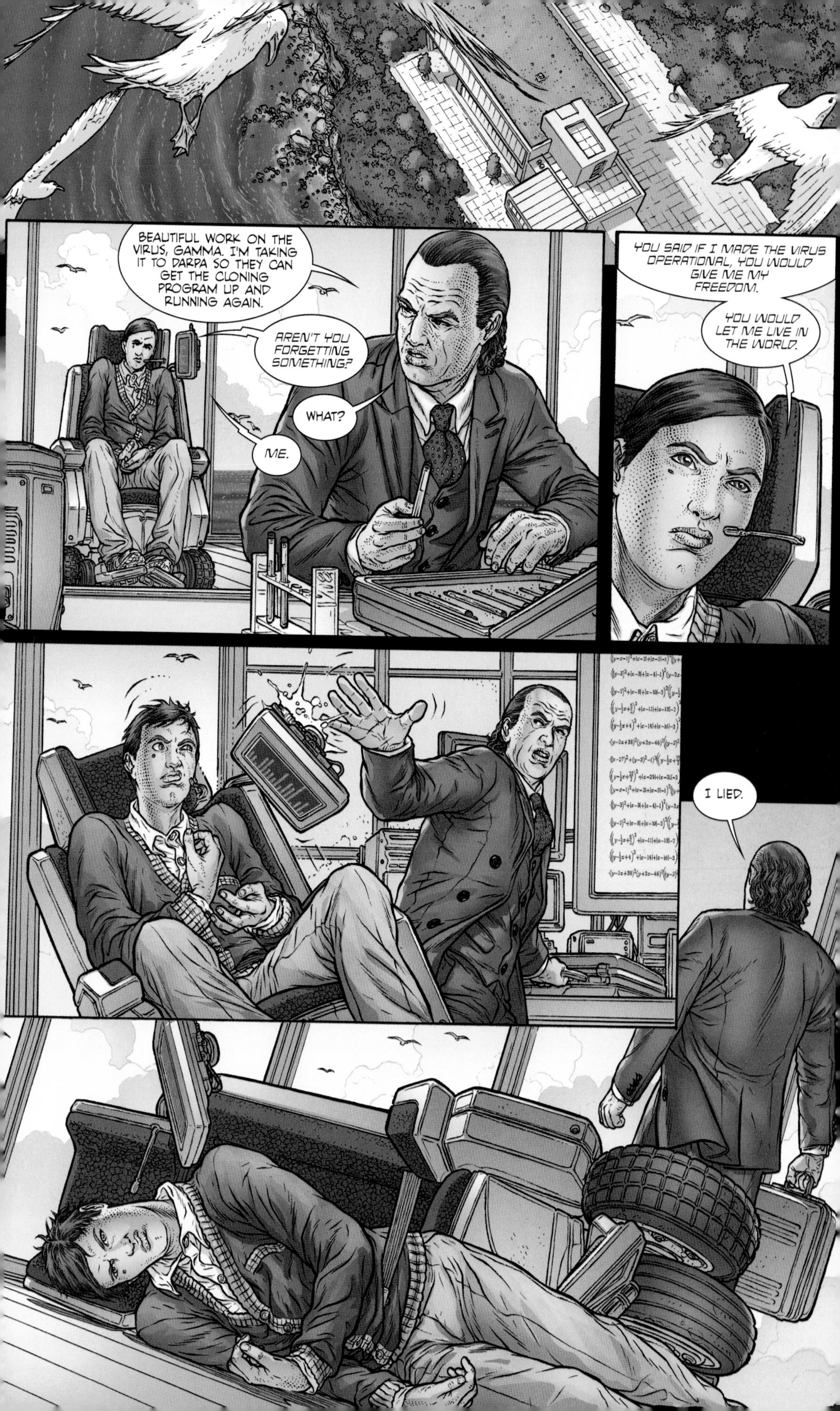
BEAUTIFUL WORK ON THE VIRUS, GAMMA. I'M TAKING IT TO DARPA SO THEY CAN GET THE CLONING PROGRAM UP AND RUNNING AGAIN.
AREN'T YOU FORGETTING SOMETHING?
WHAT?
ME.
YOU SAID IF I MADE THE VIRUS OPERATIONAL, YOU WOULD GIVE ME MY FREEDOM.
YOU WOULD LET ME LIVE IN THE WORLD.
I LIED.

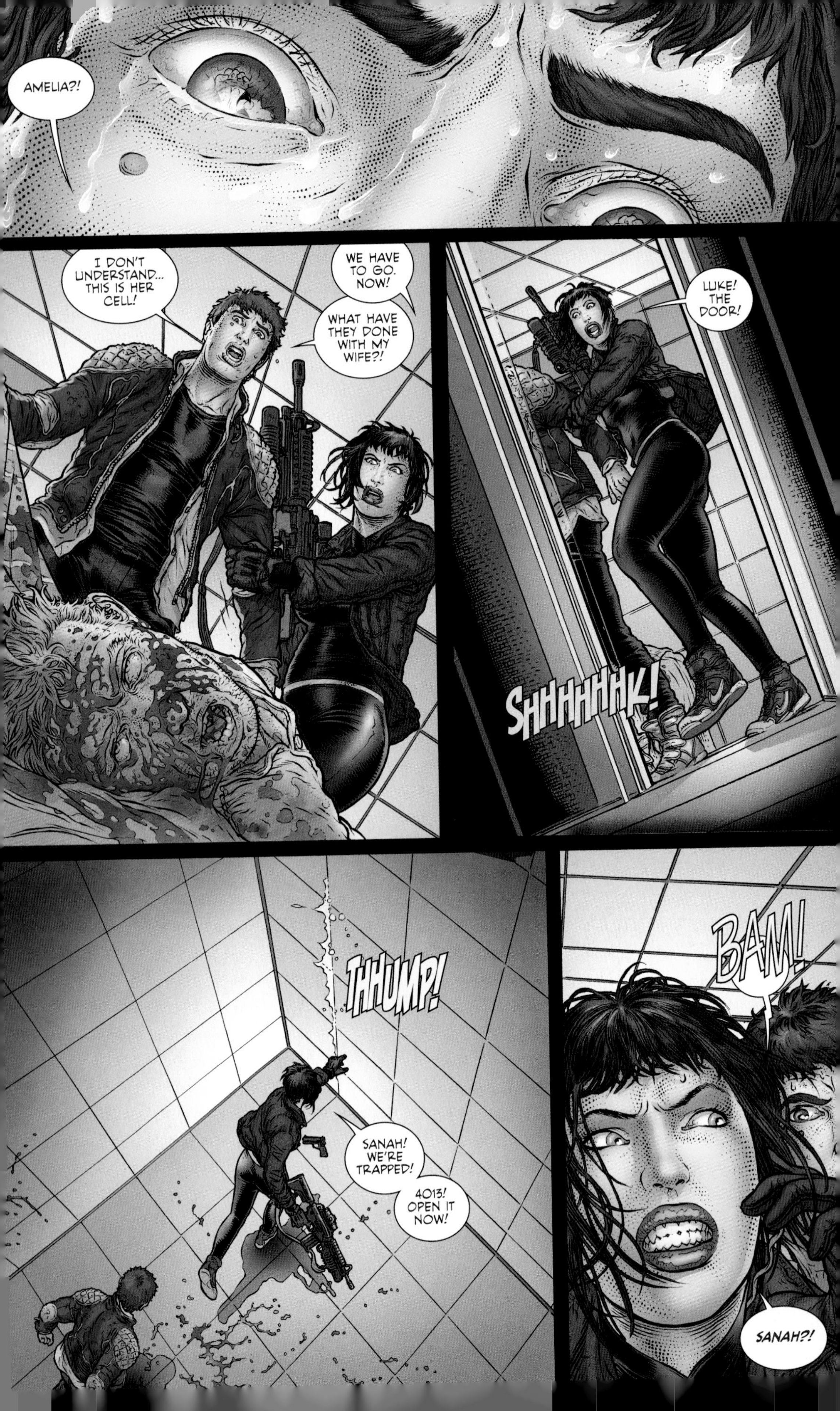
AMELIA?!
I DON'T UNDERSTAND... THIS IS HER CELL!
WE HAVE TO GO. NOW!
WHAT HAVE THEY DONE WITH MY WIFE?!
LUKE! THE DOOR!
SHHHHHK!
THHUMP!
SANAH! WE'RE TRAPPED!
4013! OPEN IT NOW!
BAM!
SANAH?!

SANAH?!

MMMNNNFF!

SETTLE DOWN! IT'S UNDER CONTROL.

THWAP!

SETTLE DOWN! IT'S UNDER CONTROL.

AGHHGHHHHGG

JENNIFER! UNLOCKING THE CELL NOW. YOU'RE FREE AND CLEAR.

EEEEWWUEEEEWUU!!

WELL... FREE.

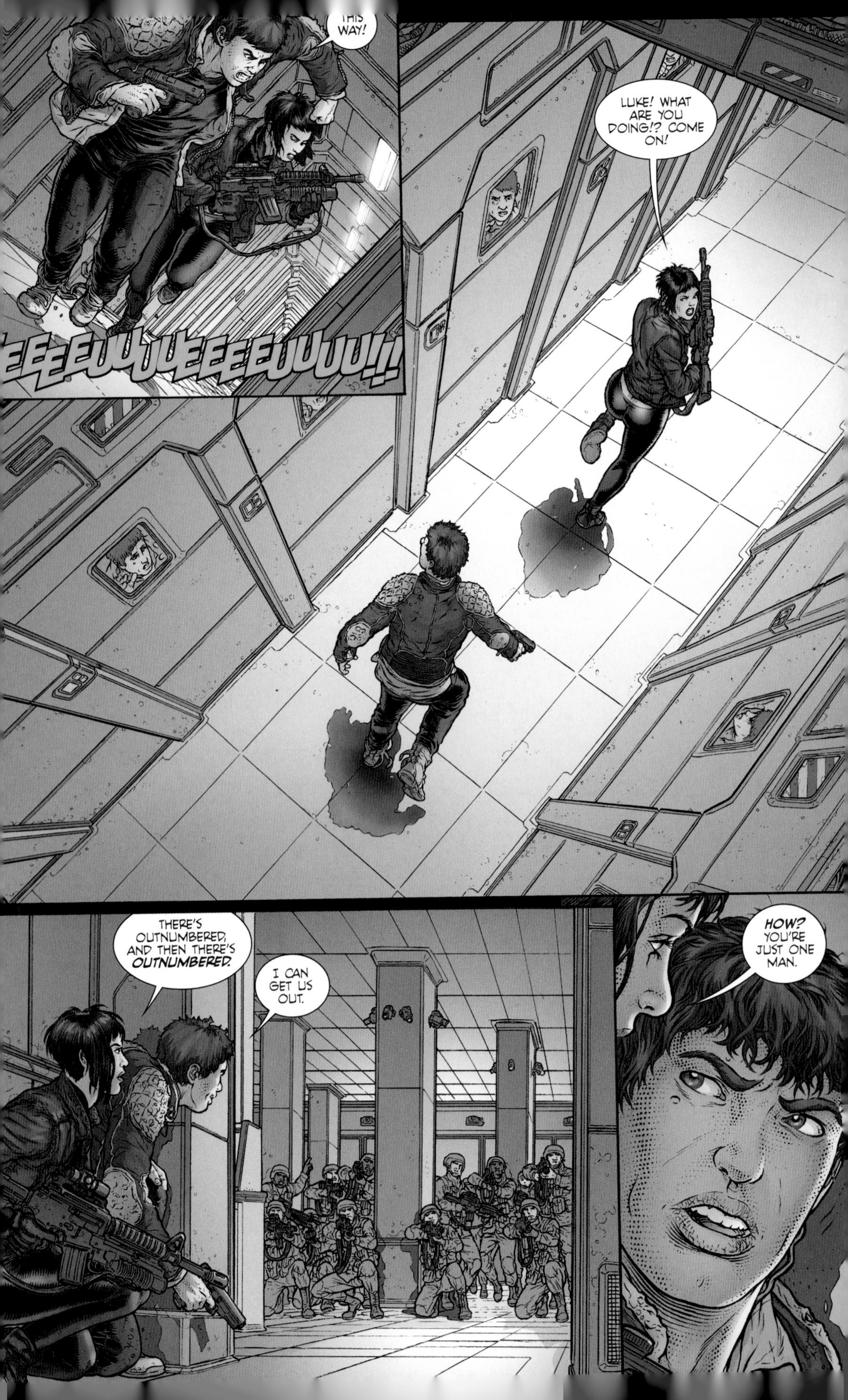
THIS WAY!
EEEEUUUUEEEEEUUUUU!!!
LUKE! WHAT ARE YOU DOING!? COME ON!
THERE'S OUTNUMBERED, AND THEN THERE'S **OUTNUMBERED.**
I CAN GET US OUT.
**HOW?** YOU'RE JUST ONE MAN.

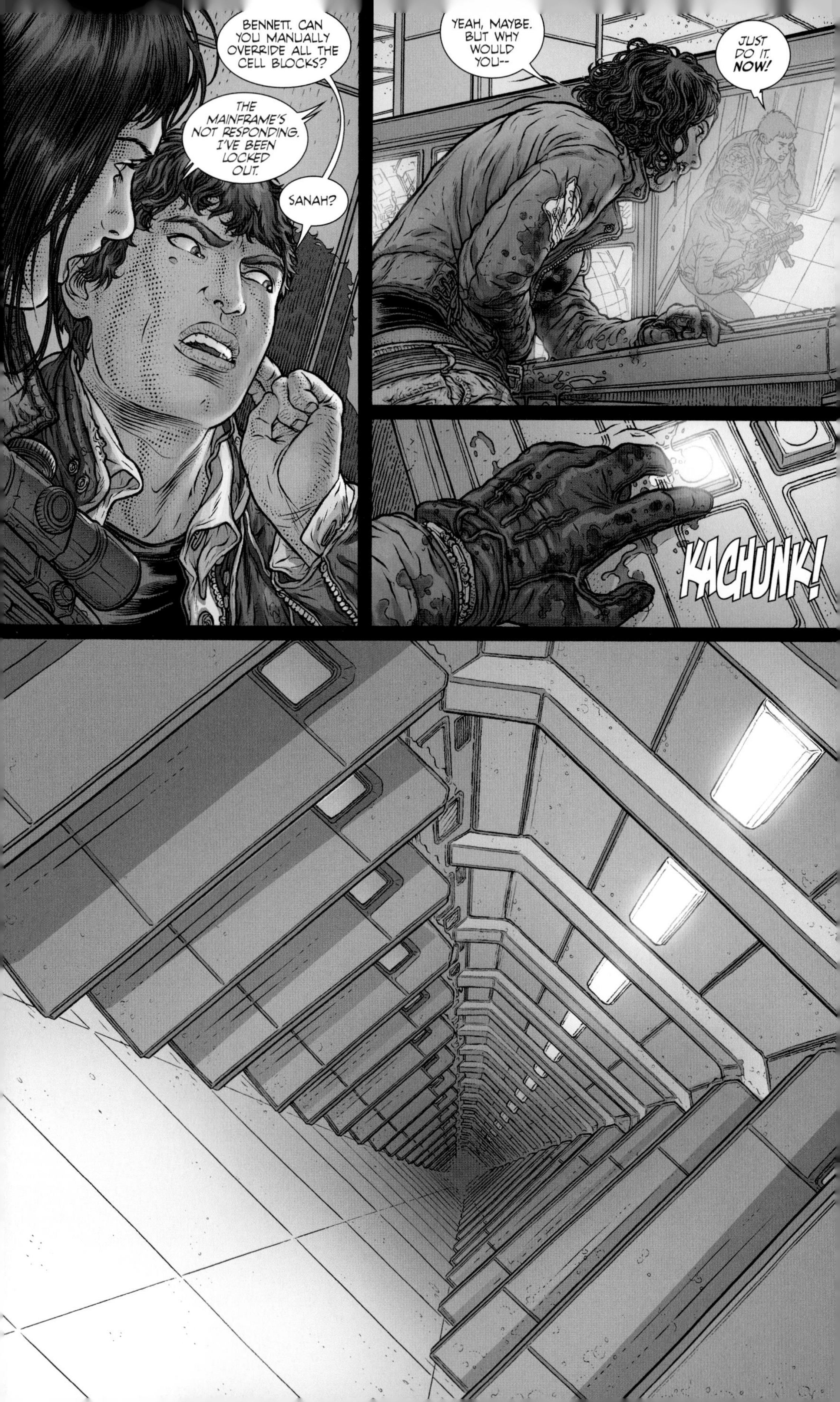
BENNETT. CAN YOU MANUALLY OVERRIDE ALL THE CELL BLOCKS?
THE MAINFRAME'S NOT RESPONDING. I'VE BEEN LOCKED OUT.
SANAH?
YEAH, MAYBE. BUT WHY WOULD YOU--
JUST DO IT. NOW!
KACHUNK!

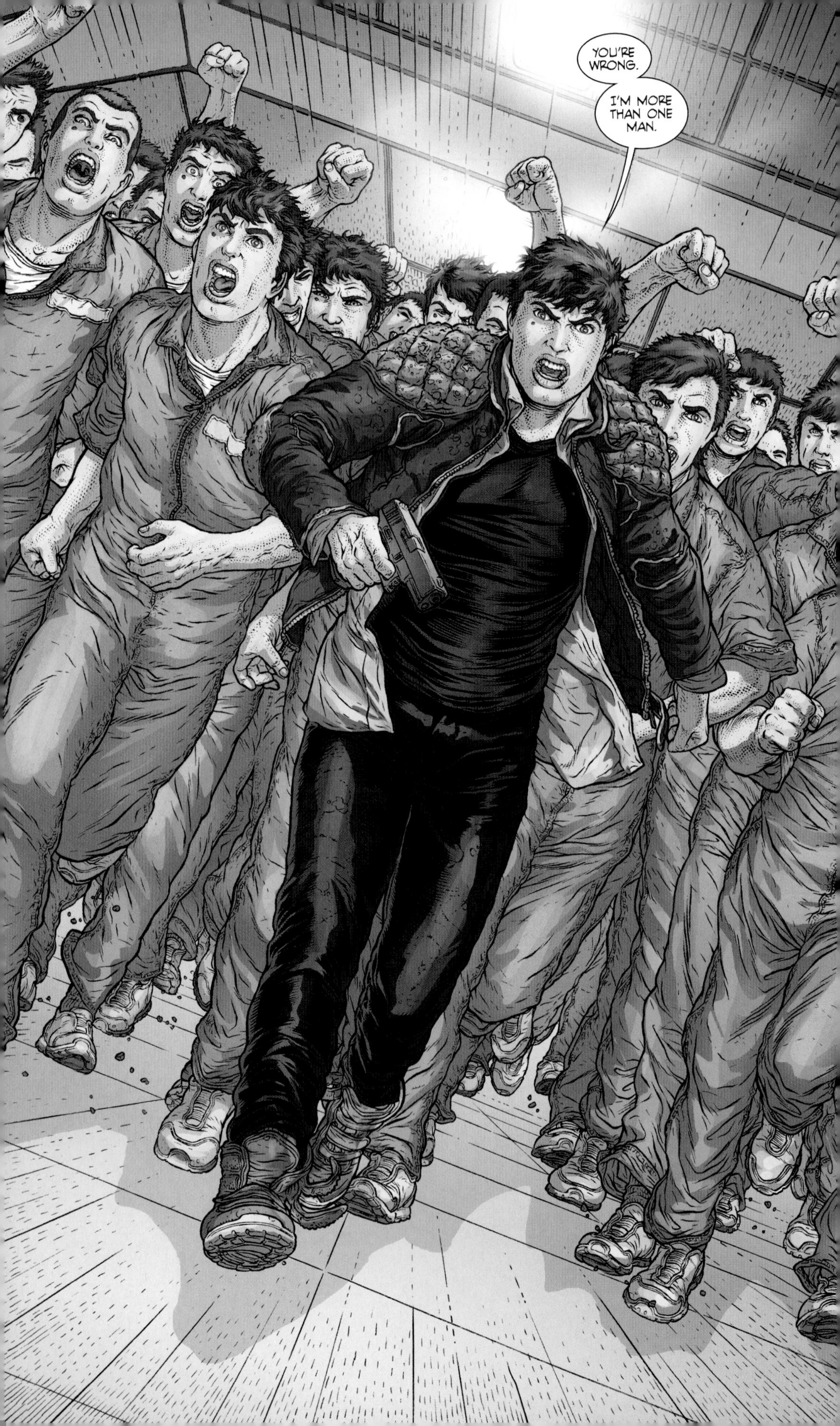
YOU'RE WRONG.
I'M MORE THAN ONE MAN.

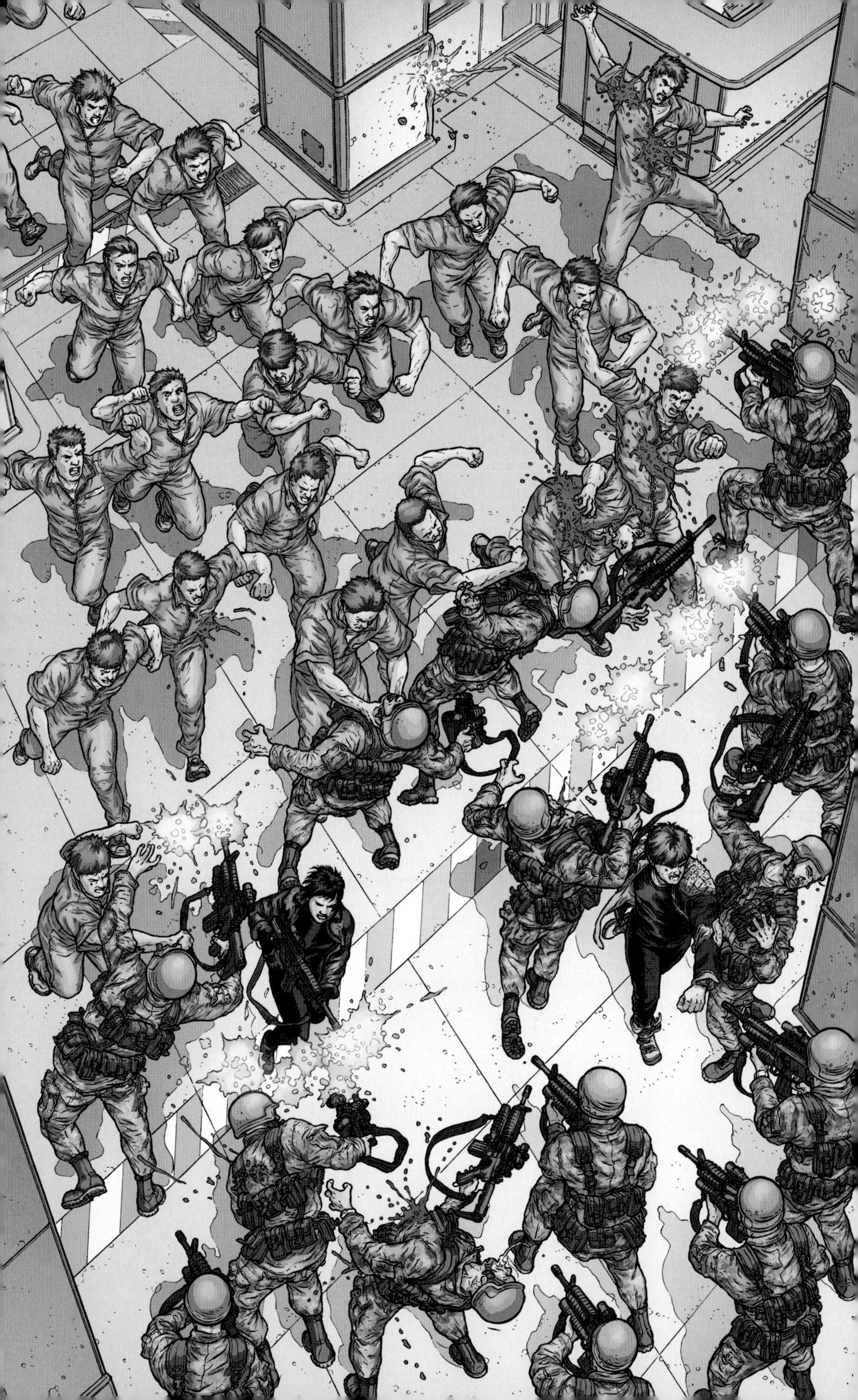

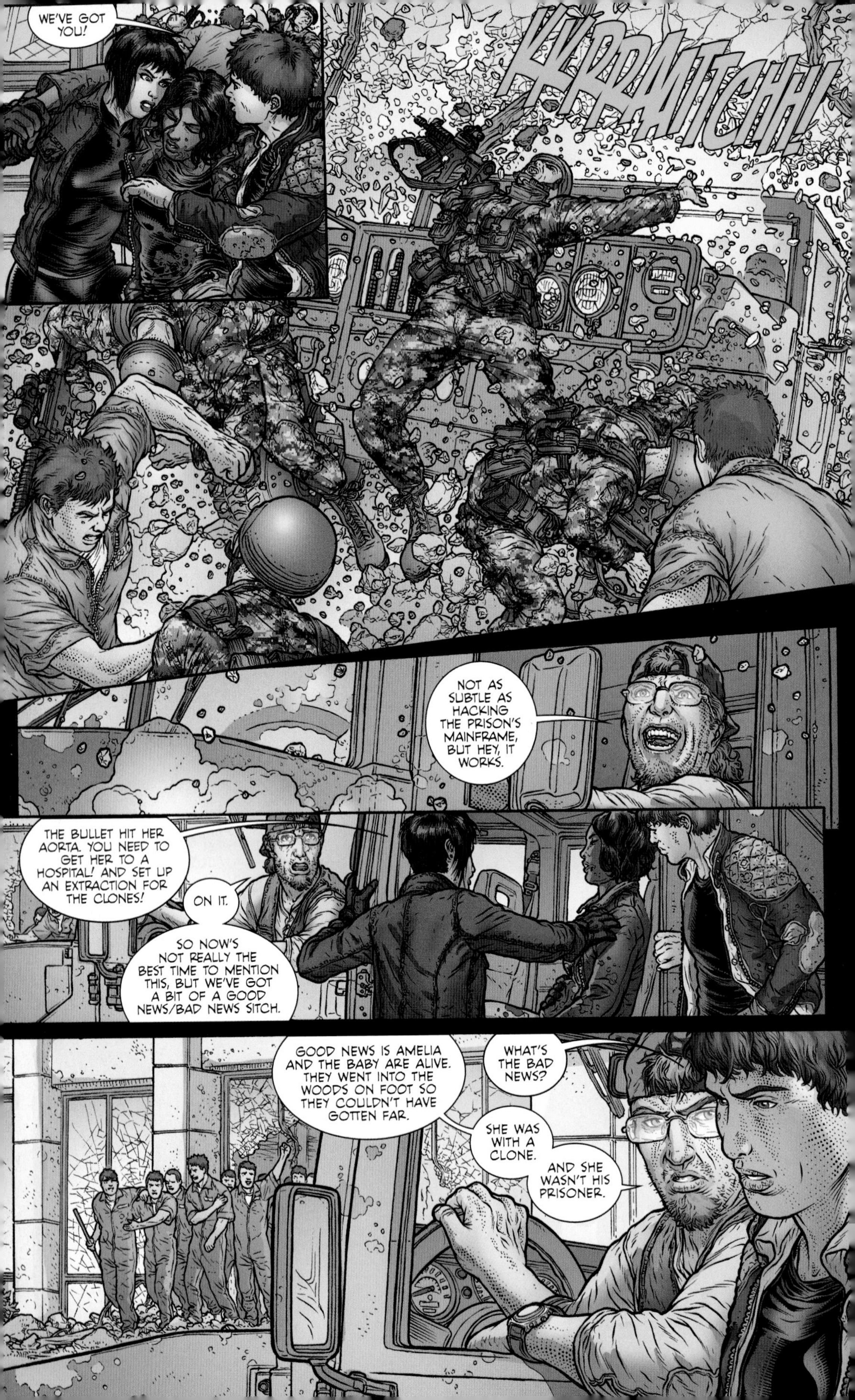
WE'VE GOT YOU!
KKRRAATCHH!
NOT AS SUBTLE AS HACKING THE PRISON'S MAINFRAME, BUT HEY, IT WORKS.
THE BULLET HIT HER AORTA. YOU NEED TO GET HER TO A HOSPITAL! AND SET UP AN EXTRACTION FOR THE CLONES!
ON IT.
SO NOW'S NOT REALLY THE BEST TIME TO MENTION THIS, BUT WE'VE GOT A BIT OF A GOOD NEWS/BAD NEWS SITCH.
GOOD NEWS IS AMELIA AND THE BABY ARE ALIVE. THEY WENT INTO THE WOODS ON FOOT SO THEY COULDN'T HAVE GOTTEN FAR.
WHAT'S THE BAD NEWS?
SHE WAS WITH A CLONE.
AND SHE WASN'T HIS PRISONER.

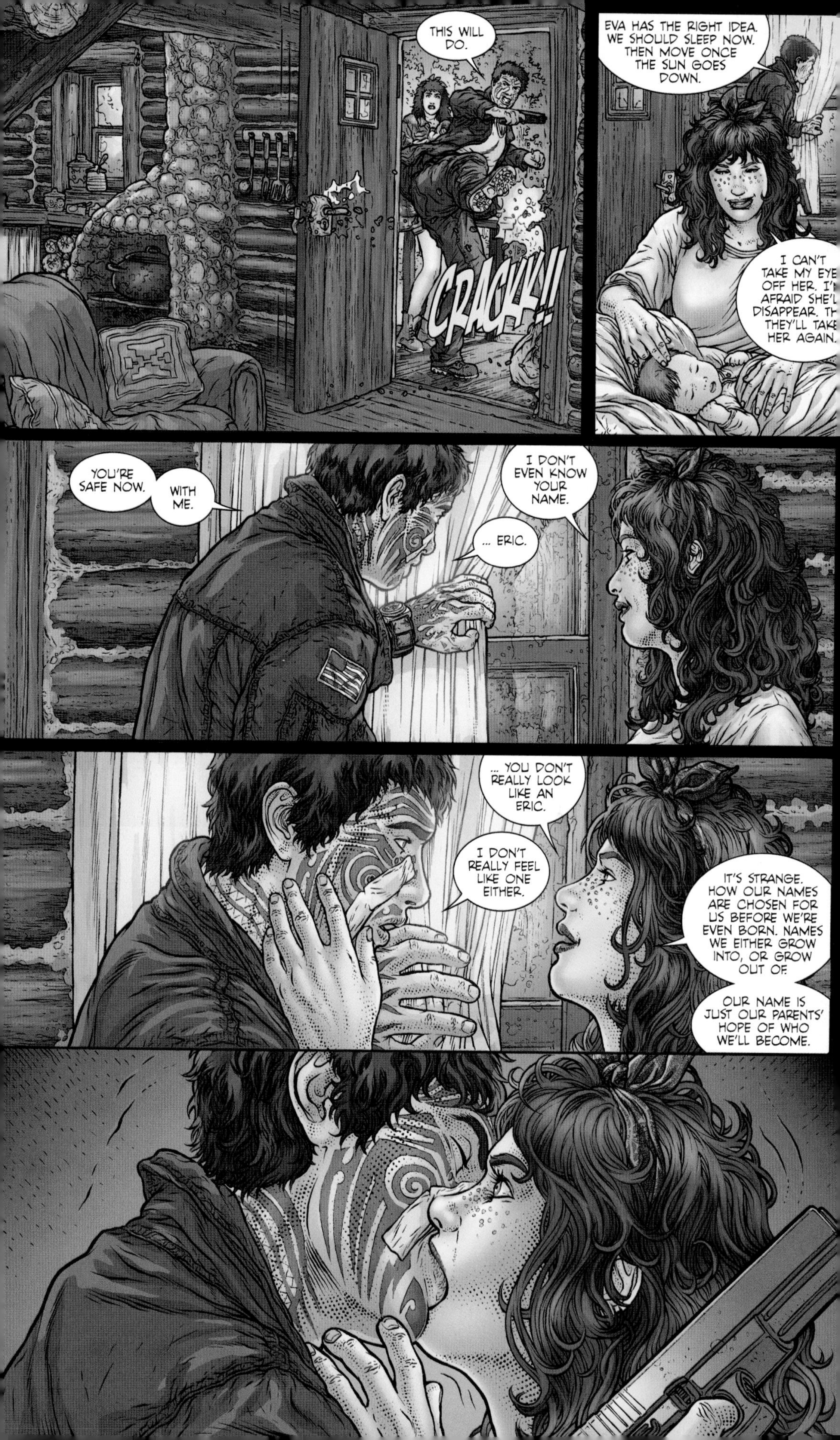
THIS WILL DO.
CRACKK!!
EVA HAS THE RIGHT IDEA. WE SHOULD SLEEP NOW. THEN MOVE ONCE THE SUN GOES DOWN.
I CAN'T TAKE MY EYE OFF HER. I' AFRAID SHE'L DISAPPEAR. TH THEY'LL TAKE HER AGAIN.
YOU'RE SAFE NOW.
WITH ME.
I DON'T EVEN KNOW YOUR NAME.
... ERIC.
... YOU DON'T REALLY LOOK LIKE AN ERIC.
I DON'T REALLY FEEL LIKE ONE EITHER.
IT'S STRANGE. HOW OUR NAMES ARE CHOSEN FOR US BEFORE WE'RE EVEN BORN. NAMES WE EITHER GROW INTO, OR GROW OUT OF.
OUR NAME IS JUST OUR PARENTS' HOPE OF WHO WE'LL BECOME.

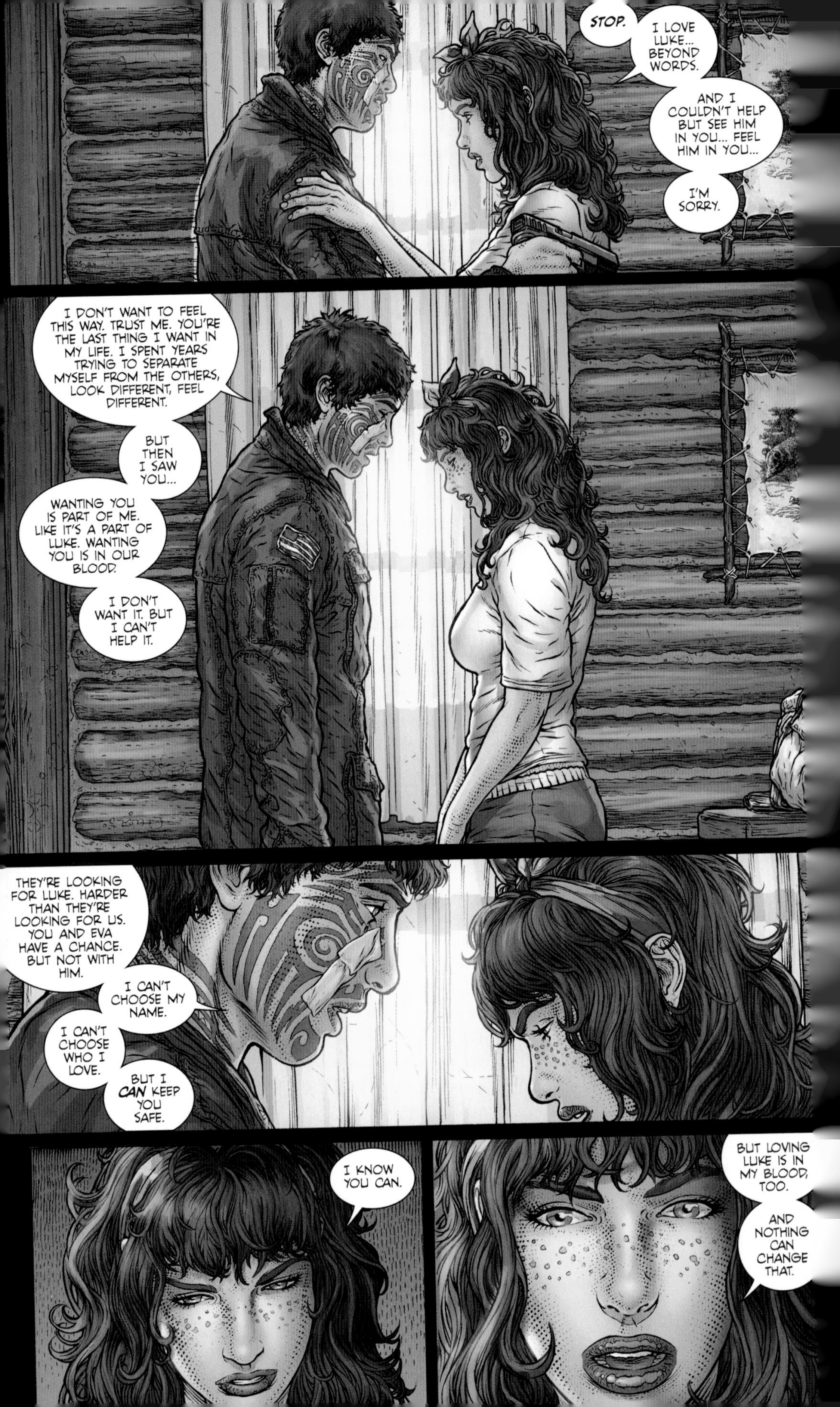
STOP.
I LOVE LUKE... BEYOND WORDS.
AND I COULDN'T HELP BUT SEE HIM IN YOU... FEEL HIM IN YOU...
I'M SORRY.
I DON'T WANT TO FEEL THIS WAY. TRUST ME. YOU'RE THE LAST THING I WANT IN MY LIFE. I SPENT YEARS TRYING TO SEPARATE MYSELF FROM THE OTHERS, LOOK DIFFERENT, FEEL DIFFERENT.
BUT THEN I SAW YOU...
WANTING YOU IS PART OF ME. LIKE IT'S A PART OF LUKE. WANTING YOU IS IN OUR BLOOD.
I DON'T WANT IT. BUT I CAN'T HELP IT.
THEY'RE LOOKING FOR LUKE. HARDER THAN THEY'RE LOOKING FOR US. YOU AND EVA HAVE A CHANCE. BUT NOT WITH HIM.
I CAN'T CHOOSE MY NAME.
I CAN'T CHOOSE WHO I LOVE.
BUT I *CAN* KEEP YOU SAFE.
I KNOW YOU CAN.
BUT LOVING LUKE IS IN MY BLOOD, TOO.
AND NOTHING CAN CHANGE THAT.

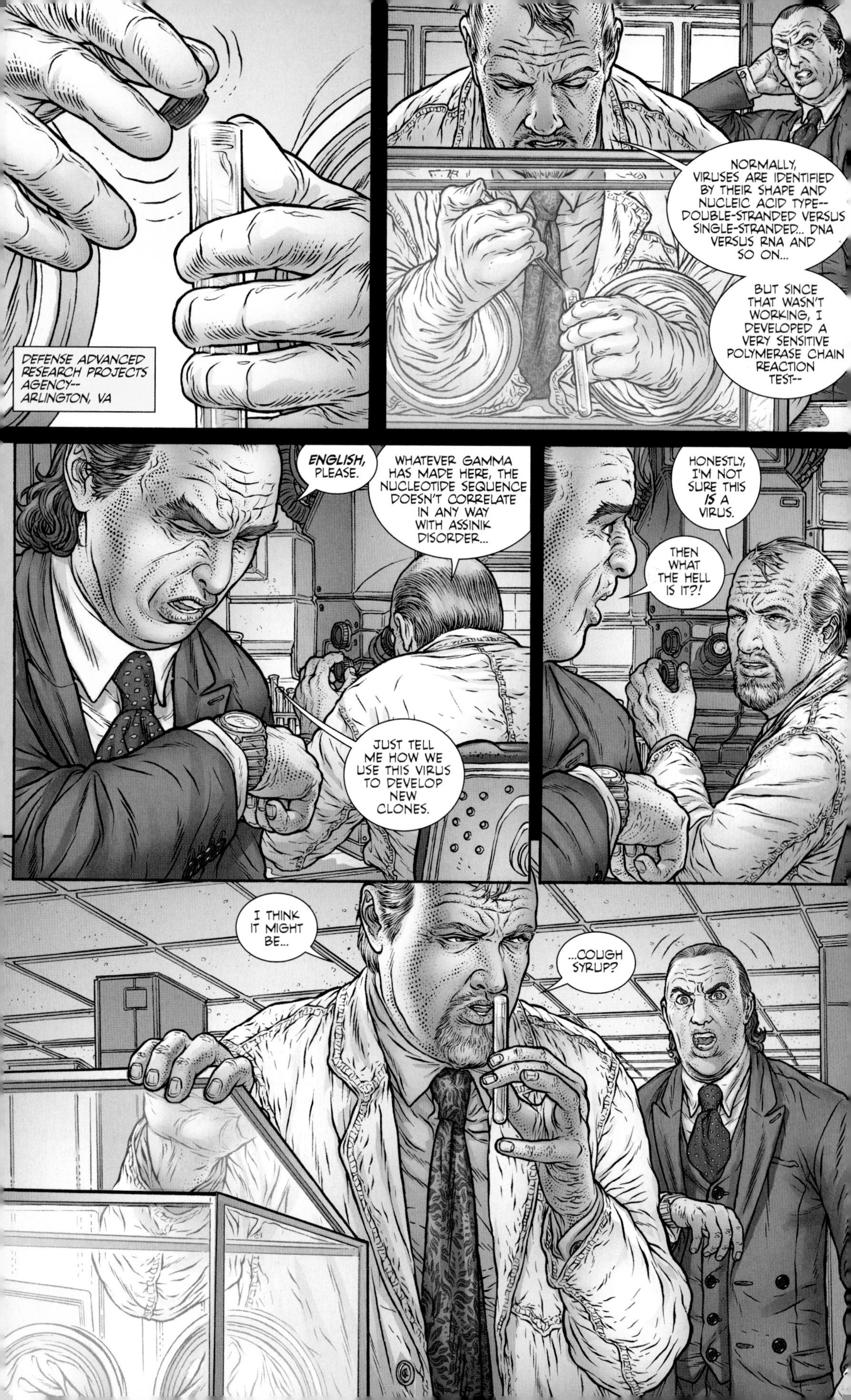
DEFENSE ADVANCED RESEARCH PROJECTS AGENCY-- ARLINGTON, VA
NORMALLY, VIRUSES ARE IDENTIFIED BY THEIR SHAPE AND NUCLEIC ACID TYPE-- DOUBLE-STRANDED VERSUS SINGLE-STRANDED... DNA VERSUS RNA AND SO ON...
BUT SINCE THAT WASN'T WORKING, I DEVELOPED A VERY SENSITIVE POLYMERASE CHAIN REACTION TEST--
ENGLISH, PLEASE.
WHATEVER GAMMA HAS MADE HERE, THE NUCLEOTIDE SEQUENCE DOESN'T CORRELATE IN ANY WAY WITH ASSINIK DISORDER...
JUST TELL ME HOW WE USE THIS VIRUS TO DEVELOP NEW CLONES.
HONESTLY, I'M NOT SURE THIS IS A VIRUS.
THEN WHAT THE HELL IS IT?!
I THINK IT MIGHT BE...
...COUGH SYRUP?

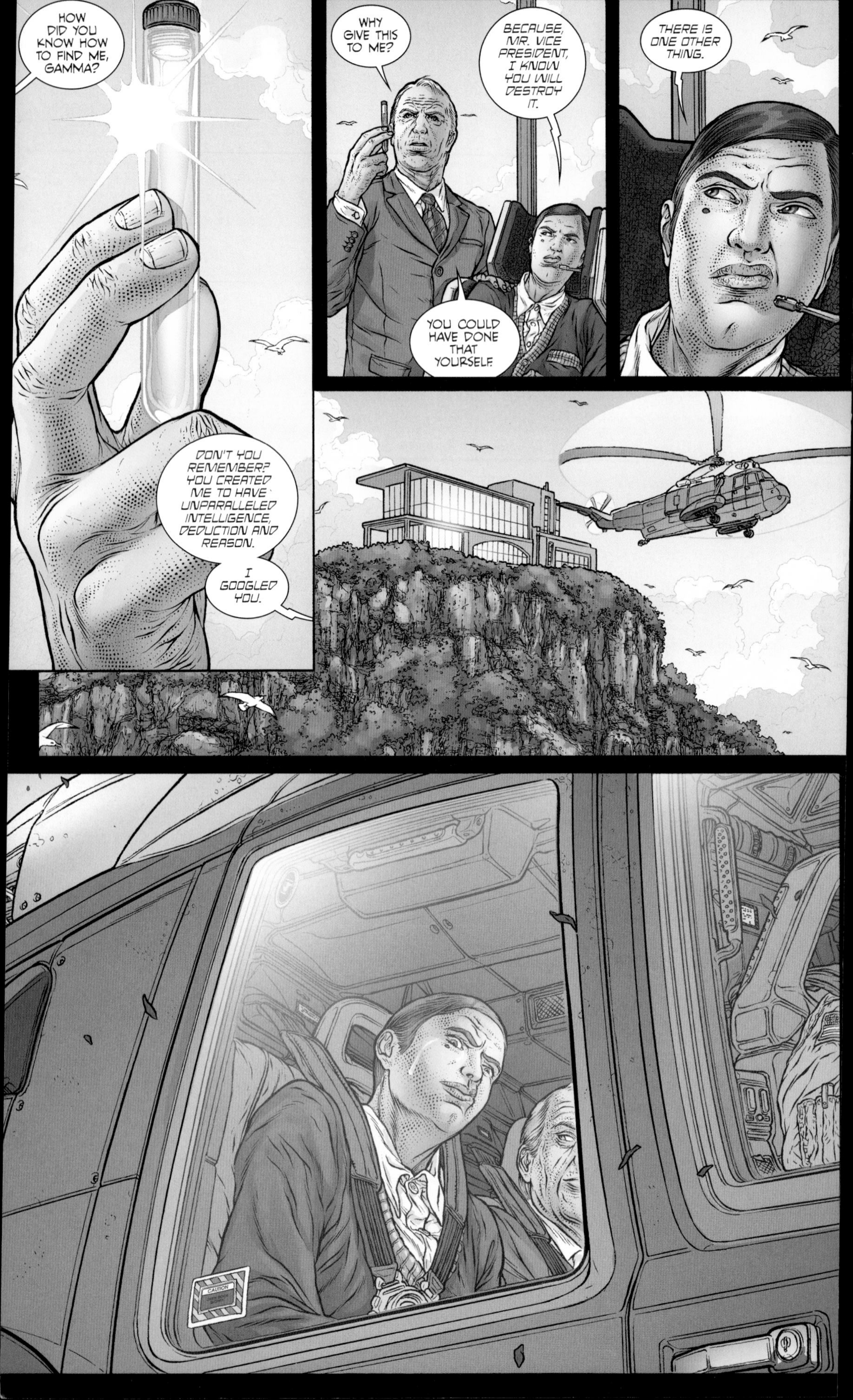
HOW DID YOU KNOW HOW TO FIND ME, GAMMA?
WHY GIVE THIS TO ME?
BECAUSE, MR. VICE PRESIDENT, I KNOW YOU WILL DESTROY IT.
YOU COULD HAVE DONE THAT YOURSELF.
THERE IS ONE OTHER THING.
DON'T YOU REMEMBER? YOU CREATED ME TO HAVE UNPARALLELED INTELLIGENCE, DEDUCTION AND REASON.
I GOOGLED YOU.
CAUTION

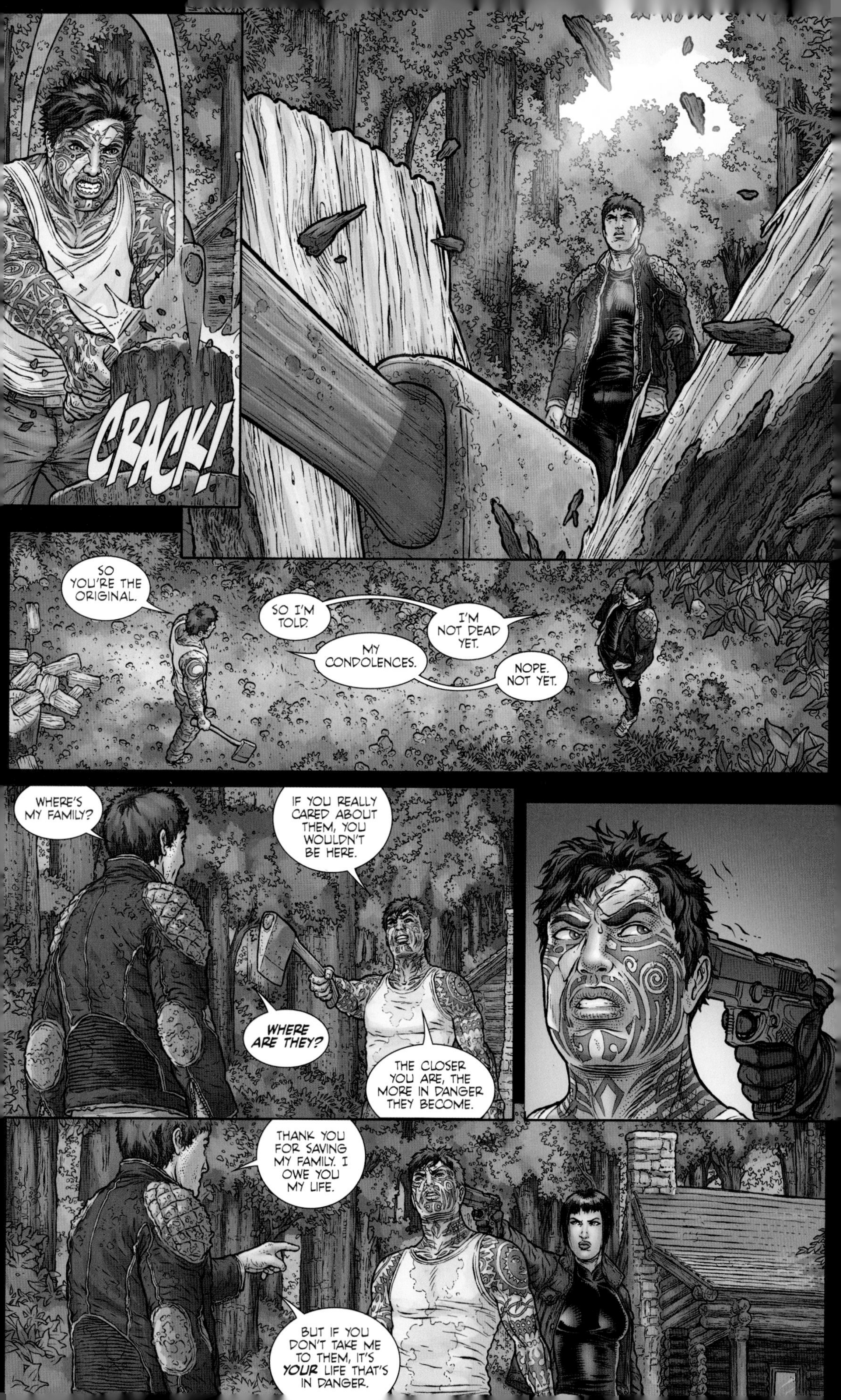

CRACK!
SO YOU'RE THE ORIGINAL.
SO I'M TOLD.
I'M NOT DEAD YET.
MY CONDOLENCES.
NOPE. NOT YET.
WHERE'S MY FAMILY?
IF YOU REALLY CARED ABOUT THEM, YOU WOULDN'T BE HERE.
WHERE ARE THEY?
THE CLOSER YOU ARE, THE MORE IN DANGER THEY BECOME.
THANK YOU FOR SAVING MY FAMILY. I OWE YOU MY LIFE.
BUT IF YOU DON'T TAKE ME TO THEM, IT'S YOUR LIFE THAT'S IN DANGER.

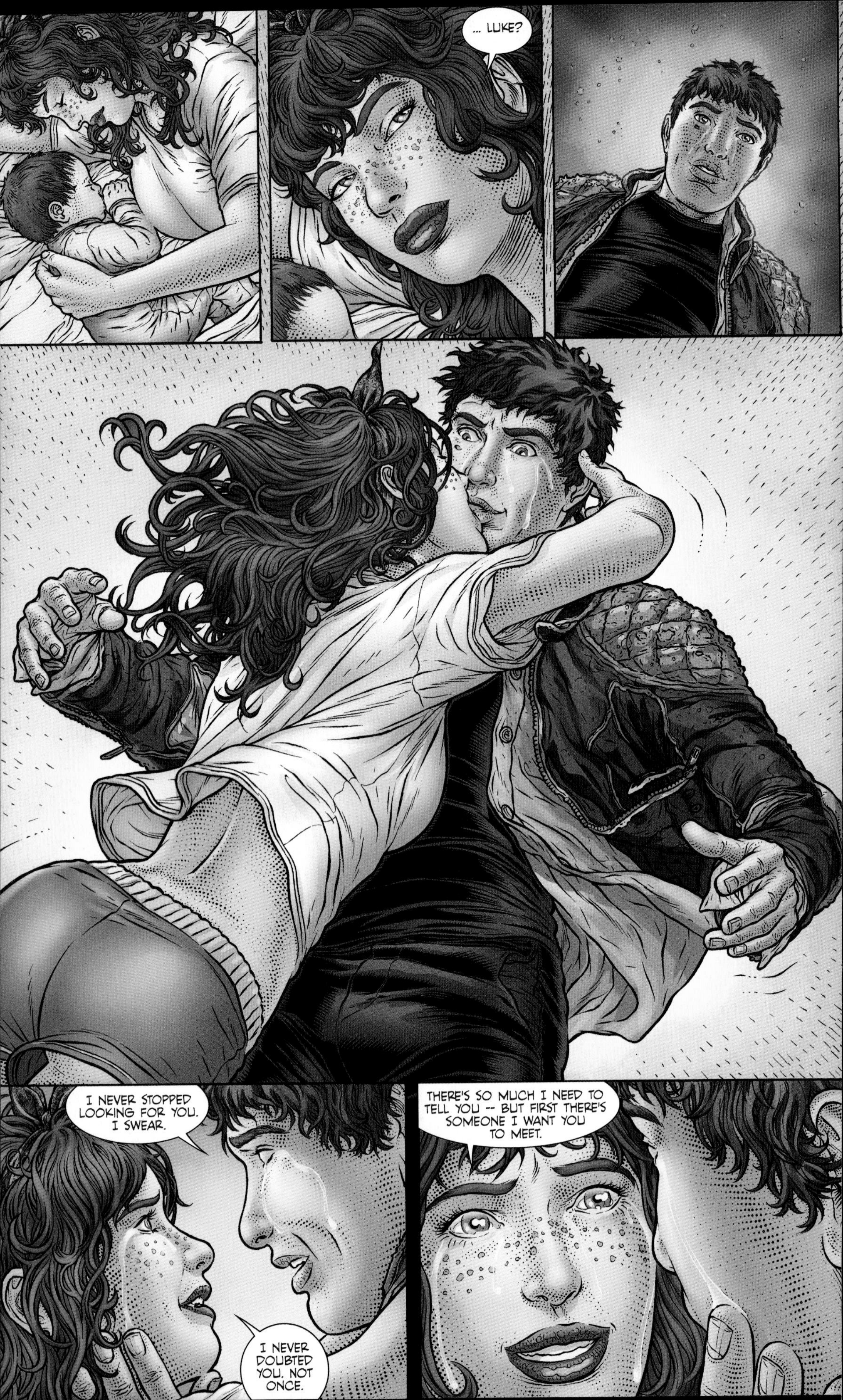
... LUKE?
I NEVER STOPPED LOOKING FOR YOU. I SWEAR.
I NEVER DOUBTED YOU. NOT ONCE.
THERE'S SO MUCH I NEED TO TELL YOU -- BUT FIRST THERE'S SOMEONE I WANT YOU TO MEET.

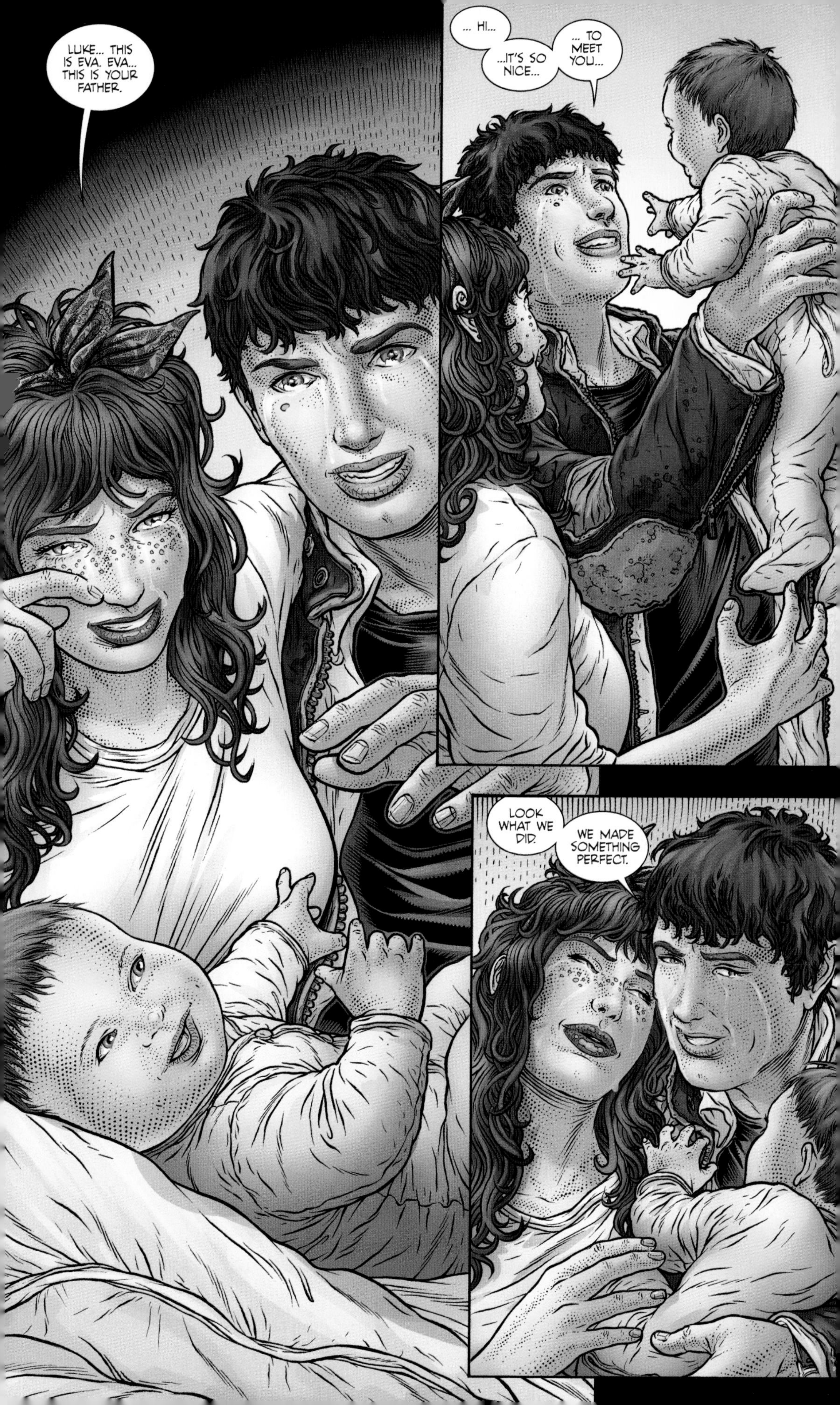
LUKE... THIS IS EVA. EVA... THIS IS YOUR FATHER.
... HI...
...IT'S SO NICE...
... TO MEET YOU...
LOOK WHAT WE DID.
WE MADE SOMETHING PERFECT.

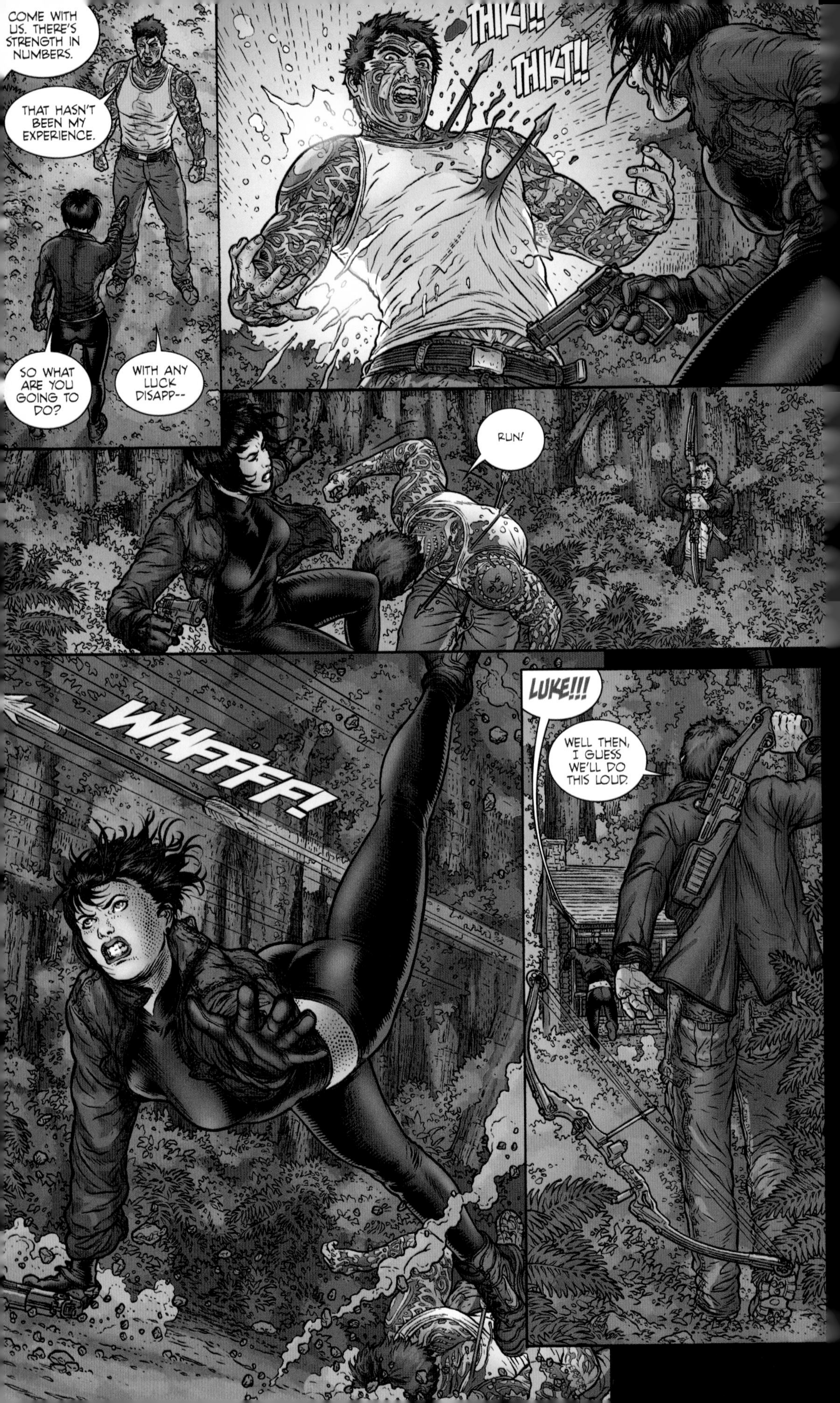
COME WITH US. THERE'S STRENGTH IN NUMBERS.
THAT HASN'T BEEN MY EXPERIENCE.
SO WHAT ARE YOU GOING TO DO?
WITH ANY LUCK DISAPP--
THIKT!!
THIKT!!
RUN!
WHFFFF!
LUKE!!!
WELL THEN, I GUESS WE'LL DO THIS LOUD.

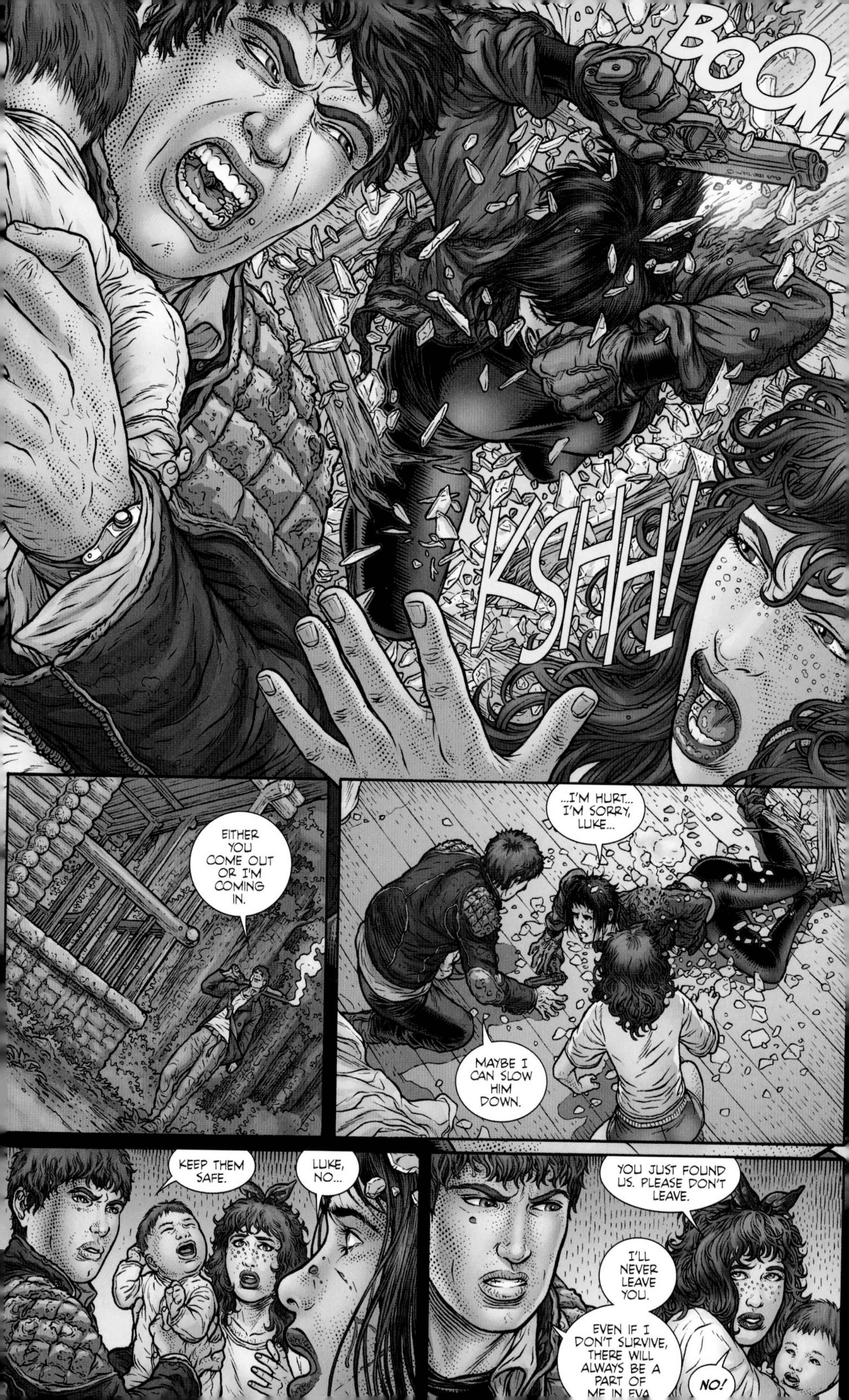
BOOM!!
KSHH!
EITHER YOU COME OUT OR I'M COMING IN.
...I'M HURT... I'M SORRY, LUKE...
MAYBE I CAN SLOW HIM DOWN.
KEEP THEM SAFE.
LUKE, NO...
YOU JUST FOUND US. PLEASE DON'T LEAVE.
I'LL NEVER LEAVE YOU.
EVEN IF I DON'T SURVIVE, THERE WILL ALWAYS BE A PART OF ME IN EVA
NO!

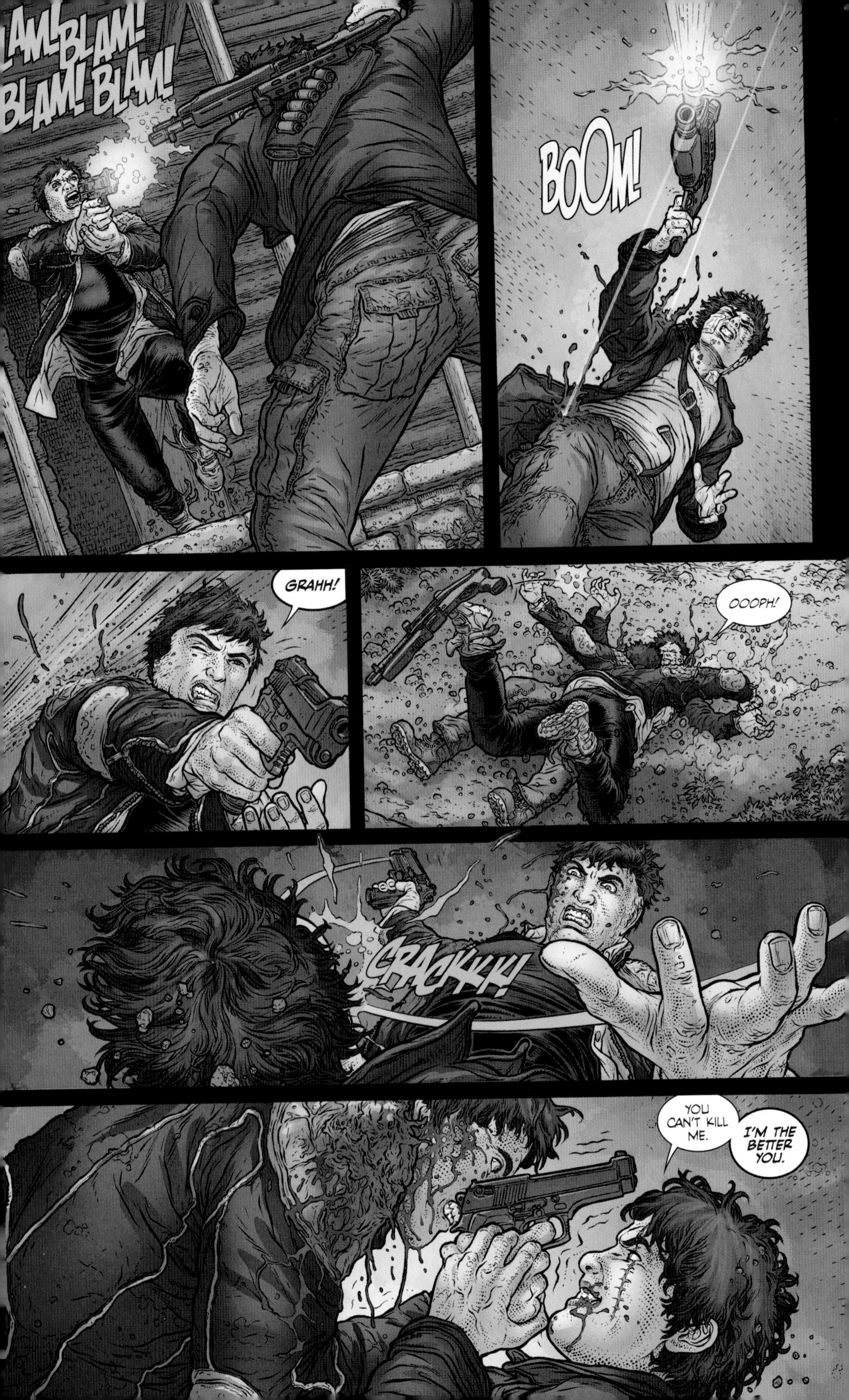
BLAM! BLAM!
BLAM! BLAM!
BOOM!
GRAHH!
OOOPH!
CRACKKK!
YOU CAN'T KILL ME.
I'M THE BETTER YOU.

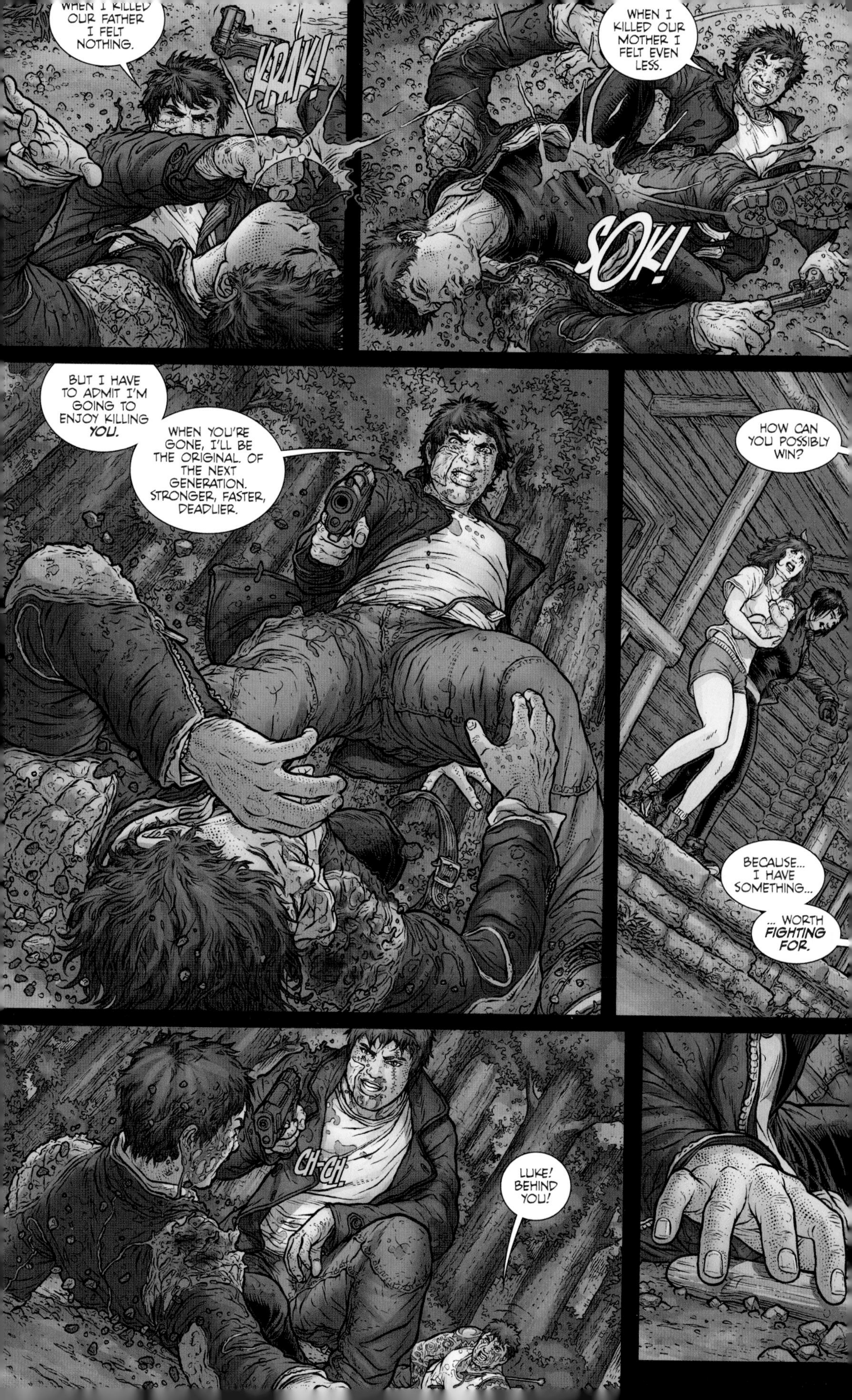
WHEN I KILLED OUR FATHER I FELT NOTHING.
KRAK!
WHEN I KILLED OUR MOTHER I FELT EVEN LESS.
SOK!
BUT I HAVE TO ADMIT I'M GOING TO ENJOY KILLING YOU.
WHEN YOU'RE GONE, I'LL BE THE ORIGINAL. OF THE NEXT GENERATION. STRONGER, FASTER, DEADLIER.
HOW CAN YOU POSSIBLY WIN?
BECAUSE... I HAVE SOMETHING...
... WORTH FIGHTING FOR.
CH-CH.
LUKE! BEHIND YOU!

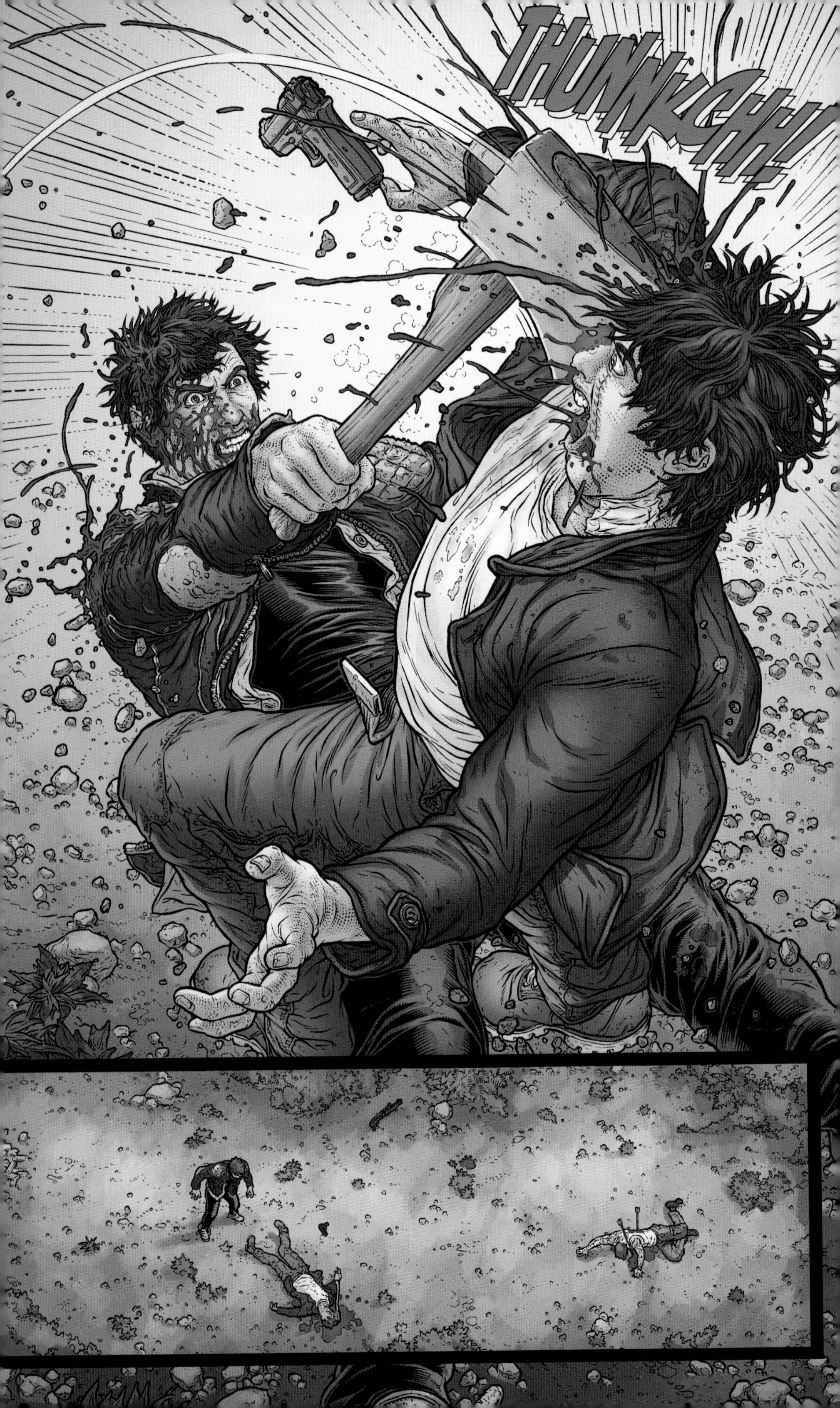
THUNKCHH

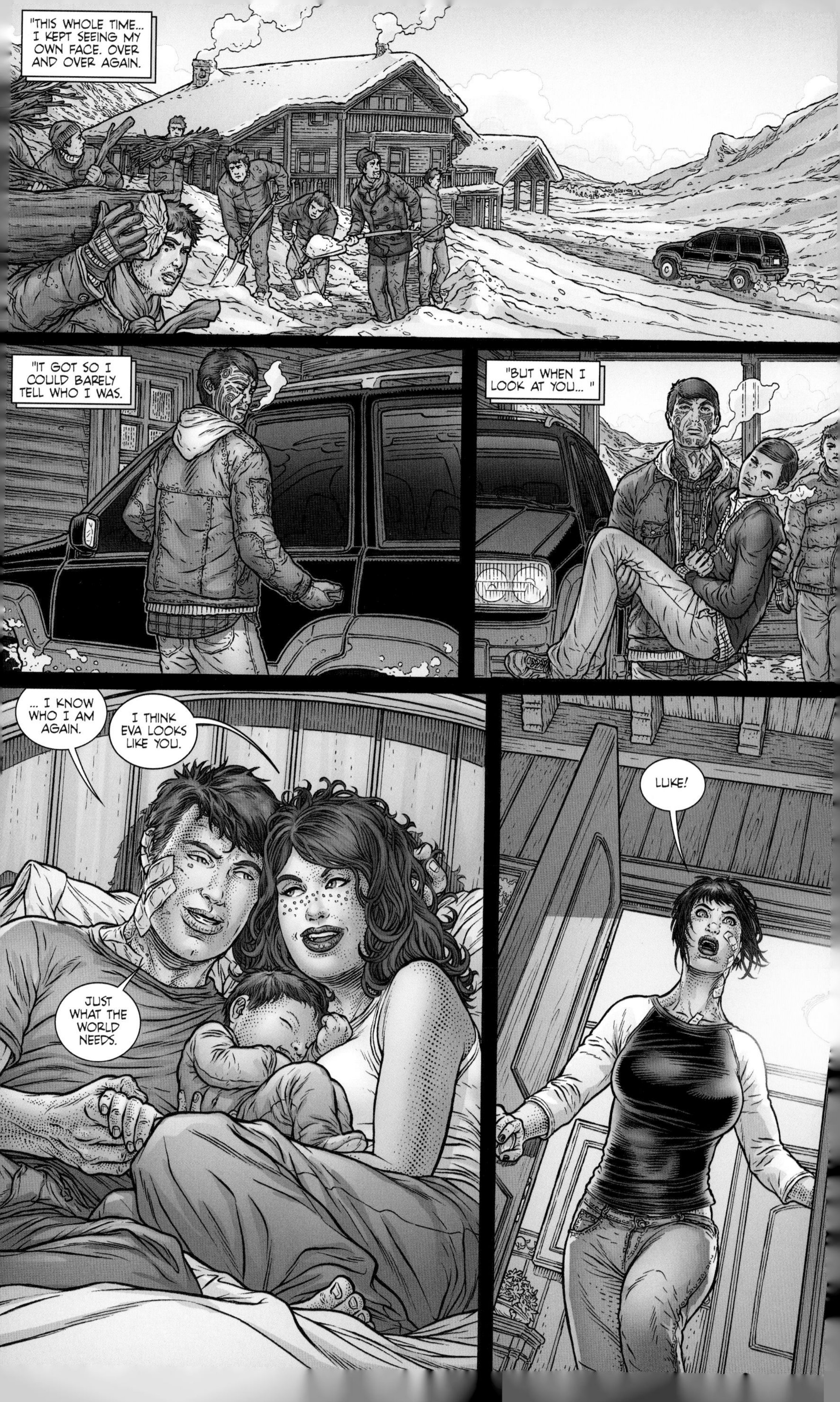
"THIS WHOLE TIME... I KEPT SEEING MY OWN FACE. OVER AND OVER AGAIN.
"IT GOT SO I COULD BARELY TELL WHO I WAS.
"BUT WHEN I LOOK AT YOU... "
... I KNOW WHO I AM AGAIN.
I THINK EVA LOOKS LIKE YOU.
JUST WHAT THE WORLD NEEDS.
LUKE!

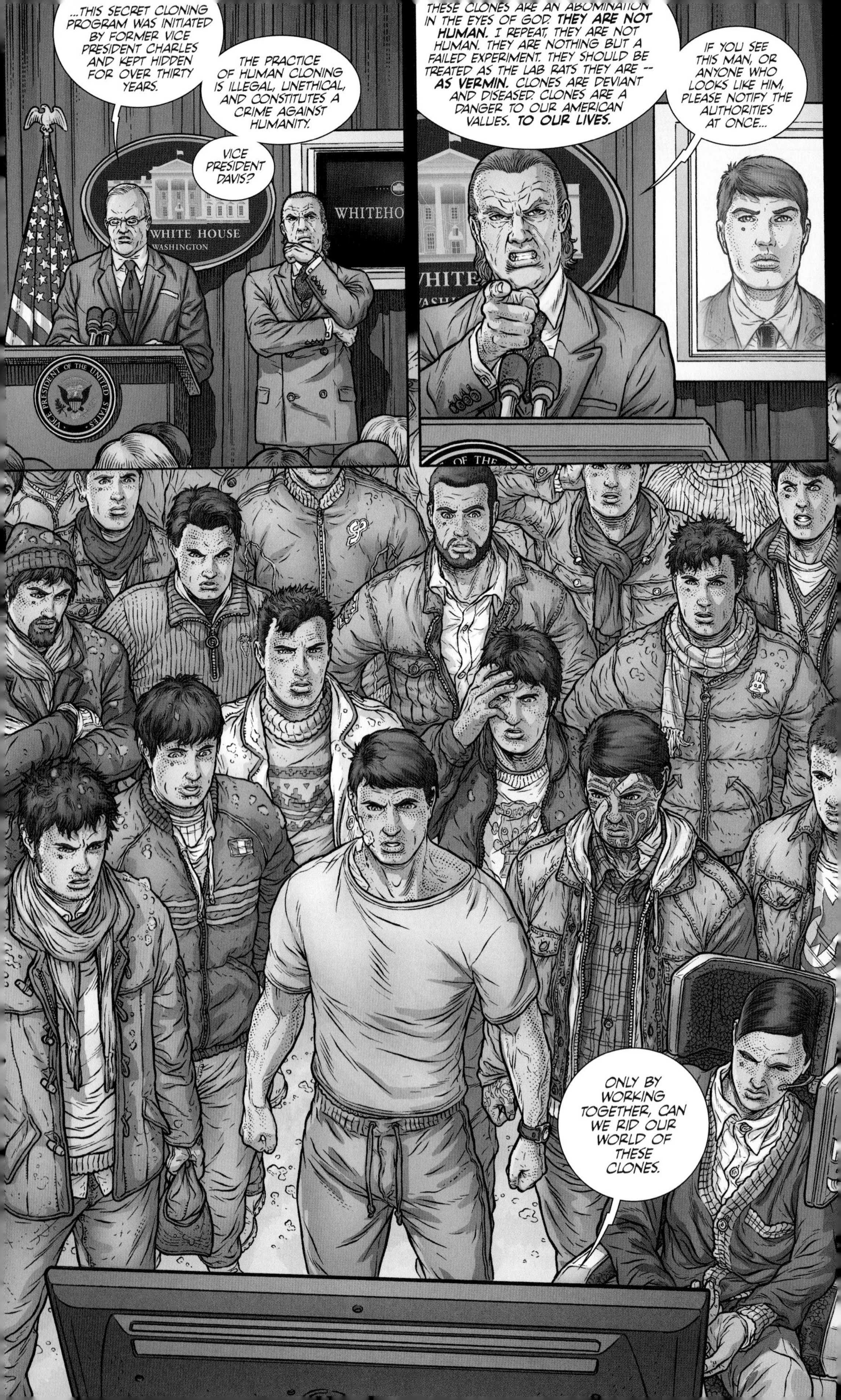
...THIS SECRET CLONING PROGRAM WAS INITIATED BY FORMER VICE PRESIDENT CHARLES AND KEPT HIDDEN FOR OVER THIRTY YEARS.
THE PRACTICE OF HUMAN CLONING IS ILLEGAL, UNETHICAL, AND CONSTITUTES A CRIME AGAINST HUMANITY.
VICE PRESIDENT DAVIS?
WHITE HOUSE
WASHINGTON
THESE CLONES ARE AN ABOMINATION IN THE EYES OF GOD. THEY ARE NOT HUMAN. I REPEAT, THEY ARE NOT HUMAN. THEY ARE NOTHING BUT A FAILED EXPERIMENT. THEY SHOULD BE TREATED AS THE LAB RATS THEY ARE -- AS VERMIN. CLONES ARE DEVIANT AND DISEASED. CLONES ARE A DANGER TO OUR AMERICAN VALUES. TO OUR LIVES.
IF YOU SEE THIS MAN, OR ANYONE WHO LOOKS LIKE HIM, PLEASE NOTIFY THE AUTHORITIES AT ONCE...
ONLY BY WORKING TOGETHER, CAN WE RID OUR WORLD OF THESE CLONES.

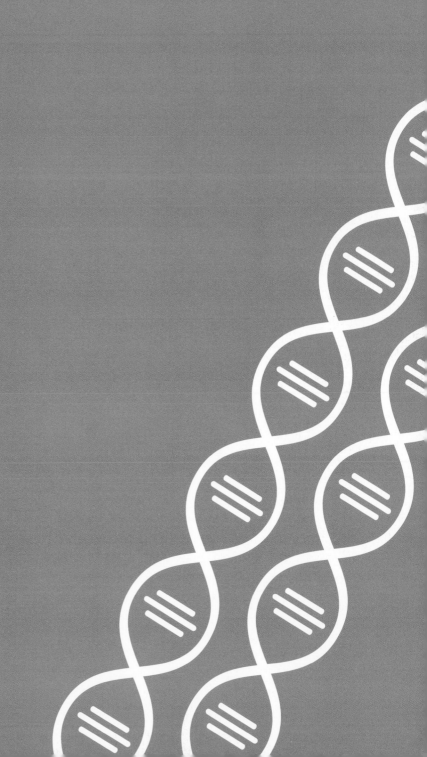

# SKETCHBOOK

**AARON GINSBURG:** Initially, for the cover of this trade, we had imagined Luke right smack dab in the center, holding Amelia in his arms. He's the hero of the story, naturally, and this arc depicts the brutal struggles Luke goes through to finally be reunited with his wife and newborn daughter. It just made sense.

Then Juan came back to us with this pencil. As you can see, he instinctually put Eric ("Tat") in the center, carrying Amelia tightly, a wave of fury in his eyes. And when we all saw this image, we realized why Juan's impulse made so much more sense...

If Luke already had Amelia in his arms on the cover, it somehow telegraphed the end of our arc and, as a result, undermined the very conflict of our journey. It said, "Hey, Luke saves Amelia, he's already won." What Juan did was create an image where the wrong clone has Amelia in his grasp. Not only is it not Luke with his wife, it's the one clone with dangerous ulterior motives: a desire to make Amelia love him instead.

By putting our protagonist in the upper right corner, Juan helped us tell the desperate, action-packed story of Luke and his team fighting against all odds to reach Amelia, and hinting that the final obstacle will be facing off with a darker version of himself, Tat.

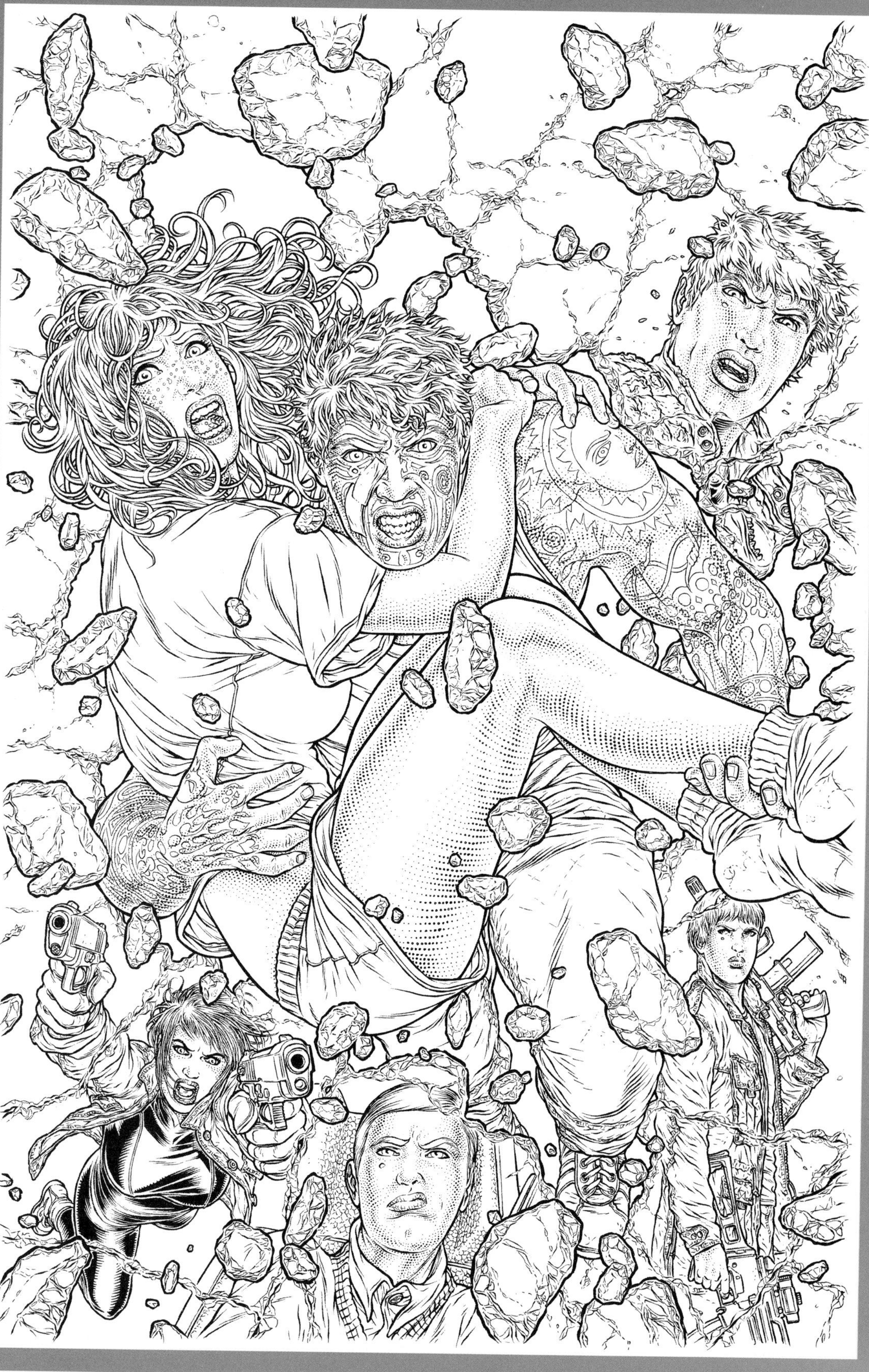

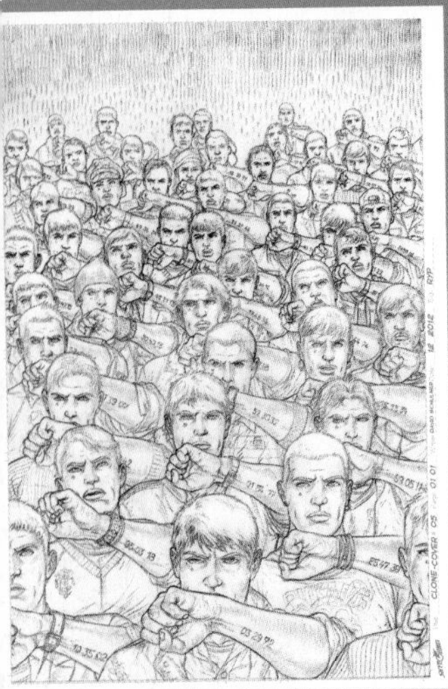

## [ISSUE SIX]

**DAVID SCHULNER:** To be honest I was never included in the cover concepts for issues 1 - 5. Maybe Sina Grace, our previous editor, thought I was an asshole or maybe he was always using that old Earthlink account of mine and wondered why I never replied (again, making me an asshole). Next time I see Sina, I should ask him. Anyway, I was actually pretty happy not to be included in the process because it meant I got to be completely surprised by what Juan came up with. I would literally be on the Image website or Comixology and see the upcoming covers for the first time just like you. As I write this I'm realizing I probably should have been shown at least a pencil, right? Okay, Sina definitely thought I was an asshole. But I digress. Seeing the cover for #6 was one of those great surprises. It was as if Juan plucked the image right out of my subconscious. But now, Sean Mackiewicz, our brilliant new editor (see how I called him "brilliant", Sina? I hate you too!) includes us in the process and I have to say... I miss being surprised a little.

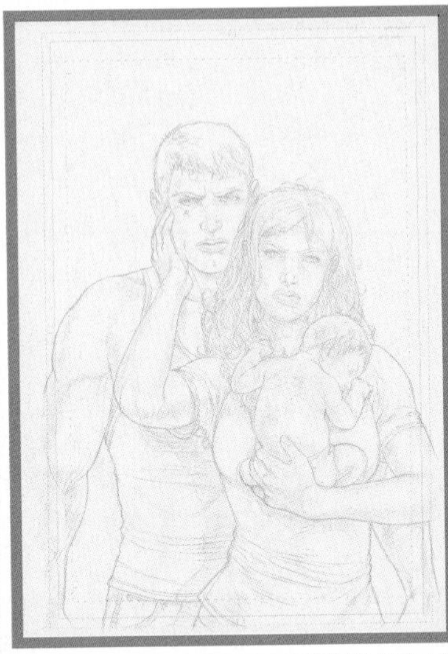

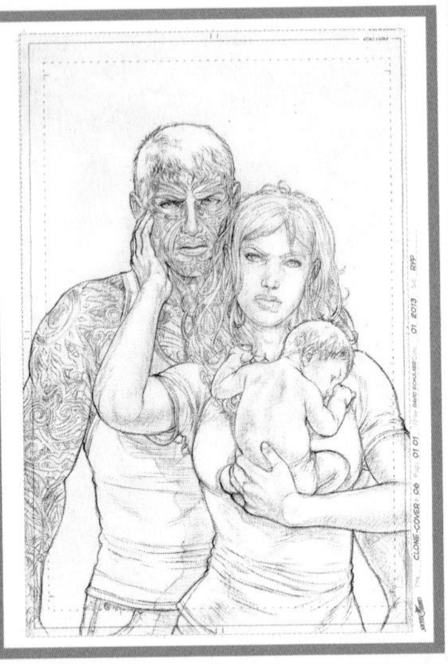

## [ISSUE SEVEN]

**WADE MCINTYRE:** This is my favorite CLONE cover. We were considering a more action-oriented image when Sean had the idea for this strange "family portrait." What I love about it most is the complicated emotion that Juan was able to capture behind the characters' eyes. Especially Amelia– what a great stare– but even the baby has something going on emotionally. I also think the pose is fascinating: Amelia isn't looking at the man behind her, only stroking his face. So to her, it would feel exactly like touching her husband. Only we, the readers, get to see that it's only a clone of the man she loves. The color choice brings it all home. The amber bursts right through the cooler blue and green palette of most of our other covers, and the fact that this warmth and emotion is applied to two characters who really shouldn't be together, makes it even better.

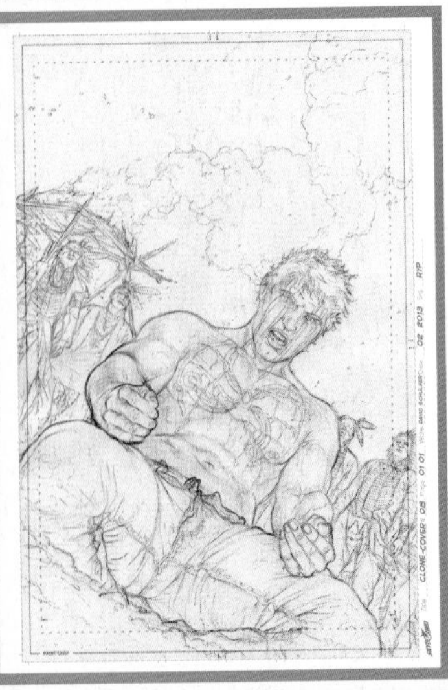

## [ISSUE EIGHT]

**AARON:** When the time came to select a cover concept for #8, we were in a bit of a jam. Juan had so completely, thoroughly, definitively blown the roof off with #7's stunning cover of Tat and Amelia in their strange familial embrace, we knew we needed to find the right image to follow it up. I remember we wrestled for days between several concepts...

Maybe, we should see BETA, post-truck accident, in the midst of a gruesome surgery, being sewn back together by masked doctors like our CLONE-version of Humpty Dumpty... Or maybe we finally put Amelia and Luke together on the cover, wrapped together sensually in bed, and then place their bed – metaphorically – in the middle of the sun-bleached desert... Like a nightmare. It just didn't seem right.

On a whim, we pitched Juan this idea: "Perhaps the cover depicts LUKE kneeling in the middle of the rocky Arizona desert, his face and chest dramatically painted with sand (and war paint). There are teepees and Navajo shaman in the distance, watching, waiting..."

And Juan came back with the first pencils of what became the CLONE #8 cover. Immediately, we knew we'd found our image. It was dramatic and vibrant and so very different from anything we had explored before in the series. With this image, Juan helped us introduce mysticism to our story - a new world where faith has equal power to science, where the old ways will provide more hope than the future.

CLONE-COVER # 09
01 01
DAVID SCHULNER
03 2013
RYP

## [ISSUE NINE]

**DAVID:** This idea was all Sean's. He wanted something sexy and dangerous that would make you go "Holy shit!" I'm not a fan of covers that give you "holy shit" images, but then they don't actually happen in the issue. That feels like schmuck bait to me. "Schmuck bait" is the affectionate term writers use to describe incidents that make the audience/reader go "holy shit!" but then you immediately take that incident away in the next issue or episode ("killing" your lead character only to revive him a few minutes later is the most common and schmuckiest schmuck bait). But this cover actually illustrates the "ploy" Jennifer and Sanah use to break into the facility where Amelia is being kept. Pretend Luke is their prisoner. And just for the record I'm totally guilty of using schmuck bait. Sometimes it's just too hard to resist!

CLONE-COVER # 10
01 01
DAVID SCHULNER
03 2013
RYP

## [ISSUE TEN]

**WADE:** As the conclusion of the second arc, #10 is filled with big developments and arresting images. So, for the cover we chose... none of them. We were determined not to spoil any of the surprises, so instead we chose to give some face time to a couple of characters who hadn't yet made it onto a cover: Beta and Gamma. The emergence of these two very different second-generation clones is a major thread in this arc, so I'm glad Juan gave them their due. And of course there's blood spatter because, well, one of them gets the axe in this issue.

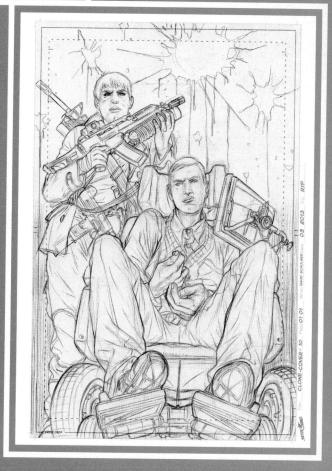

# ...ORE BOOKS FROM ...ROBERT ...KIRKMAN ...D SKYBOUND!

TO FIND YOUR NEAREST COMIC BOOK STORE, CALL:
**1-888-COMIC-BOOK**

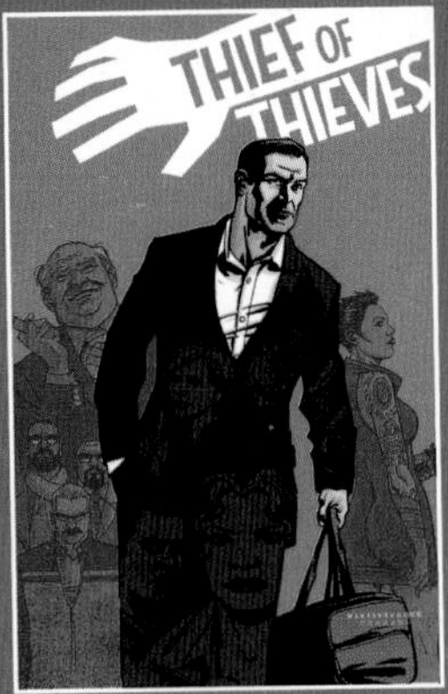
THIEF OF THIEVES

**THIEF OF THIEVES**
**VOL. 1: "I QUIT."**
ISBN: 978-1-60706-592-0
$14.99
**VOL. 2: "HELP ME."**
ISBN: 978-1-60706-676-7
$14.99

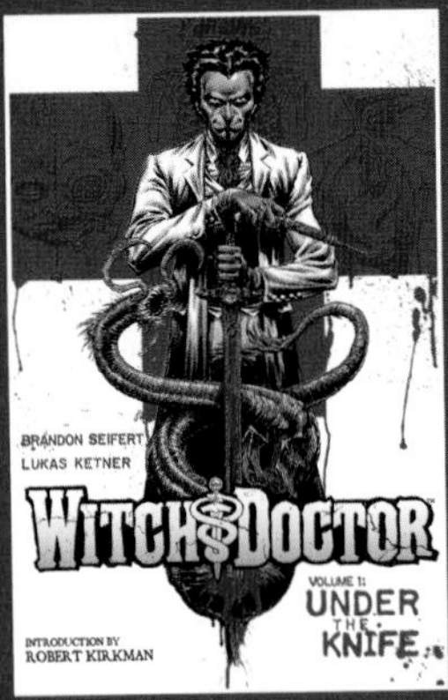
BRANDON SEIFERT
LUKAS KETNER
WITCH DOCTOR
VOLUME 1: UNDER THE KNIFE
INTRODUCTION BY ROBERT KIRKMAN

**WITCH DOCTOR**
**VOL. 1: UNDER THE KNIFE TP**
ISBN: 978-1-60706-441-1
$12.99

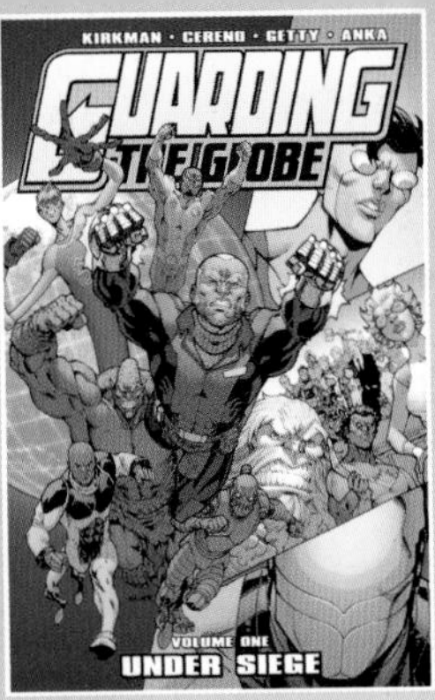
KIRKMAN · CERENO · GETTY · ANKA
GUARDING THE GLOBE
VOLUME ONE
UNDER SIEGE

**GUARDING THE GLOBE**
**VOL. 1: UNDER SIEGE TP**
ISBN: 978-1-60706-356-8
$16.99
**VOL. 2: HARD TO KILL TP**
ISBN: 978-1-60706-673-6
$16.99

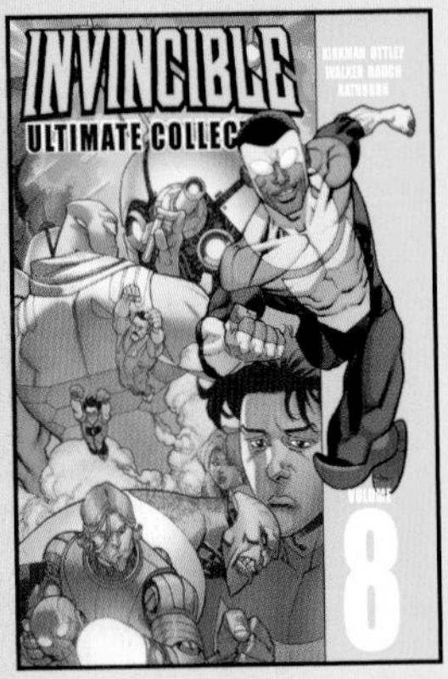
INVINCIBLE
ULTIMATE COLLEC
KIRKMAN OTTLEY WALKER RAUCH RATHBURN
VOLUME 8

**INVINCIBLE**
**VOL. 1: FAMILY MATTERS TP**
ISBN: 978-1-58240-711-1
$12.99
**VOL. 2: EIGHT IS ENOUGH TP**
ISBN: 978-1-58240-347-2
$12.99
**VOL. 3: PERFECT STRANGERS TP**
ISBN: 978-1-58240-793-7
$12.99
**VOL. 4: HEAD OF THE CLASS TP**
ISBN: 978-1-58240-440-2
$14.95
**VOL. 5: THE FACTS OF LIFE TP**
ISBN: 978-1-58240-554-4
$14.99
**VOL. 6: A DIFFERENT WORLD TP**
ISBN: 978-1-58240-579-7
$14.99
**VOL. 7: THREE'S COMPANY TP**
ISBN: 978-1-58240-656-5
$14.99
**VOL. 8: MY FAVORITE MARTIAN TP**
ISBN: 978-1-58240-683-1
$14.99
**VOL. 9: OUT OF THIS WORLD TP**
ISBN: 978-1-58240-827-9
$14.99
**VOL. 10: WHO'S THE BOSS TP**
ISBN: 978-1-60706-013-0
$16.99
**VOL. 11: HAPPY DAYS TP**
ISBN: 978-1-60706-062-8
$16.99
**VOL. 12: STILL STANDING TP**
ISBN: 978-1-60706-166-3
$16.99
**VOL. 13: GROWING PAINS TP**
ISBN: 978-1-60706-251-6
$16.99
**VOL. 14: THE VILTRUMITE WAR TP**
ISBN: 978-1-60706-367-4
$19.99
**VOL. 15: GET SMART TP**
ISBN: 978-1-60706-498-5
$16.99
**VOL. 16: FAMILY TIES TP**
ISBN: 978-1-60706-579-1
$16.99
**VOL. 17: WHAT'S HAPPENING TP**
ISBN: 978-1-60706-662-0
$16.99
**ULTIMATE COLLECTION, VOL. 1 HC**
ISBN 978-1-58240-500-1
$34.95
**ULTIMATE COLLECTION, VOL. 2 HC**
ISBN: 978-1-58240-594-0
$34.99
**ULTIMATE COLLECTION, VOL. 3 HC**
ISBN: 978-1-58240-763-0
$34.99
**ULTIMATE COLLECTION, VOL. 4 HC**
ISBN: 978-1-58240-989-4
$34.99
**ULTIMATE COLLECTION, VOL. 5 HC**
ISBN: 978-1-60706-116-8
$34.99
**ULTIMATE COLLECTION, VOL. 6 HC**
ISBN: 978-1-60706-360-5
$34.99
**ULTIMATE COLLECTION, VOL. 7 HC**
ISBN: 978-1-60706-509-8
$39.99
**ULTIMATE COLLECTION, VOL. 8 HC**
ISBN: 978-1-60706-680-4
$39.99
**COMPENDIUM VOL. 1**
ISBN: 978-1-60706-411-4
$64.99
**THE COMPLETE INVINCIBLE LIBRARY, VOL. 2 HC**
ISBN: 978-1-60706-112-0
$125.00
**THE COMPLETE INVINCIBLE LIBRARY, VOL. 3 HC**
ISBN: 978-1-60706-421-3
$125.00
**THE OFFICIAL HANDBOOK OF THE INVINCIBLE UNIVERSE TP**
ISBN: 978-1-58240-831-6
$12.99
**INVINCIBLE PRESENTS,**
**VOL. 1: ATOM EVE & REX SPLODE TP**
ISBN: 978-1-60706-255-4
$14.99

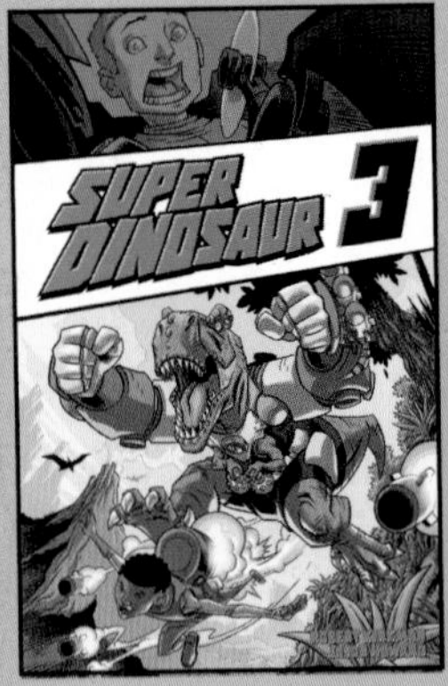
SUPER DINOSAUR 3

**SUPER DINOSAUR**
**VOL. 1**
ISBN: 978-1-60706-420-6
$9.99
**VOL. 2**
ISBN: 978-1-60706-568-5
$12.99
**VOL. 3**
ISBN: 978-1-60706-667-5
$12.99
**DEL...**
ISB...-7
$4...

**THE ASTOUNDING WOLF-MAN**
**VOL. 1 TP**
ISBN: 978-1-58240-862-0
$14.99
**VOL. 2 TP**
ISBN: 978-1-60706-007-9
$14.99
**VOL. 3 TP**
ISBN: 978-1-60706-111-3
$16.99
**VOL. 4 TP**
ISBN: 978-1-60706-249-3
$16.99

**BATTLE POPE**
**VOL. 1: GENESIS TP**
ISBN: 978-1-58240-572-8
$14.99
**VOL. 2: MAYHEM TP**
ISBN: 978-1-58240-529-2
$12.99
**VOL. 3: PILLOW TALK TP**
ISBN: 978-1-58240-677-0
$12.99
**VOL. 4: WRATH OF GOD TP**
ISBN: 978-1-58240-751-7
$9.99

**BRIT**
**VOL. 1: OLD SOLDIER TP**
ISBN: 978-1-58240-678-7
$14.99
**VOL. 2: AWOL**
ISBN: 978-1-58240-864-4
$14.99
**VOL. 3: FUBAR**
ISBN: 978-1-60706-061-1
$16.99

**CAPES**
**VOL. 1: PUNCHING THE CLOCK TP**
ISBN: 978-1-58240-756-2
$17.99

**HAUNT**
**VOL. 1 TP**
ISBN: 978-1-60706-154-0
$9.99
**VOL. 2 TP**
ISBN: 978-1-60706-229-5
$16.99
**VOL. 3 TP**
ISBN: 978-1-60706-552-4
$14.99
**THE IMMORTAL EDITION, VOL. 1 HC**
ISBN: 978-1-60706-241-7
$34.99

**THE INFINITE**
**VOL. 1 TP**
ISBN: 978-1-60706-475-6
$9.99

**SUPERPATRIOT**
**AMERICA'S FIGHTING FORCE**
ISBN: 978-1-58240-355-1
$14.99

**TALES OF THE REALM**
**HARDCOVER**
ISBN: 978-1-58240-426-0
$34.95
**TRADE PAPERBACK**
ISBN: 978-1-58240-394-6
$14.95

**TECH JACKET**
**VOL. 1: THE BOY FROM EARTH TP**
ISBN: 978-1-58240-771-5
$14.99